Politics of Peace Agreement Implementation

Sajib Bala

Politics of Peace Agreement Implementation

A Case Study of the Chittagong Hill Tracts (CHT) in Bangladesh

Sajib Bala
Department of International Relations
Jahangirnagar University
Dhaka, Bangladesh

ISBN 978-981-16-1943-4   ISBN 978-981-16-1944-1 (eBook)
https://doi.org/10.1007/978-981-16-1944-1

© The Editor(s) (if applicable) and The Author(s), under exclusive license to Springer Nature Singapore Pte Ltd. 2022
This work is subject to copyright. All rights are solely and exclusively licensed by the Publisher, whether the whole or part of the material is concerned, specifically the rights of translation, reprinting, reuse of illustrations, recitation, broadcasting, reproduction on microfilms or in any other physical way, and transmission or information storage and retrieval, electronic adaptation, computer software, or by similar or dissimilar methodology now known or hereafter developed.
The use of general descriptive names, registered names, trademarks, service marks, etc. in this publication does not imply, even in the absence of a specific statement, that such names are exempt from the relevant protective laws and regulations and therefore free for general use.
The publisher, the authors and the editors are safe to assume that the advice and information in this book are believed to be true and accurate at the date of publication. Neither the publisher nor the authors or the editors give a warranty, expressed or implied, with respect to the material contained herein or for any errors or omissions that may have been made. The publisher remains neutral with regard to jurisdictional claims in published maps and institutional affiliations.

This Palgrave Macmillan imprint is published by the registered company Springer Nature Singapore Pte Ltd.
The registered company address is: 152 Beach Road, #21-01/04 Gateway East, Singapore 189721, Singapore

Dedicated to
my academic supervisors and family members
who supported me in accomplishing my goal.

PREFACE

Although hundreds of peace agreements have been signed between conflicting parties in different parts of the world, many of these efforts have not been successful, particularly in the implementation phase. In the current academic parlance of peace and conflict research, implementing a peace agreement is one of the most critical and challenging issues. For lack of proper implementation, many peace agreements are yet to result in effective peace-making in post-conflict societies. To address this core problem in peace studies, I decided to deal with the implementation aspect of the Chittagong Hill Tracts (CHT) Peace Agreement of Bangladesh which was signed in 1997 and find out the reasons for its improper and ineffective implementation. More than 24 years have passed since the CHT Peace Agreement was signed, but till to date, the number of casualties from killing, mutilation, abduction and kidnapping of hundreds of CHT people continues to rise. With the methodological triangulation of both primary and secondary data, I have discovered that the CHT Peace Agreement is not successful owing to different political interests between the signing parties. My aim has primarily been to study the non-implementation syndrome of a peace agreement due to the political dimension of controlling power, the asymmetrical distribution of power and unequal sections/clauses in the peace agreement. I intend that this book will reduce the dearth of research on the topic of the politics of peace agreement implementation. The basis of this book is my PhD dissertation carried out at Hiroshima University, Japan, with Monbukagakusho scholarship.

Most earlier research has attempted to address the root causes of the CHT conflict, and some studies have addressed the post-conflict situation from the state-level perspective (here, the Government of Bangladesh is the key actor) and the CHT-based local-level analysis. However, an attempt is made in this book to analyse the case of the CHT Peace Agreement's implementation by exploring the political views (also, addressing the root causes of the conflict) at three levels—state, local and international. This analysis is expected to give the issue a holistic outlook which has rarely been provided in the prior literature. On the one hand, the knowledge in the field of the politics of peace agreement implementation is accumulated by analysing the concepts of 'politics', 'peace', 'peace agreement', 'implementation of peace agreement' through the theoretical prisms of realism and liberalism. On the other hand, the non-implementation syndrome of the CHT Peace Agreement is analysed through interviewing some notable persons who are direct stakeholders in the implementation of politics. To cross-check the secondary data, their narratives are essential for understanding the politics in implementing a peace agreement in general. The book also explores the CHT Peace Agreement's linkages, if any, with other post-conflict cases, that is, northeastern India (e.g. Mizo and Nagaland's peace initiatives), the Tamil crisis in Sri Lanka and the Free Aceh Movement in Indonesia.

This is expected to pave the way for framing connections between the politics of interest and policies which affect the implementation of peace agreements, in general, and the CHT case, in particular. This book is intended for undergraduate, graduate as well as post-graduate students in various disciplines, like, political science, peace and conflict studies, international relations, anthropology, public administration, psychology, history and sociology, with the aim of developing an understanding of the implementation of peace agreements as well as the non-implementation syndrome. It will be helpful for policy framers, implementers, peace agreement beneficiaries, practitioners, researchers and other stakeholders interested in and/or wanting to work in areas such as peace studies, South Asian studies, politics, peace agreement implementation, conflict management, ethnic conflict and peace-building. Moreover, the findings will help to create effective strategies for the formation of new peace agreements and the implementation of existing peace agreements. It may also draw the attention of academics and other researchers to conducting more comprehensive and intensive research regarding the different disputes of the CHT Peace Agreement as well as of other peace agreements. Thus, the book is likely to be used as a guide to many secondary sources.

Dhaka, Bangladesh   Sajib Bala

Contents

1 **Introduction** 1
  1.1 *Chapter Introduction* 1
  1.2 *Demographic Composition of Bangladesh* 3
  1.3 *Overview of the Chittagong Hill Tracts (CHT)* 4
  1.4 *Background of the Research Question* 6
  1.5 *Research Question, Objectives and Hypotheses* 9
  1.6 *Originality* 9
  1.7 *Research Method* 11
  1.8 *Overview of Chapters* 13
  References 16

2 **Politics of Peace Agreement Implementation: Theoretical Reflections** 19
  2.1 *Chapter Introduction* 19
  2.2 *Theoretical and Conceptual Analysis* 21
  2.3 *Analytical Framework* 34
  2.4 *Theoretical and Analytical Design* 37
  2.5 *Chapter Conclusion* 38
  References 39

3 **From Eruption of the Conflict to Its Management** 41
  3.1 *Chapter Introduction* 41
  3.2 *Pre-colonial Period: Beginning of the Erosion of the Hill People's Autonomy* 42

3.3	British Period (1760–1947): Beginning of the Marginalisation of the Hill People	44
3.4	Pakistan Period (1947–1971): Continued Marginalisation	51
3.5	Bangladesh Period (1971–1997)	56
3.6	Chapter Conclusion	63
References		65

4 Assessment of the Implementation Status of the CHT Peace Agreement — 67
- 4.1 Chapter Introduction — 67
- 4.2 Factors Underlying Signing of the CHT Peace Agreement — 68
- 4.3 Key Features of the CHT Peace Agreement and Its Major Subjects — 69
- 4.4 Implementation Status: A Dispute — 73
- 4.5 Chapter Conclusion — 91
- References — 92

5 State Actors and Implementation of the CHT Peace Agreement — 95
- 5.1 Chapter Introduction — 95
- 5.2 Response at the Governmental Level — 96
- 5.3 Role of the Army in the CHT's Affairs — 106
- 5.4 Bureaucracy in the CHT-Based Local Administration — 112
- 5.5 Chapter Conclusion — 116
- References — 117

6 Empirical Study at CHT-Based Local Level — 119
- 6.1 Chapter Introduction — 119
- 6.2 Intra-Community Rivalries — 120
- 6.3 Inter-Community (Bengali Settlers vs. Hill People) Relationships Affecting the CHT Peace Agreement — 128
- 6.4 Factional Rivalries of the CHT People — 130
- 6.5 Brief Analysis of Group Dynamics in the Chittagong Hill Tracts (CHT) — 131
- 6.6 Chapter Conclusion — 132
- References — 133

7	Empirical Study at International Level	135
	7.1 Chapter Introduction	135
	7.2 Chittagong Hill Tracts (CHT) Case at the International Level	136
	7.3 India's Role Regarding the CHT Case	137
	7.4 Role of the International Chittagong Hill Tracts Commission	140
	7.5 Development Initiatives of the CHT and the United Nations Development Programme (UNDP)	145
	7.6 Undesirable Examples of International Organisations' Involvement	148
	7.7 Chapter Conclusion	149
	References	150
8	Dynamics of Peace Agreement Implementation: Research Findings	151
	8.1 Chapter Introduction	151
	8.2 Findings Through Comprehensive Analysis	152
	8.3 Revisiting the Hypotheses, Objectives and Research Question	161
	8.4 Chapter Conclusion	162
9	Conclusion	165
	9.1 Revisiting the Findings: Politics in Actors' Interests	166
	9.2 Policy Recommendations	169
	9.3 Implications	172
	9.4 Comparative Analysis of the CHT Peace Agreement with Other Peace Agreements	173
	9.5 Avenues for Further Research	175
Appendix 1: Semi-Structured Questionnaire (Checklist)		177
Appendix 2: List of Interviewees		181
Appendix 3: Map of the Chittagong Hill Tracts (CHT)		187
Appendix 4: Chittagong Hill Tracts Peace Agreement of 1997		189
Index		207

Acronyms

ADB	Asian Development Bank
AL	Awami League
BD	Basic Democracies
BDR	Bangladesh Rifles (Now Border Guards Bangladesh)
BGB	Border Guards Bangladesh
BHDC	Bandarban Hill District Council
BIPF	Bangladesh Indigenous Peoples' Forum
BNP	Bangladesh Nationalist Party
CHT	Chittagong Hill Tracts
CHTDB	Chittagong Hill Tracts Development Board
CHTDF	Chittagong Hill Tracts Development Facility
CHTRC (shortened to RC)	Chittagong Hill Tracts Regional Council
DC	Deputy Commissioner
DFs	District Forests
EC	European Commission
ECOSOC	Economic and Social Council (of the United Nations)
EU	European Union
GoB	Government of Bangladesh
GOC	General Officer Commanding
HDC	Hill District Council
HWF	Hill Women's Federation
IDPs	Internally Displaced Peoples
ILO	International Labour Organization
ISPR	Inter Services Public Relation Directorate

IWGIA	International Work Group for Indigenous Affairs
JI	Jamaat-e-Islami (A Fundamentalist Political Party)
JP	Jatiya Party
JSS	Jana Samhati Samiti (See PCJSS Below)
KHDC	Khagrachhari Hill District Council
KII	Key Informant Interview
LGCs	Local Government Councils
LTTE	Liberation Tigers of Tamil Eelam
MoCHTA	Ministry of Chittagong Hill Tracts Affairs
MP	Member of Parliament
NCCHT	National Committee on Chittagong Hill Tracts
NGO	Non-Governmental Organisation
NIP	National Indicative Programme
OCCHTC	Organising Committee Chittagong Hill Tracts Campaign
PCJSS (shortened to JSS)	Parbatya Chattagram Jana Samhati Samiti (United People's Party of CHT)
PCP	Pahari Chattra Parishad (Hill Students' Council)
PFs	Protected Forests
PGP	Pahari Gono Parishad (Hill People's Council)—Hill people's led organisation
PGP	Parbattya Gano Parishad (Council of Hill Peoples)—Bengali settlers' led organisation
RAW	Research and Analysis Wing (The Primary Foreign Intelligence Agency of India)
RC	Regional Council (See CHTRC Above)
RFs	Reserve Forests
RHDC	Rangamati Hill District Council
SAARC	South Asian Association for Regional Cooperation
SB	Shanti Bahini (Peace Force)
SDO	Sub-Divisional Officer
SP	Superintendent of Police
UCDP	Uppsala Conflict Data Program
UN	United Nations
UNDP	United Nations Development Programme
UNFPA	United Nations Population Fund
UNHCR	United Nations High Commissioner for Refugees (United Nations Refugee Agency)
UNWGIP	United Nations Working Group on Indigenous Populations
UPDF	United People's Democratic Front

USFs	Unclassified State Forests
VDP	Village Defence Party
WGIP	Working Group on Indigenous Populations (See UNWGIP Above)

List of Figures

Fig. 1.1　Distribution of population by religion (in Percentage) (2011 Census) (*Source* Developed by author based on the Bangladesh Bureau of Statistics (2015), p. 86)　4
Fig. 2.1　Theoretical and analytical framework (*Source* Developed by author based on the above analysis)　38
Fig. 6.1　CHT-based local-level group dynamics (*Source* Developed by author based on the earlier discussion)　131
Fig. 8.1　Levels of influence in implementing the CHT peace agreement (*Source* Developed by author based on earlier arguments)　162

List of Tables

Table 1.1	Area and population of the Chittagong Hill Tracts (CHT)	4
Table 2.1	Scope of theoretical and applied politics	24
Table 3.1	Demographic account of the Hill people and the Bengali (settlers) inhabited in the Chittagong Hill Tracts (CHT)	55
Table 4.1	Data of implementation status claimed by the Government of Bangladesh (GoB)	73
Table 4.2	Data of implementation status claimed by the PCJSS	75
Table 4.3	A.1 (keeping up tribal-inhabited characteristics of the CHT)	79
Table 4.4	B.26 (special provision relating to the land management regarding HDCs' permission)	80
Table 4.5	B.34 (transferred subjects under the jurisdiction of HDCs)	82
Table 4.6	C.9.a (supervision and coordination of HDCs' functions through CHTRC)	83
Table 4.7	C.13 (prerogatives of CHTRC in formulating and amending law)	84
Table 4.8	D.1 (rehabilitation of India-returnee tribal refugees and Internally Displaced Peoples)	85
Table 4.9	D.3 (settlement of lands to the landless tribal families)	86
Table 4.10	D.4 (land dispute resolution through Land Commission)	87
Table 4.11	D.17 (withdrawal of temporary camps and handover of abandoned lands)	88
Table 5.1	Strengths of military forces in Bangladesh	107

Table 6.1	Composition of Adivasi representation on CHTRC	122
Table 6.2	Religious composition of the CHT people	129

CHAPTER 1

Introduction

1.1 Chapter Introduction

After signing a peace agreement, its implementation becomes an intractable challenge to most peacebuilders worldwide. This is particularly true in case of intra-state conflict in a multi-ethnic state. In such type of country, non-implementation of a peace agreement whatever is more visible and prevalent. Implementing a peace agreement involves a range of measures adopted by various actors at different levels that are targeted at reducing the risk of lapsing or relapsing into conflict. The peace agreement's signing parties, for example, the state's government and its counterpart, are the primary actors with the responsibility for implementing the agreement. Moreover, at the state level, the government and, more broadly, other state agencies (e.g. the bureaucracy and the army) have the authoritative power to implement the agreement. Political, army and bureaucratic elites are sensitive to their own interests—interest in assuming power, economic interest or other interests. In a sovereign state, the government is usually one of the key actors in implementing the peace agreement as it has the ultimate authority for formulating, as well as defining, the laws for implementing the agreement's provisions. At the same time, local as well as international actors may have their own views about the implementation process of the peace agreement. For example, the beneficiary of a peace agreement, the marginalised ethnic people, may have differences with the

© The Author(s), under exclusive license to Springer Nature
Singapore Pte Ltd. 2022
S. Bala, *Politics of Peace Agreement Implementation*,
https://doi.org/10.1007/978-981-16-1944-1_1

government regarding the implementation policies initiated by the state. In many cases, domestic issues do not exclude the concerns of the international community, many of which are involved in human rights causes and share ideas in common with the marginalised groups. These international networks play a wider role in signing the peace agreement and its implementation process through motivating (or, in some cases, exerting pressure on) the government to fulfil their demands. These international actors have been successful mostly when the willingness of the primary parties in conflict to implement the agreement flows in a promising direction. This mostly depends on the domestic political culture of the state concerned as well as on the peace agreement beneficiary/ies.

Considering the politics of interest at the three levels described above, the efforts in implementing the Chittagong Hill Tracts (CHT) Agreement (popularly known as, and hereafter, the CHT Peace Agreement) in Bangladesh offer a typical case worthy of research. In the CHT, the Peace Agreement was signed in 1997 between the representatives of the Government of Bangladesh (GoB) (more, specifically, National Committee on Chittagong Hill Tracts [NCCHT]) and the Parbatya Chattagram Jana Samhati Samiti (PCJSS) (United People's Party of CHT), the political representatives of the Hill people,[1] to end nearly two decades of conflict between the mainstream Bengali elites and ethnic minorities living in the area. However, effective peace has not yet taken a concrete and active form. Presently, the major obstacle to achieving peace is the partial (or weak) implementation of the CHT Peace Agreement which is greatly intensified by the dispute about the implementation status of the sections (provisions/clauses) of the Agreement. In this book, answers have been sought to the following research question: why do the GoB, the Hill people and the international actors hold different views about the implementation of the CHT Peace Agreement? In other words, the political stances of the respective actors are implied by their various positions. The answer to this question is explored through analysing the current dispute of the implementation of the Agreement which is mostly

---

[1] The people, with the particular exception of the Bengalis (or Bengali settlers), living in the CHT are generally addressed using varying terminology: Pahari (Hill people), Hill communities, Hill ethnic communities, Hill ethnic people, CHT indigenous people, Upajati (tribal people), Adivasi (indigenous or aboriginal people), etc. The debates over terminology evolved as a result of scholars' different justifications for using the word or the English translation of the Bengali word or due to conceptual differences between the people of Bangladesh and Western countries. In this book, the above terminology has been used, indicating the differences as expressed by the Bengali ethnic community.

determined by the politics of interest, that is, political, economic, social power, etc., of the different actors mentioned above.

After the 'chapter introduction', this chapter deals with the following issues in various sections in a logical and coherent manner, they are, demographic composition of Bangladesh, an overview of the CHT, the background of the research question, objective and hypothesis relating to the research question, originality of the work, research method and finally, an overview of the chapters taken for discussion in overall body of the book.

1.2 Demographic Composition of Bangladesh

According to the *Statistical Pocket Book Bangladesh 2019*, as of July 2018, Bangladesh, with a total area of 147,570 square kilometres, had a population of about 164.6 million (Bangladesh Bureau of Statistics, 2020, pp. 3–4). Based on the most recent Census of 2011, of the total population, the highest number, ethnically, was the Bengali ethnolinguistic people except for the tiny 1.10% (Bangladesh Bureau of Statistics, 2015, p. 153) of other ethnic (tribal[2]) population, with these people located all over the country. Based on the 2011 Census, excluding the Bengalis, the total number of the ethnic population throughout Bangladesh is 1,586,141[3] (from 27[4] different ethnic communities), of which 845,541 (calculated from Table 1.1) people are living in the CHT[5] (Bangladesh Bureau of Statistics, 2019, p. 98).

---

[2] The Bengali version of the word 'tribal' is Upajati which means sub-nation. The ethnic people, except the Bengalis, are not willing to be termed 'tribal', preferring the term 'Adivasi' (indigenous people). In addition, they are demanding constitutional recognition in line with the United Nations' conventions to protect their cultural, traditional, language and land rights.

[3] The indigenous communities claim to have a population exceeding three million.

[4] The state authority mentioned 27 ethnic communities (or groups); however, different sources acknowledged different data. For example, the Bangladesh Indigenous Peoples' Forum (BIPF) published a list of 45 indigenous communities all over Bangladesh (Bleie, 2005, p. 13). On the same page, Bleie also discussed the existence of some 30 ethnic communities. Mohsin (2003), in her book (p. 91), mentioned about 45 different communities apart from Bengalis.

[5] There are 64 districts in Bangladesh and, as with other districts, Rangamati, Bandarban and Khagrachhari are three separate districts. Despite its vast history, presently, in general, the CHT are constituted as comprising these three districts. In the territorial administrative set-up, the district (*zilla*) is the second administrative tier after the divisional levels.

Table 1.1 Area and population of the Chittagong Hill Tracts (CHT)

District	Area (sq. km.)	Population	Adivasi (number)	Adivasi in percentage (calculated)	Total Bengali population
Bandarban	4,479	388,335	172,401	44.39	752,690 (47.1%) (calculated)
Khagrachhari	2,749	613,917	316,987	51.63	
Rangamati	6,116	595,979	356,153	59.76	
Total (calculated)	13,344	1,598,231	845,541	52.90	

Source Developed by author based on the *Statistical Pocket Book Bangladesh 2018*, published by Bangladesh Bureau of Statistics (2019), pp. 50, 71, 74, 98

The Bangladeshi people mainly believe in four religions, with their respective percentages presented below (Fig. 1.1):

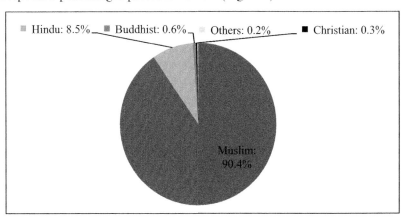

Fig. 1.1 Distribution of population by religion (in Percentage) (2011 Census) (*Source* Developed by author based on the Bangladesh Bureau of Statistics (2015), p. 86)

1.3 Overview of the Chittagong Hill Tracts (CHT)

Geographically, the CHT are covered with abundant hill and forest areas in the south-eastern part of Bangladesh. The CHT comprise seven central valleys formed by the Feni, Karnafuli, Chengi, Myani, Kassalong, Sangue and Matamuhuri rivers and their tributaries, and numerous hills, ravines and cliffs covered with dense vegetation abound the region. This is in complete contrast to most other districts of Bangladesh, where the lands mainly consist of alluvial plains (Shelley, 1992, p. 35). The CHT are surrounded by the Indian states of Tripura and Mizoram to the north and east, respectively; by Chittagong and the plain of Cox's Bazar stretching along the Bay of Bengal to the west; and by the Arakan territory of Myanmar to the south and south-east. In 1984, the CHT were divided into three administrative districts, viz. Khagrachhari (north), Rangamati (middle) and Bandarban (south) (Royhan, 2016, p. 130). For readers' convenience in gaining an understanding of the location of the CHT, a map is attached in Appendix 3. These three districts occupy a physical area of about 13,344 square kilometres, constituting approximately 10% of the total land area of Bangladesh. Of the total CHT population of 1,598,231, the Hill people comprise approximately 52.90% (refer to Table 1.1 for details).

The CHT are inhabited by 11[6] ethnic communities, namely the Chakma, Marma, Tripura, Tanchangya, Mrung, Lushai, Bawm, Pankho, Chak, Khami [Khumi] and Kheyang (Mohsin, 2003, p. 16). Many of these communities also have alternative names. Most people in these ethnic communities are Buddhists with a family structure similar to that in the Hindu religion. These Hill ethnic communities are of Sino-Tibetan descent belonging to the Mongolian racial group; thus, they are ethnically different from the settled populace in Bangladesh. The Hill people closely resemble the people of north-east India, Myanmar and Thailand rather than the Bengali ethnic population of Bangladesh which is made up of people of a "mixed [race] comprising proto-Australoid, Mongoloid, Caucasoid and Dravidian strains" (Ahmed, 1993, as cited in Mohsin, 2002, p. 11). Each group has its own customs, language and dress; therefore, it is presupposed that every group has its own culture. Moreover, these groups can be roughly distinguished by two categories: the groups living in the valley—comprising Chakma, Marma and Tripura—and the other groups who live on the ridges of the hills. This variation in the location of habitation led the British administrator (Deputy Commissioner) Captain T. H. Lewin (who had initially served

---

[6] These 11 ethnic communities were included in the content of the 1997 CHT Peace Agreement with a few changes in spelling of the concerned ethnic communities as mentioned above.

from 1866 to 1869, and again from 1871 to 1874) to categorise the Hill people into Khyoungtha and Toungtha which, in the Burmese-Arakanese language, means 'Children of the River and Children of the Hills', respectively (Lewin, 1869/2011, p. 34). The Chakma, Marma and Tripura are not only the numeric majority of these communities, but they have also assumed power as evidenced by their socio-economic, political and educational advancement. Among many differences, the administrative structure of the CHT and the types of land, including its ownership patterns, differ from plain areas of Bangladesh. This is addressed in detail in Chapter 3.

A segment of Bengali population (the majority ethnic population of Bangladesh) is now living in the Chittagong Hill Tracts (CHT). In the CHT, in 1872, the population comprised 98% Adivasi and 2% Bengali, but the latter has now increased to 47.1% of the CHT population (see Table 1.1 of this chapter and Table 3.1 for details in Chapter 3). Considering the increasing proportion of the Bengali community in the CHT, many Hill people perceive that the Bengalis will become the majority population in the CHT in the near future. The percentages of Hill people and Bengali people (mostly settlers) are also presented in Table 3.1. The CHT have immense geo-strategic and economic importance for Bangladesh. The region is endowed with resources, and its frontiers and boundaries are adjacent to the Indian Ocean that touches Bangladesh via the Bay of Bengal. This opening in the south carries significant geo-strategic importance for an India-locked country like Bangladesh. The CHT touch India's territory which is reckoned with great concern by India in the context of its domestic problem in Seven Sister States.[7]

1.4 Background of the Research Question

The long-standing CHT ethnic conflict began in 1972 during the Bangladesh period (government by Bangladesh) and was between the mainstream Bengali elites and political representatives of the Chittagong Hill Tracts (CHT). Although its roots were laid beginning from the British colonial administration and through the Pakistan regime, the

---

[7] The Seven Sister States comprise the adjacent states (provinces) in north-eastern India: Arunachal Pradesh, Assam, Meghalaya, Manipur, Mizoram, Nagaland and Tripura.

PCJSS, particularly after Bangladesh's independence in 1971, started their claim, asserting the Hill people's distinct socio-cultural and political rights in the CHT which they claimed as their ancestral land (this is addressed in detail in Chapter 3). Collective ownership of land had been a long-term custom in this particular area, a unique feature that differed from other regions of Bangladesh. Along with various other measures, the successive governments of Bangladesh deployed military power to annihilate the PCJSS's opposition. During this protracted conflict, to counter the hegemony of the GoB, the PCJSS resorted to armed struggle under the banner of Shanti Bahini (SB) (Peace Force)—an armed force of the PCJSS—the struggle taking a heavy toll of lives including rebels, soldiers and civilians in the Chittagong Hill Tracts (CHT). Provisionally, the conflict came to an end through the two primary parties—the GoB and the PCJSS—signing the CHT Peace Agreement on 2 December 1997. The CHT Peace Agreement was established under the framework of the Constitution of Bangladesh and maintained full and firm confidence in Bangladesh's sovereignty and integrity. The Agreement consisted of four parts and 72 sections and had the aspiration of upholding the political, economic, social, cultural and educational rights of all citizens of the CHT (for details, see Sect. 4.3 in Chapter 4 and the CHT Peace Agreement attached in Appendix 4). More than two decades have passed since signing the Agreement. However, the PCJSS remains unhappy about the promises made by the GoB in its implementation of the Agreement. Of the total 72 sections/clauses of the Agreement, PCJSS, in a leaflet, claimed that only 25 were fully implemented as against the government's claim of 48 ("Govt Conspires," 2021). These debates are addressed in detail in Chapter 4. Moreover, Jyotirindra Bodhipriya Larma (alias, Santu Larma), President of the PCJSS, mentioned that the CHT Peace Agreement had not been implemented owing to the government's interests (Roy, 2016), with the country's bureaucracy and the army still not willing for the Agreement to be fully implemented ("Full Implementation," 2016).

After signing the CHT Peace Agreement, a sustainable resolution of the conflict foundered on the rock of mutual incompatibility of interests between the parties, that is, the government and the PCJSS. While the former subscribed to the politics of interest, in other words, political, economic, social power, etc., the latter remained plagued by various factions or groups with different conflicting interests. In the sovereign state of Bangladesh, the government has the legislative power as well as the authority to formulate the laws (or to amend the laws) for implementation of the CHT Peace Agreement. At the state level, civil administrators, the army, opposition political parties, public opinion, etc., also have influential power to affect the government's decisions. Along with the GoB, the other state institutions are much concerned about their interests in assuming power (their political interests) and their economic interests or are very much aware of the unitary character of the state. Conversely, the Hill people, particularly the PCJSS, have differences with the GoB regarding the initiatives undertaken to implement the CHT Peace Agreement; for example, the restoration of land rights is one of the prime concerns. Locally, in the CHT, intra-tribal and Bengali–tribal rivalries continue to affect the Agreement's implementation process. On the one hand, the Bengali settlers, who live in the CHT, are not supportive of the Agreement; on the other hand, the post-Agreement CHT-based political party—the United People's Democratic Front (UPDF)—is demanding full autonomy for the region. Meanwhile, to establish some form of self-rule, the PCJSS's struggle has wooed support from the international community, and its various logistical activities have attracted international attention. For example, at the international level, with the formation of the Working Group on Indigenous Populations (WGIP) at the United Nations (UN) in 1982, indigenous people's movements have gained distinctiveness and more space in major global governance institutions. Various private individuals, groups and government and non-governmental organisations (NGOs) have been undertaking initiatives to build up world public opinion for a beneficial solution to the CHT case.

This book has sought to analyse the politics concerned within the dispute of the implementation of the CHT Peace Agreement from a liberal and realist view (this theoretical discussion is addressed in Chapter 2). More explicitly, the political nature of assuming power or of groups' interests is addressed in this research work. To undertake this effort, three levels of analysis have been incorporated, that is, the state level (e.g. the government [GoB], including political parties, the army and the bureaucracy); the local level (e.g. the PCJSS, the UPDF and Bengali settlers); and the international level (including state actors and non-state actors).

1.5 Research Question, Objectives and Hypotheses

After exploring the background of this study, the following research question has been articulated: why do the Government of Bangladesh (GoB), the Hill people and international actors hold different views about the implementation of the CHT Peace Agreement? To explore the research question, the following objectives are specifically examined. The primary (first) objective is to identify the spectrum of interests of the actors in the implementation of the Agreement. Secondly, the other objectives are to critically analyse how those interests have determined the implementation of the Agreement, and, thirdly, to discuss the consequences of the varying interests involved in the implementation of the CHT Peace Agreement. The following hypotheses are formulated and tested: firstly, gaps in interests between the actors in the Agreement's implementation are commonly responsible for different views which remain as obstacles towards its successful implementation, and secondly, the level of influence on the CHT Peace Agreement's implementation differs depending on the actors.

1.6 Originality

Studies in the literature on this specific topic—peace agreement implementation and politics, and particularly the CHT case of Bangladesh—are rare. The earlier studies have mostly analysed the CHT case from historical, socio-cultural, political and economic perspectives as a way to investigate the marginalisation (and alienation) of the Hill people whether in the pre- or post-development phase of the CHT Peace Agreement. These studies reflect the deficiencies in the discourse of politics and peace agreement implementation. As a result, scholars have urged that a new study should be undertaken in this area. A few studies have addressed the topic of implementation after signing the CHT Peace Agreement, with many agreeing on importance of full implementation of all sections of the Agreement. Most authors have attempted to discover some of the causes responsible for the partial implementation of the Agreement. They have then discussed this issue under the ambit of the state-level (here, the government [GoB] is the key actor) and the CHT-based local-level analysis. Although the CHT case is an intra-state conflict in Bangladesh, it has attracted international attention. This could be due to the Hill people's attempts to gain support from the international community, international actors' involvement in the human rights cause or international actors' own interests. This matter has rarely been addressed in the previous literature.

The book attempts to address the implementation of dispute from the perspectives of the state, local and international spheres with the ultimate aim being to analyse this case holistically. In doing so, the politics behind the implementation of the CHT Peace Agreement have been explored. In the political discourse, the interest of assuming power (or other interests) is a central concern in a sovereign state where the government, the army, the bureaucracy, etc., are willing to assume power in the realist sense. In connection with this point, the aspects of politics and peace agreement implementation that have been undertaken are discussed in detail in Chapter 2. The study also addressed the CHT-based local group dynamics that are affecting the CHT Peace Agreement's implementation, as well as the international community's involvement in the case. However, almost all authors in the literature have agreed that the sooner all provisions of the Agreement were implemented, the sooner the problem would be solved, the quicker the peace process would evolve.

On three major counts, the book is unique when compared with the other works of similar nature. First, in the various disciplines of Social Sciences, the specific topics—'politics' and 'peace agreement implementation', and particularly the CHT case of Bangladesh—are found to be absent or, at best, rare. Readers will be able to enrich their epistemological as well as practical knowledge between the nexus of politics and implementation of a peace agreement including its concepts and theories, for example, 'politics', 'peace', 'peace agreement', 'implementation of peace agreement', 'realism', 'liberalism', etc. Second, the case study of the CHT Peace Agreement is analysed from a holistic approach by taking into account a three-tier analysis, that is, state, local and international, whereas earlier studies mostly addressed the CHT case from state-level and CHT-based local-level research. Thus, the study becomes holistic in nature instead of being a narrow one. Third, one significant strength is the collection of primary data through appointments and interviews with notable people who are direct stakeholders in the implementation politics of the CHT Peace Agreement. Their narratives are fundamental in analysing the politics of interest in implementing a peace agreement, in general, and the CHT case, in particular. The information collected from the interviewees will help the global peace researchers/promoters to find out the probable drawbacks of the non-implementation syndrome of a peace agreement.

In summary, the strengths and originality of this book are that it analyses the case of the CHT Peace Agreement's implementation by exploring the political view at the three levels—state, local and international. The logical, analytical perspective adopted here is further elaborated in Chapter 2. Furthermore, in considering interviewees' direct connections and long-term research expertise on the CHT case (details are included in the next section, Sect. 1.7), the strong position taken on the subject matter in this study is warranted.

1.7 Research Method

The research method is the logical explanation of how a study will be conducted, including the techniques (or tools) used for its performance. The study documented in this book is exploratory in nature as it has sought to primarily examine the political interests among the three levels as mentioned earlier that are involved in the case of the CHT Peace Agreement's implementation. Moreover, this empirical field research is conducted both in Bangladesh and in the areas extending beyond its borders. Primarily based on qualitative research, the book considers the social settings of the research object; moreover, quantitative data are also incorporated for further substantiation. For the collection of data, the study relies on existing content, relevant for the analysis of the case of the CHT Peace Agreement's implementation. The relevant analysis has been conducted by reviewing secondary sources, that is, books, research articles from journals or publications, newspapers, magazines, annual reports, on-line documents, documents from the Ministry of Chittagong Hill Tracts Affairs (MoCHTA) and the PCJSS, important documents collected from interviewees, etc. To substantiate these data by content analysis, the primary data, collected using the key informant interview (KII) method with the people concerned, were incorporated.

During the fieldwork in the CHT and other parts of Bangladesh in May–June 2016, this work was arranged in a representative manner with purposive interviews conducted with 30 people. Despite the passage of time, their narratives still add weight as no mentionable or qualitative development has occurred in implementing the CHT Peace Agreement until now; for example, one of the crucial issues of the Agreement, the dispute about the number of implemented sections, continues to remain virtually unchanged. Interviewees came from different professions and were from ethnic backgrounds that incorporated CHT inhabitants as well as people from other parts of Bangladesh. Most respondents participated in an in-depth interview: of the 30 interviews, all except one were conducted in the Bengali language. In the one exception with a scholar from India in Japan, the interview was conducted in the English language. First, the interviewees' narratives were mostly organised and then translated into English from the Bengali language by the author and then incorporated in the text to substantiate the relevant issues of discussion. Of the 29 interviewees from Bangladesh, 18 were CHT-based local people including those with different professional backgrounds, also interviewing those in leadership positions among the PCJSS and UPDF members. The remaining 11 interviewees were Bengali ethnic people: their roles included civil society members, NGO workers, university professors, autonomous organisations' employees, political leaders, Members of Parliament, army, bureaucrats and expert researchers with years of experience of their equivalents. Also, numerous informal conversations were conducted with stakeholders in various societal fields, ranging from those participating in political and civil society activities through to members of religious institutions, and the general public. A self-administered, semi-structured questionnaire (or checklist) was developed to collect data from respondents (see Appendix 1).

In a representative way, the sample interviewees were purposively selected considering their long-term research expertise and empirical experience in the CHT case. Their in-depth knowledge, direct connectedness with the issue and respective position vis-à-vis implementation and/or non-implementation of the CHT Peace Agreement are the factors to be reckoned with great significance. The primary parties that were intensively interviewed by the author consist of persons belonging to policy (decision making) level authority. For example, Jyotirindra Bodhipriya Larma, popularly known as Santu Larma—President of the PCJSS and Chairman of the Chittagong Hill Tracts Regional Council (CHTRC)—who signed the Agreement on behalf of the CHT inhabitants, was personally interviewed by the author. At the government (GoB) policy level, for example, Members of Parliament, Ministers and the Chairman of the Parliamentary Standing Committee on the Ministry of the Hill Tracts were all personally interviewed by the researcher. Raja Devasish Roy—Chief of Chakma Circle, Member of UN Permanent Forum on Indigenous Issues, Member (ex-officio) of Advisory

Committee MoCHTA—was interviewed by the author to analyse the implementation politics of a peace agreement at the national level as well as at international level. Moreover, interviews were conducted with army officers who were posted to the CHT, bureaucrats in the CHT and CHT-based local people. The interviewee cluster also includes many common and general people with direct or indirect linkage with the conflict. Conducting these interviews and analysing the secondary data led to the initiative being taken to explore the politics (or interest) behind the case of the CHT Peace Agreement's implementation. The list in Appendix 2 substantiates this point by presenting their professional background, experience and involvement in the CHT case.

As mentioned above, the study reported in this book is primarily qualitative in nature with content analysis and key informant interviews that constitute the primary sources of data to find answer to the research question while targeting the objectives. To achieve this, subsequent chapters have been organised to include analysis of their content while also presenting comparative discussion. As secondary data may not always be effective in exposing the real scenario, here, for example, on the issue of the CHT Peace Agreement's implementation, the study's use of primary data is considered valuable. In this way, the in-depth key informant interviews have been incorporated to find out the underlying relevant facts about the politics of implementation. The interviewees' narratives were extensively evaluated and included as references to substantiate the content analysis (as presented mainly in Chapters 5, 6 and 7). Based on the primary and secondary data, the analysis and findings are presented in Chapter 8, followed by the conclusion in Chapter 9.

1.8 OVERVIEW OF CHAPTERS

This book is organised into nine chapters, with each chapter presented from a different perspective. However, the chapters are closely connected through their scrutiny of the relationships between the CHT Peace Agreement's implementation and the politics between the various actors. These chapters are briefly discussed below.

After the introduction in this first chapter, the next chapter (Chapter 2) sheds light on the theoretical and conceptual discussion as well as presenting the analytical framework developed to address the politics of peace agreement implementation in the CHT case. Two broad theoretical approaches, namely realism and liberalism, are applied for direction, with a discussion of neorealism and neoliberalism, respectively. In the theoretical approach of realism, the discussion of the struggle for power or political interest is at the centre. Also, liberalism has been associated with creating favourable conditions for peace (Garner et al., 2009, p. 361). The relevant concepts, namely 'politics', 'peace', 'peace agreement' and 'implementation of peace agreement', are also analysed in this chapter. The second section of Chapter 2 presents an analytical framework that has been developed based on three levels of analysis, that is, the state level (e.g. the GoB, the army and the bureaucracy); the local level (e.g. the PCJSS, the UPDF and Bengali settlers); and the international level (e.g. state actors and non-state actors).

Chapter 3 takes a systematic approach to outlining the background of the CHT conflict and its apparent management through the signing of the CHT Peace Agreement in 1997. Although the Hill people were mostly politically independent during the pre-colonial period, the process of their marginalisation mostly had its origin under the British colonial rulers. The marginalisation process and the plight of these Hill communities continued under the Pakistan and Bangladesh regimes, either through different new projects or following on from previous measures. Following these bitter experiences, the Hill people demanded constitutional autonomy, including their own legislature, on the verge of the formation of the Constitution of Bangladesh; however, their demand was subsequently rejected. The later history involved two decades of armed conflict between the PCJSS insurgents and the Bangladesh security forces: this ended with the signing of the CHT Peace Agreement in 1997 through a long negotiation process. As the Agreement and its crucial provisions are not yet fully implemented, the questions are becoming more complicated. These queries relate to the implementing agencies' real intentions and their respective interests.

Chapter 4 presents the comparative discussion about the dispute over the current implementation status of the sections of the CHT Peace Agreement. As the Agreement's implementation status is very much connected with understanding the implementing agencies' real motives, the acute need is to analyse the gap in the implementation status as claimed by the two primary signatory parties—the GoB and the PCJSS. Moreover, Chapter 4 briefly discusses two interrelated issues, that is: (1) contributory factors responsible for the signing of the 1997 CHT Peace Agreement and (2) key features of the Agreement. Although the Agreement was signed (and negotiated) between the GoB and the PCJSS, some actors in Bangladesh and internationally had incentives to become involved in the process.

Following the foundation laid in the earlier chapters, the empirical discussions in Chapters 5, 6 and 7 address the three levels of analysis.

Chapter 5 mostly addresses the empirical discussion at the state level through the analysis of the primary and secondary data collected from various sources. At the state level, the GoB has the authoritative power to formulate new laws and define existing laws for the CHT Peace Agreement's implementation. Moreover, in the implementation process, the GoB (specifically, the mainstream Bengali political party which formed the government) must frequently consider various issues, for example, the willingness to assume the state's power, opposition political parties' reaction, the state's sovereignty, constitutional supremacy, etc. The involvement of the army and the bureaucracy in the CHT case is also inseparable as the CHT problem was under the Bangladesh army's direct control until the signing of the Peace Agreement in 1997, and the bureaucracy was/is one of the implementing agencies at the CHT-based local level. Each of these groups (e.g. the GoB, opposition political parties, the army and the bureaucracy) have viewed the Agreement with their own respective interests in mind, that is, the assumption of power, political interests, economic interests and/or other interests; these interests are mostly analysed from the perspective of realist view.

Chapter 6 presents the empirical study of the primary and secondary data in seeking to address how the CHT Peace Agreement's implementation is concerned with the CHT-based local-level group (also community) dynamics. Here, the CHT Peace Agreement's beneficiaries are primarily the Hill people and more specifically the PCJSS. Therefore, the acute need is to address the group dynamics between (Bengali–tribal) and within (intra-tribal) the ethnic communities and how these rivalries are affecting the Agreement's implementation.

Chapter 7 explores international actors' involvement in the CHT case using primary data and secondary data from various sources. In today's globalised society, many sub-nationalist movements, like those that have arisen over the CHT case, have an international connection, with the involvement of both state and non-state actors. The involvement of these international actors is generally due to the Hill communities seeking their support, the international actors' encouragement on human rights causes or the international actors pursuing their interests.

Chapter 8 mainly comprises the study's analysis with the significant findings presented based on the exploration in the earlier chapters. In doing so, this chapter firstly aims at broad analysis to scrutinise the reasons why gaps in recognising the status of the CHT Peace Agreement's implementation have occurred at the above three levels. The chapter briefly revisits the earlier chapters and then draws the study's significant findings. To answer the research question, the hypotheses are tested in the second section of this chapter. The hypotheses were formulated to find out if wider gaps in the interests (whether political, economic or other areas of interest) of the actors were responsible for different views that presented obstacles accountable for the partial implementation of the CHT Peace Agreement. Through its summary of the main stages of the arguments, Chapter 8 also addresses the research objectives.

Finally, the conclusion is presented in Chapter 9 by reviewing the politics in actors' interests. This chapter presents the policy recommendations, implication of the study and avenues for further research. In the section of comparative analysis with other peace agreement, this chapter includes a discussion encompassing north-eastern India (e.g. Mizo and Nagaland's peace initiatives), Tamil crisis in Sri Lanka and the Free Aceh Movement in Indonesia, where the state/government authorities' supremacy is markedly present in signing the peace agreements or implementing existing peace agreements.

References

Bangladesh Bureau of Statistics. (2015). *Bangladesh population and housing census 2011, national report, volume-1, analytical report*. Ministry of Planning, Government of the People's Republic of Bangladesh.

Bangladesh Bureau of Statistics. (2019). *Statistical pocket book Bangladesh 2018*. Ministry of Planning, Government of the People's Republic of Bangladesh.

Bangladesh Bureau of Statistics. (2020). *Statistical pocket book Bangladesh 2019*. Ministry of Planning, Government of the People's Republic of Bangladesh.

Bleie, T. (2005). *Tribal peoples, nationalism and the human rights challenge: The adivasis of Bangladesh*. The University Press Limited.

Full implementation of CHT accord: Frustrations over failure in 19 years. (2016, December 2). *The Daily Star*. https://www.thedailystar.net/frontpage/full-implementation-cht-accord-frustrations-over-failure-19-years-1323913. Accessed 1 October 2020.

Garner, R., Ferdinand, P., & Lawson, S. (2009). *Introduction to politics*. Oxford University Press Inc.

Govt conspires against CHT peace accord: Santu Larma. (2021, December 3). *New Age*, p. 2.

Lewin, T. H. (2011). *The hill tracts of Chittagong and the dwellers therein, with comparative vocabularies of the hill dialects*. Khudra Nrigoshthir Cultural Institute. (Original work published 1869).

Mohsin, A. (2002). *The politics of nationalism: The case of the Chittagong hill tracts, Bangladesh*. The University Press Ltd.

Mohsin, A. (2003). *The Chittagong hill tracts, Bangladesh: On the difficult road to peace*. Lynne Rienner Publishers Inc.

Roy, P. (2016, December 2). CHT peace accord: Only 26 of 72 clauses implemented. *The Daily Star*. https://www.thedailystar.net/frontpage/only-26-out-72-clauses-implemented-1323907. Accessed 1 October 2020.

Royhan, S. A. (2016). *The Chittagong hill tracts*. Kalikolom Prokashona.

Shelley, M. R. (Ed.). (1992). *The Chittagong hill tracts of Bangladesh: The untold story*. Centre For Development Research.

CHAPTER 2

Politics of Peace Agreement Implementation: Theoretical Reflections

2.1 CHAPTER INTRODUCTION

The primary aim of this chapter is to develop a theoretical framework that is applicable for analysing the politics of the CHT Peace Agreement's implementation. Following this aim, in addition to the introduction and conclusion, this chapter is organised into three sections. Section 2.2 begins with the analysis of theoretical approaches and concepts relating to the book. This section starts with the discussion of two theoretical approaches—liberalism and realism—and extends to discuss neoliberalism, neorealism and International Society theories. The current study focuses a realist view in its analysis of the interest of assuming (controlling of) power (a core concept of politics) and a liberal way of thinking towards achieving some of the demands of the CHT Peace Agreement's beneficiaries through its implementation. Here, several concepts, such as 'politics', 'peace', 'peace agreement' and 'implementation of peace agreement', are discussed in seeking to answer the research question, that is, why do the Government of Bangladesh (the GoB), the Hill people and international actors hold different views about the implementation of the CHT Peace Agreement? In the academic parlance of peace agreement implementation, the discussion of the liberal view of peace is essential as the willingness to implement is mainly motivated by liberal thinking. However, in the realist view, the primary concern of states is to maximise their relative power and to protect their interests domestically and internationally. In this way, the study of peace or peace agreement implementation is closely linked with the theoretical approaches of liberalism and realism, or neoliberalism and neorealism, respectively.

Political thinkers, for example, Lasswell (1950), defined politics (or political science) as the study of "influence or the influential", and he synonymously used the terms "power and the powerful" (pp. 3–19): these are core concepts in the discussion of realism (or neorealism). Moreover, in the discussions of Lasswell (1950) and Lord Bryce (Bryce, as cited in Carpenter, 1936), the probability of the few getting more (e.g. from the government at the state level) acknowledges the political character of the state's supremacy, with this probability profound in analysing the real intentions of agencies implementing a peace agreement, for example, the CHT Peace Agreement. Garner added his view, along the same lines, to the discussion that power and authority are the centres in the study of politics with the state being the ultimate source of authoritative power in formulating new laws (or amending existing laws) for implementing a peace agreement (Garner et al., 2009, pp. 5–7). These academic discussions are broadened in Sect. 2.2 of this chapter (theoretical and conceptual analysis). The CHT Peace Agreement's beneficiaries (here, primarily, the PCJSS) might have emphasised on implementing all sections of the Agreement. Mostly, in the liberal view, this party owned the Agreement so it could fulfil many of its demands. In today's globalised society, some national issues draw international attention as, in many cases, domestic politics relate to international politics. In the case of the CHT Peace Agreement, the international community is mostly involved through its concern about the human rights cause, but other examples are of international actors being involved in due to their interests. This can, therefore, be discussed in both the liberal and realist views. However, in Sect. 2.3, an analytical framework is developed, where three levels of analysis—the state, the CHT-based local and the international levels—are developed. Section 2.4 presents the theoretical and analytical design, with these illustrated in Fig. 2.1, with this section followed by the chapter's conclusion.

2.2 THEORETICAL AND CONCEPTUAL ANALYSIS

Realism and liberalism offer ways of thinking about politics, not only by academics but also by politicians and citizens of states. According to the discussion of Jackson and Sorensen (2013), the state is the major actor, with the power of the state strongly noted, and the strong can dominate the weak (p. 121). Classical realism is considered a traditional approach to the analysis of politics in the international sphere as well as in the national sphere. Basically, this normative approach considers the focal point to be the core political principles of national security and state sovereignty. On the other hand, liberals have emphasised the need for a distinction that peace is not merely the absence of war, as most realists believe. Various dimensions are associated with the concept of peace. A relevant understanding is that peace is more than merely the absence of war. However, in many cases, state interests are the ultimate arbiter in judging or formulating policy concerning peace or peace agreement implementation. To scrutinise the politics relating to the CHT Peace Agreement's implementation, it is essential to analyse the relevant theories and concepts in the context of this research, as addressed in the following sub-sections.

2.2.1 *Liberalism, Realism, Neoliberalism and Neorealism*

The liberal approach is closely connected with the emergence of the modern constitutional state, and liberal thinkers perceive that significant potential exists for humanitarian reasons in the modern state to secure individual liberty. As noted by Lawson, "[a]s we have seen, liberalism has also been closely associated with ideas about creating positive conditions for peace" (Garner et al., 2009, p. 361). Early liberal thinkers, for example, Locke (1632–1704), Kant (1724–1804) and Bentham (1748–1832), focused on freedom, cooperation, peace and progress in the academic discourse of classical liberalism (Locke, Kant and Bentham, as cited in Jackson & Sorensen, 2013, p. 102). On the other hand, classical realists, such as Thucydides, Machiavelli and Hobbes, discussed realism in a way in which the grammar and vocabulary of power were central. Here, power is possessed not only as a dimension of political life but also as the substance of political responsibility. According to E. H. Carr, the sharp critic of liberal idealism, philosophical conflicts of interest are present both between countries and between people (Carr, as cited in Jackson & Sorensen, 2013, p. 39). The book, *Politics among Nations:*

The Struggle for Power and Peace, by Morgenthau, the leading classical realist of the twentieth century, is one of the best works in interpreting the summary of realism's core arguments. Briefly, the classical realism of Morgenthau and Carr denotes a pessimistic view of human nature associated with the notion of power politics between states that subsists in international anarchy.

> According to Morgenthau (1965), men and women are by nature political animals: they are born to pursue power and to enjoy the fruits of power. Morgenthau speaks of the *animus dominandi*, the human 'lust' for power (Morgenthau 1965: 192). The craving for power dictates a search not only for relative advantages but also for a secure political space—i.e., territory— to maintain oneself and to enjoy oneself free from the political dictates of others. The ultimate political space within which security can be arranged and enjoyed is, of course, the independent state. (Morgenthau, 1965, as cited in Jackson & Sorensen, 2013, pp. 72–73)

Realism contested liberalism and remained the dominant theoretical approach in political analysis. Within this theoretical contest, liberal thinkers sought to formulate an alternative to realist thinking which would avoid the utopian phenomenon of earlier liberalism. Scholars termed it 'neoliberalism' which is considered to be the renewed approach to liberal thinking. Neoliberalism also shares old liberal thoughts about the possibility of development and change, but it puts idealism aside. In a nutshell, within the debate between liberalism and realism, post-Second World War liberalism, well known as neoliberalism, was analysed as four main strands of thinking: sociological liberalism; interdependence liberalism; institutional liberalism; and republican liberalism (Nye, Keohane, Zacher and Matthew, as cited in Jackson & Sorensen, 2013, p. 102). In current neoliberalism, for example, sociological liberalism emphasises transnational relationships, that is, relationships between people, groups, organisations and societies belonging to different countries as these are more cooperative as well as more supportive of peace than are relationships between national government. In the view of Rosenau (1980), "the concept of transnational relations ... suggest[s] dynamic processes initiated and suggested by people" (p. 1). Interdependence liberals pay special attention to economic ties between people and government, believing that this would lead to political integration and peace. Institutional liberals illustrate that international institutions would promote cooperation between states. Democratic liberalism is the idea that liberal democracies improve the potential for peace as they do not have the mobility to engage in war against each other. Conversely, Waltz's (2010) book, *Theory of International Politics*, sets forth a significantly different realist theory which is most often referred to as 'neorealism'.

Waltz departs sharply from the classical realist argument based on human nature viewed as 'plain bad' and thus leading to conflict and confrontation. For Waltz, states are power-seeking and security conscious not because of human nature but rather because the structure of the international system compels them to be that way. (Waltz, as cited in Jackson & Sorensen, 2013, p. 49)

This point of Waltz's analysis is essential as it is the basis for neorealism's counter-attack against neoliberalism. Also, neorealists do not deny the potential for cooperation between states; however, within this cooperation, neorealists argue that states will always fight to maximise their relative power and to protect their autonomy.

2.2.2 Synthesis of Neoliberalism and Neorealism

During the 1980s, some neoliberals and neorealists initiated the sharing of a common analytical point which is mostly neorealist in character, namely that states are the central actors and they continually pursue their own best interest. Similarly, during the 1990s, scholars, for example, Robert Keohane, and Martin and Barry Buzan, endeavoured to formulate a synthesis of neoliberalism and neorealism coming from both the neoliberal and neorealist sides. Nevertheless, no complete synthesis has been achieved between the two theoretical approaches, and the debate continues. According to scholars from the International Society (also known as the English School), conflict and cooperation are simultaneously present in a society, that is, the state and individual citizens. These different relative aspects cannot be simplified and abstracted into a single theory underlining one explanatory variable—that is, power. In reviewing these aspects, International Society scholars called attention to the simultaneous presence of both liberal and realist elements. The next sub-section discusses the concepts relevant to this study, as mentioned in this chapter's introductory section.

2.2.3 Politics

It is difficult to give one definition of politics. Politics is defined from various perspectives. The study of politics dates back to the Greeks: the Greek philosophers—Plato and Aristotle—have made a significant contribution in this field with Aristotle credited as being the founding father of political science. In the words of Sabine (1964), "[f]or Aristotle ... political science became empirical, though not exclusively descriptive; and the art included the improvement of political life even though this has to be done on a modest scale" (p. 116). The term 'politics' is derived from the Greek word *polis*—meaning a city-state—with its derivatives, *polites*—a citizen—and the adjective, *politikos*—civic. The concept of politics has been divided into two broad subdivisions: (i) political philosophy, or theoretical or deductive politics, and (ii) historical, applied or inductive politics. The English author Sir Frederick Pollock divided these sections as presented in Table 2.1.

The first subdivision, theoretical politics, is concerned with the discussion of the fundamental characteristics of the state or with the formulation of the ends and limits of state authority, without specific reference to the actions of the government. The state is an abstractive subject which is often substituted by its visible existence—the government of the concerned state. Therefore, the government is the format through which the purposes of the state seek to be attained.

Table 2.1 Scope of theoretical and applied politics

Theoretical Politics	Applied Politics
A. Theory of the State	A. The State (actual forms of government)
B. Theory of Government	B. Government (the working of governments, administration, etc.)
C. Theory of Legislation	C. Laws and Legislation (procedures, courts, etc.)
D. Theory of the State as an artificial person	D. The State personified (diplomacy, peace, wars, international dealings)

Source Pollock, as cited in Gilchrist, 1952, p. 1

It [theoretical politics] asks: What are the purposes of political organization and what are the best means of realizing them? The individual wants to realize his best self; to what extent can the State help him in this, his natural endeavour? What is the nature of the authority of the State? Has the State, for instance, unlimited power to regulate the thought and activities of individuals or are there limitations to its powers? Has the individual rights against the State ... and inter-State relations are also of great importance to political theory. (Appadorai, 1952, pp. 3–4)

Naturally, the study of politics should then include an analysis of government, as well as its activities. In this connection, the second subdivision, applied politics, incorporates the actual activities of the state through its governmental bodies and with its various organisations (or institutions). The principle of the state may be as varied as its forms, and the workings of governmental bodies have not always been to the same pattern. By applying the inductive process and studying the past and the present, political thinkers are often able to formulate the principles regarding the organisations of the government concerned, its structure and activities. For example, a systematic study of government including their past and present history tells us that "[p]ower tends to corrupt and absolute power corrupts absolutely".[1] Such a study builds an understanding of the principles of governmental organisations as well as the knowledge that incorporates comparative discussion of the types of the legislature, executive and judiciary. However, the subject matter of these two subdivisions often incorporates discussion of the other, as both centre on the state or the government.

Moreover, the discussion of politics is comprehensive and practical: in the modern era, it covers the state, the government, citizens, institutions, etc., which together have overtaken the only etymological meaning of the Greek word—*polis*. As noted by Appadorai:

> Politics may therefore be defined as 'the science concerned with the State and of the conditions essential to its existence and development'; or, in the words of Janet, 'that part of social science which treats of the foundations of the State and the principles of government'. (Appadorai, 1952, p. 4)

As the subject of politics covers the entire field of political science, the term 'political science' is often substituted for the term 'politics'. As addressed by Gilchrist:

---

[1] The quoted phrase is attributed to nineteenth-century British politician Lord Acton.

Sidgwick, for example, declares that the study of Political Science, or, as he calls it Politics, "is concerned primarily with constructing, on the basis of certain psychological premises, the system of relations which ought to be established among the persons governing, and between them and the governed, in a society composed of civilised men, as we know them". (Sidgwick, as cited in Gilchrist, 1952, p. 3)

As with other sciences categorised into the social sciences, political science also includes the discussion of the relationships of men in society, and as each man is essentially connected with the state (this is a particular subject matter of political science), each social science is, to some extent, political science. Although it is not possible for the absolute separation of the social sciences, it is possible to separate the various branches of the discipline. For example, economics or political economy deal with wealth; sociology with the forms of social phenomena—unions, social laws and ideals; and political science with the state and the government in general. Political thinkers generally agree that politics deal with the state or the government, meaning, by that term, the people or group of people organised by law within a fixed territory. However, the specific types of the subject matter of these social sciences are not watertight; they often touch one another at various points of research.

Lasswell (1950), in his famous book, *Politics: Who Gets What, When, How*, stated that "the study of politics is the study of influence and the influential" (p. 3). Moreover, he applied the term 'political science' as a substitute for the term 'politics'. For example, he wrote that "[p]olitical science, then, is the study of influence and the influential. Influence is determined based on shares in the values which are chosen for purposes of the analysis" (Lasswell, 1950, p. 25). In the interpretation of "influence and the influential", he synonymously used the concepts of "power and the powerful" (Lasswell, 1950, p. 19). The influential are not to be satisfactorily described by using a single index but with selected terms, for example, class, skill, personality and attitude. It is mentioned again that the influential cannot be defined in the explanation of John Adams as "the rich, the well-born, and the able" (Adams, as cited in Carpenter, 1936, p. 1175). And, in this analysis, the government continues to exist. In this connection, we may emphasise Lord Bryce's analysis of government by the few, but "it is impossible to locate the few without considering the many" (Bryce, as cited in Carpenter, 1936, p. 1175). In this discussion, the current study agrees with Lasswell and Bryce's arguments about the probability that the few (e.g. the government) will gain more than the many.

In this connection, Garner noted that the question of the power and authority of a state is central to the study of politics (Garner et al., 2009, pp. 5–7). Moreover, he also mentioned Barbara Goodwin's view that "[p]olitical theory may … be defined as the discipline which aims to explain, justify or criticize the disposition of power in society" (Goodwin, 2007, as cited in Garner et al., 2009, p. 7). However, authority is very much related to sovereignty. The state is a sovereign body in the sense that it has the supreme authority to making laws within a specific territory. Ultimately, the state has assumed the power to exercise or implement, rules over individuals ('the many') as, in a state (or government), the term 'authority' is often used interchangeably with the term 'power'. However, some scholars have drawn much wider boundaries for political power with these extending beyond the state: they incorporate the politics found in various groups ranging from the family to international societies. The perspective of politics applied in the current research work is analysed in sub-Sect. 2.2.7.

2.2.4 Conceptualisation of Peace

Peace, like an umbrella, conceptually covers a vast area from the individual to the national and international spheres. A general expression of human desires is that people are eager to have a peaceful life, yet it is quite difficult to achieve peace. Moreover, it is challenging to conceptualise the term 'peace' as it is a relative phenomenon that involves multifaceted dimensions of analysis depending on, among others, an ideological, socio-cultural or political sense; and the interpretation of peace may differ from person to person as well as between conflicting parties. While in understanding with most philosophers' view that peace is a complex, long-term and multi-layered process, the attempt has been made in the current study to conceptualise the term 'peace' from different angles.

In academic parlance, the term 'peace', as a concept, was analysed in detail by Johan Galtung—the founder of the discipline of peace and conflict studies. The properties of peace thinking are indicated by Galtung (1967) as: "it [peace] is usually vague, confused and contradictory" (p. 6). He compared the terms 'peace' and 'happiness', considering that happiness would be used more at the individual level, while peace could attract global, collective concern. Galtung (1967) addressed three directions (or concepts) of peace, the first of which is the old idea of peace as a synonym for stability or equilibrium. According to him, "[i]t also covers the 'law and order' concept, in other words the idea of a predictable social order even if this order is brought about by means of force and the threat of force" (Galtung, 1967, p. 12). He then discussed peace under two broad concepts—positive peace and negative peace. The second concept, 'negative peace',

> is the idea of peace as the absence of organized collective violence, in other words, violence between major human groups; particularly nations, but also between classes and between racial and ethnic groups because of the magnitude internal wars can have. (Galtung, 1967, p. 12)

Here, the word 'violence' is used mainly in the "sense of biological and physical force" or as the "efforts to cause bodily harm to other human beings". Then, the third concept—positive peace—is addressed as:

> This is peace as a synonym for all other good things in the world community, particularly cooperation and integration between human groups, with less emphasis on the absence of violence. ... the concept would exclude major violence, but tolerate occasional violence. (Galtung, 1967, p. 12)

This concept of positive peace seems to be particularly widespread in underprivileged groups—groups that are less oriented to the status quo. Conversely, both the first and the second concepts would meet with more ready acceptance in over-privileged groups: these groups are interested in stability (or equilibrium), and law and order, and uninterested in violence as any violence would be perpetrated against them (Galtung, 1967, p. 12).

McDougal (1991) again defined the concept as "peace is the least application of violence and coercion to the individual and to the freedom of access of the individual to cherished values" (p. 139). On the other hand, Laue (1991) described peace as not only a cherished value desired by individuals or states, but also.

> a process of continuous and constructive management of differences toward the goal of more mutually satisfying relations, the prevention of escalation of violence and the achievement of those conditions that exemplify the universal well-being of human beings and their groups from the family to the culture and the state. (p. 301)

It is evident from this definition that Laue (1991) analysed the peace discourse from the viewpoint of the micro-level to the macro-level, that is, from the family to the state level. Moreover, according to him, peace includes the condition where everyone in the global arena lives gently, and every person has an equal opportunity to have access to the world's resources and amenities. This leads to a question in society: how would peace prevail when a privileged group of people (a section of the total population of a society) live in advantaged circumstances while the vast majority of citizens are struggling to escape from poverty? This group rivalry is also addressed and discussed in detail in Galtung's writings, with this concisely incorporated in the earlier paragraph. The proponents of social positive peace have emphasised the elimination of poverty and the establishment of social justice as these positive phenomena are the true conditions for achieving a peaceful society. In connection with this point, Galtung (1967) mentioned the following ten examples for positive peace: presence of cooperation; freedom from fear; freedom from want; economic growth and development; absence of exploitation; equality; justice; freedom of action; pluralism; and dynamism (p. 14). However, if critically examined, the positive and negative concepts of peace are not unrelated. For example, human experiences reveal that the absence of violence (or conflict) may promote economic development, social justice, political stability, etc. Thus, the concept of peace not only deals with the integration of human society but also with the very forces and stipulations that cause the minimisation of significant violence (at times, occasional violence/conflict is used as a way forward for underprivileged groups).

2.2.5 Definition of Peace Agreement

In conflict-prone societies, particularly in areas of armed conflict, a deal for a peace agreement between rival parties is sought. The peace agreement often exhibits specific negotiation capability for the provisions and commitments of the parties in conflict to achieve a durable peace. These arrangements are sought by the rival parties before they commit themselves to the object of realising peace. Following Galtung's (1964) discussion about negative and positive peace, that is, "negative peace which is the absence of violence, absence of war — and positive peace which is the integration of human society" (p. 2), a peace agreement can be considered as successful if it has been durable throughout the process of addressing the grievances of underprivileged groups. In connection with this point, emphasis can be placed on the negative aspect of peace and, in particular, focusing on the conflictive behaviour of belligerent nations to address the conditions under which violence (or conflict) can be reduced. More than the absence of violence (or conflict), peace can also be attained through emphasising the positive aspect of peace and taking into account some measures, for example, the provisions for the well-being of the parties in conflict or the ten examples as introduced by Galtung.

However, a peace agreement is defined "as an arrangement entered into by warring parties to explicitly regulate or resolve the basic incompatibility" (Wallensteen & Sollenberg, 1997, p. 357). Bell (2000) classified three main types of peace agreements, that is, pre-negotiation, framework/substantive and implementation (p. 25). With regard to a state-based definition, according to the Department of Peace and Conflict Research (n.d.), Uppsala University, "[a] peace agreement is a formal agreement between warring parties, which addresses the disputed incompatibility, either by settling all or part of it, or by clearly outlining a process for how the warring parties plan to regulate the incompatibility". In defining the peace agreement, Stedman et al. (2002) incorporated the role of international mediators along with the conflicting parties within the state territory. To define a peace agreement, Stedman (2002) emphasised a standard that would serve as a formal marker of commitment to war termination and would allow a focus on the ability of outsiders (international mediators or international peace implementers) to get parties to comply with formal commitments (p. 22). In the end, Stedman et al. (2002) agreed on the definition, proposed by Peter Wallensteen and Margareta Sollenberg (1997), as mentioned above.

2.2.6 Implementation of Peace Agreement

Following a peace deal, sustainable peace is assured by the successful implementation of the peace agreement. Before focusing on the discussion of implementing a peace agreement, academics have mainly emphasised getting rival parties to sign an agreement to end their specific conflict. This view nearly overlooks the importance of the phase after the deal is signed, the implementation of the agreement. A peace agreement may be well-drafted and incorporate appropriate provisions; however, if these resources are not dedicated to its implementation, the strong possibility is that it will be unsuccessful. For example, a willingness to implementing the agreement should be required from both sides, and the agreement should seek their initiatives in this regard. A peace agreement is like a theory (or a document): it details in writing what should be done. However, the implementation of a peace agreement is more practical; it deals with what is happening in accordance with the provisions of the agreement. Without looking at the implementation status, a vital phase in the peace process, the real destination of promoting peace would have no context. Placing importance on implementation is one of the best ways to enhance the peace agreement, giving it room to grow and mature.

A peace agreement is signed not only to stop violence (or conflict): it should also address the root causes to stop the fighting between the parties in conflict, allowing them to solve future problems in a friendly way. The subjects that can affect the implementation process are varied and display a wide range of factors that need to be considered with the intention of developing a durable peace. When an agreement is signed, all measures need to be incorporated with the aim being to ensure the conflicting parties do not return to the conflict situation that marked the pre-agreement period. Hampson's (1996) *Nurturing Peace: Why Peace Settlements Succeed or Fail* was the first book that addressed in detail the reasons why some peace agreements fail while others succeed in ending civil wars. According to his analysis, the following four answers are contributing factors for the successful implementation of the peace agreement:

> (1) the role of third-party interventions in facilitating dispute resolution; (2) the structural characteristics of [the] conflict process; (3) the changing dynamics of regional and/or systemic power relationships; and (4) the range of issues covered by the peace settlement in question. (Hampson, 1996, pp. 8–9)

Likewise, Stedman and Rothchild (1996) argued that the following six recurrent problems negatively affected the implementation of peace agreements:

> incomplete, vague and expedient agreements; lack of coordination between mediators and those who have to implement an agreement; lack of coordination between implementing agencies; lack of sustained attention by the international community; incomplete fulfilment of agreements by warring parties; and the presence of 'spoilers' who seek to destroy any incipient peace. (p. 17)

In their edited book titled *Ending Civil Wars: The Implementation of Peace Agreements*, Stedman et al. (2002) incorporated various issues that needed addressing for the successful implementation of peace agreements including evaluation of international actors' roles, in some states, as case studies. In the theoretical aspect of case studies, issues ranging from demobilisation, disarmament, human rights, mediation, strategic coordination, transitional authority, elections, refugee repatriation, reconciliation, building local capacity, etc., have been addressed (including their relationships) in the writings of renowned peace study researchers. In the above book, Stedman (2002) mentioned that "[p]eace implementation is the process of carrying out a specific peace agreement" (p. 2). Moreover, he noted that:

> ... [w]hen peace agreements leave important matters undecided, then the warring parties are much more likely to hedge their bets, take advantage when provisions of an agreement are not specified, and interpret ambiguous terms in ways that benefit them during implementation. (Stedman, 2002, p. 9)

In the preceding discussion, the works of Hampson (1996); Stedman and Rothchild (1996); and Stedman et al. (2002) have been analysed with these authors mentioning some factors that are possibly responsible for the successful (or failed) implementation of the peace agreement. Comparing these studies in the peace agreement discourse, the CHT Peace Agreement is typical in primarily two aspects, that is: the absence of international mediators in the peace agreement negotiating process and that, unlike the case in some African regions, the CHT case was not a civil war. For example, according to the Uppsala Conflict Data Program [UCDP] (n.d.), the political and economic marginalisation of the CHT's indigenous people was responsible for the armed conflict in the Chittagong Hill Tracts (CHT).

If the implementation aspect of an agreement fails, the progress of getting the parties in conflict to be peaceful will be useless as this conflict is likely to recur. Getting these parties back to the negotiating table should not be the focus or be considered as the whole picture.

> [W]e tend to attach to 'agreement' the idea that negotiations are over when in fact they are just beginning, and to continue they require a shift from a temporary effort to negotiate an agreement to a context-based,

permanent, and dynamic platform capable of regenerating solutions to ongoing episodes of conflict. (Borer, 2006, as cited in Ben-Porat, 2008, p. 1)

If the conflict is a resurgence, a renegotiation process may again be effective to solve the problem. Also, recurrences of armed conflict risk plunging a democratic state into anarchy, resulting in what has been termed 'the fragile state'.

2.2.7 Operationalisation of the Definitions

From these discussions, it is evident that the research question and hypotheses, formulated in Chapter 1, are much linked to those as mentioned in theoretical and conceptual discussion above. On the one hand, in discussing the peace agreement (or its implementation), the first/common view is the liberal impetus as the conflicting parties initially had the affirmative willingness to mitigate the conflict. On the other hand, it is also challenging to overcome the dominant discourse of the realist view in the national and international political arenas. The research topic—politics and peace agreement implementation—also has a close connection as the implementation issue, in many cases, is subjugated by politics. Here, the definition of politics is operationalised by interests— the interest of assuming power (or of controlling/exercising power), economic interest or other interests.

Simply speaking, the CHT Peace Agreement was signed between the GoB and the PCJSS with the hope of bringing peace to the CHT in Bangladesh. With the inclusion of many disagreements, the two primary parties, even today, have not attained consensus on how many sections of the Agreement have been implemented. As many sections (including many crucial subjects) of the Agreement have not been implemented, questions have been raised about the real motives of the implementing agencies. This is viewed as being mainly linked to their interests. On the one hand, at the state level, the GoB, the army, the bureaucracy, mainstream Bengali political parties, etc., have their interests. On the other hand, at the CHT-based local level, the PCJSS, the UPDF and Bengali settlers have viewed the CHT Peace Agreement from their perspectives which relate to their interests either in implementing the Agreement or in disagreeing with its signing. The CHT case is also connected to the international community. The reason could be that the Hill people have sought support from the international community or only it has responded due to the human rights cause, even though the international community was not directly involved in the Agreement. Although many members of the international community have liberal enthusiasm for the human rights cause, some international actors have also served their interests, that is, their political, economic or strategic interests.

This discussion has revealed that various actors hold different views about the formulation of the CHT Peace Agreement and its implementation issue. These different views are mainly derived from their own interests, whether from liberal or realist motivation. Thus, by looking at what interests are present, how these interests are associated with the CHT Peace Agreement and what the consequences of these interests are, is one way to discover the politics behind the partial (or weak) implementation of the Agreement. This research technique has been applied here at the CHT-based local, state and international levels, with the study of the CHT Peace Agreement warranting this holistic approach. Finally, this study has argued that wide gaps in interests between the different actors are responsible for the partial implementation of the CHT Peace Agreement.

2.3 ANALYTICAL FRAMEWORK

It is worth mentioning that cooperation between theories is possible as well as necessary, at times, to generate an operative analytical framework. In his book, *Theory of International Politics*, Waltz (2010) noted endeavour to seek the causes of war and to describe the conditions of peace, according to the level where these causes are located—whether in man, the state or the state system (p. 18). He also stated that: "[t]heories of international politics that concentrate causes at the individual or national level are reductionist; theories that conceive of causes operating at the international level as well are systemic" (Waltz, 2010, p. 18). In the book, *Man, the State and War: A Theoretical Analysis*, he stated in his analysis that: "[a]ccording to Hobbes, self-preservation is man's primary interest; ... There are three major variables in this analysis: the individual, his society, and the state" (Waltz, 2001, p. 85). As referred to by the theoretical and conceptual discussion above, in analysing the CHT Peace Agreement's implementation (if we consider it as a dependent variable), three levels (considered as independent variables) of analysis have been developed, that is, the state level, the local level (CHT-based) and the international level, with their logical explanations following in the sub-sections below.

2.3.1 State Level

At the state level, the Government of Bangladesh (GoB) is the key actor in implementing the CHT Peace Agreement as it has the authoritative power to formulate and define laws (or rules). The state is known to be embodied through the functions performed by the government and other executive bodies. Therefore, making the policy for signing the Agreement or for its implementation strategies is very much associated with the willingness of the GoB or the ruling political party. Domestic political phenomena are not determined by the government alone but are complicated by other institutions, such as the army, the bureaucracy and opposition political parties. Each is concerned about the interest of assuming (or exercising) power, economic interest or other interests; for example, every political party has the great intention of carrying power through winning the National Parliamentary elections. On 2 December 1997, the Awami League (AL) -led government formulated the CHT Peace Agreement with the PCJSS leadership: it is currently the governing (ruling) party in Bangladesh. Signing the Agreement to address the armed conflict is mainly the liberal view. However, in the realist point of view, mainstream Bengali political parties (whether forming the government or in opposition) much wish to ascend to state power through winning support from the CHT voters in the CHT constituencies, particularly from Bengali settlers. Since signing the Agreement, more than two decades have passed: the GoB and the PCJSS still have not reached consensus about how many sections of the Agreement have been implemented. The GoB is claiming that approximately 75% of the sections (provisions) of the Agreement have already been implemented, with the remaining sections either partially implemented or under the implementation process. In Chapter 4, some crucial sections of the Agreement have been analysed with a comparative discussion of the government (GoB)'s claim and the PCJSS's counter-arguments. The GoB asserts that the implementation of most of these crucial sections is in progress or they are partially implemented. Without full implementation of these essential sections, the GoB is facing questioning about its real motive in implementing the Agreement. This question may, therefore, emerge: is it a strategy to appease the Hill people through formulating the CHT

Peace Agreement? Or, is it consuming time by saying that we (the GoB) are sincere about implementing the remaining sections of the Agreement? Is it the GoB's realist nature of assuming (or exercising) power as discussed by Harold Lasswell, Robert Garner, Barbara Goodwin and other philosophers as analysed in earlier sections? In the subsequent chapters (particularly in Chapter 5), answers to these questions have been sought.

2.3.2 CHT-Based Local Level

The CHT ethnic people have differences with the GoB regarding the implementation policy and the rules that the GoB has formulated. For example, the PCJSS, in favour of the Hill people, has boldly disagreed with what the GoB has asserted about the CHT Peace Agreement's implementation status. Recently, the PCJSS has demanded the certainty of a roadmap for implementing the Agreement from the GoB side: if this could be done, it would be an encouraging example for building trust and confidence. However, since the signing of the Agreement, factionalism between the elite groups that represent the voice of the Hill communities has placed its implementation at risk. While the Agreement was welcomed by the PCJSS and other pro-PCJSS Hill organisations, the Agreement's formulation and signing were protested by different factions of Hill indigenous groups. Along with breakaway factions of the PCJSS, the post-Agreement CHT-based political party—the UPDF—is one glaring example. Since the CHT Peace Agreement was signed, these factions have become more visible, with some factions supporting the Agreement, while others have opposed it and have demanded full autonomy. Furthermore, the Bengali settlers were not supportive of the Agreement. In fact, in the aftermath of the Agreement, another dimension of antagonism started in the CHT, this time, intra-tribal conflict as well as the Bengali–tribal opposition. This continuation of factional rivalry has affected the weaknesses within the Agreement's implementation with this, in turn, strengthening the majoritarian dissent within the dominant Bengali ruling elites. For example, some Hill indigenous interviewees claimed that, if the PCJSS and the UPDF moved together for the CHT Peace Agreement's implementation, it would be easier to motivate (or pressurise) the GoB to implement the Agreement. This factional strife between local actors is now considered to be one of the mentionable impediments to implementing the Agreement, and successive governments may have taken an opportunity from this disunity. As discussed in Chapter 6, this study has sought answers to several questions. Still, one particular question that it has tried to answer is: how does this disunity between the local factions affect the implementation of the CHT Peace Agreement?

2.3.3 International Level

In today's globalised society, national problems, in many cases, attract international attention. International actors are mostly connected to the CHT case by seeking to uphold the human rights of the Hill people. These international activists have become associated with the CHT cause, either through the Hill people seeking the international community's support or from international actors' supportive behaviour under the motivation of the human rights cause. Conversely, some involvement of international actors is a result of being motivated by their interests. However, for the convenience of the analysis, in Chapter 7, international actors' involvement is categorised into two broad distinctions: a) state actors and b) non-state actors. The role of state actor is addressed through the connection to India as a neighbouring country, its involvement through sheltering CHT refugees and its stand at the time of signing the CHT Peace Agreement. In terms of the role of non-state actors, this has been incorporated into the general discussion of individuals, groups, NGOs, UN bodies, donor consortium countries, diasporas, etc. Finally, the study broadly addresses the role of the international Chittagong Hill Tracts Commission and the United Nations Development Programme (UNDP). Most international activism is motivated by the impetus of liberalism and especially neoliberalism. It is not always agreed that the role of international actors has been constructive as, in some cases, their role has been contrary to the Hill people's well-being. These actors may have enhanced the motivation of (or exerted pressure on) the GoB in formulating the CHT Peace Agreement or in its implementation. However, the final outcome is very much dependent on the domestic political culture of the concerned state, in this case, Bangladesh. The current study's analysis has sought to assess the efficacy of international activism in the CHT case and whether it has been (or is) successful.

2.4 THEORETICAL AND ANALYTICAL DESIGN

Figure 2.1 below provides a concise representation of the above discussion:

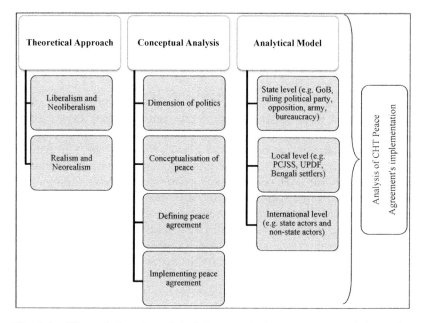

Fig. 2.1 Theoretical and analytical framework (*Source* Developed by author based on the above analysis)

2.5 Chapter Conclusion

The aims of this chapter have been twofold. The first section discussed the conceptual and theoretical approaches relevant to analysing the implementation politics of the CHT Peace Agreement. Liberalism and realism were discussed as the core theoretical approaches connected to concepts such as 'peace', 'politics' and 'implementing peace agreement'. The chapter discussed the study's attempt to determine the relationship between the discourse of politics and that of peace agreement implementation. In the second section, an analytical model has been developed based on the theoretical and conceptual discussion. In this section, the politics related to the implementation of the CHT Peace Agreement are addressed at three levels of analysis, that is, the state level, the CHT-based local level and the international level. At the state level, although the government (the GoB) is recognised as the key actor in the Agreement's implementation, in some cases, it is influenced by the army, the bureaucracy, opposition political parties, public opinion, etc. The role of the state has been mostly analysed from the realist view; on the other hand, mainly, through the liberal impetus, the Hill people (particularly the PCJSS) signed the CHT Peace Agreement to have their demands met. Although they have had to sacrifice many of their demands, they are now emphasising that all sections of the Agreement need to be fully implemented. Different views about the Agreement can be found between the CHT-based local groups. As is the case in other countries, international actors are mostly involved in the CHT's peace initiatives through their human rights concerns. In contrast, other examples reveal that international actors involved to serve their own interests. In accordance with this analytical model, the following chapters are arranged to test the hypotheses, so that evidence can be provided to answer the research question.

REFERENCES

Appadorai, A. (1952). *The substance of politics*. Oxford University Press.
Bell, C. (2000). *Peace agreements and human rights*. Oxford University Press.
Ben-Porat, G. (2008). Introduction: Implementing peace agreements. In G. Ben-Porat (Ed.), *The failure of the Middle East peace process? A comparative analysis of peace implementation in Israel/Palestine, Northern Ireland and South Africa* (pp. 1–18). Palgrave Macmillan.
Carpenter, W. S. (1936). Politics: Who gets what, when, how by Harold D. Lasswell. *The American Political Science Review*, 30(6), 1174–1176.
Department of Peace and Conflict Research. (n.d.). *UCDP definitions*. https://www.pcr.uu.se/research/ucdp/definitions/#tocjump_0571291526363102 4_38. Accessed 19 September 2020.
Galtung, J. (1964). An editorial. *Journal of Peace Research*, 1(1), 1–4.
Galtung, J. (1967). *Theories of peace: A synthetic approach to peace thinking*. International Peace Research Institute.
Garner, R., Ferdinand, P., & Lawson, S. (2009). *Introduction to politics*. Oxford University Press Inc.
Gilchrist, R. N. (1952). *Principles of political science*. Orient Longmans Ltd.
Hampson, F. O. (1996). *Nurturing peace: Why peace settlements succeed or fail*. United States Institute of Peace Press.
Jackson, R., & Sorensen, G. (2013). *Introduction to international relations: Theories and approaches*. Oxford University Press.
Lasswell, H. D. (1950). *Politics: Who gets what, when, how*. Peter Smith.
Laue, J. H. (1991). Contributions of the emerging field of conflict resolution. In W. S. Thompson, M. J. Kenneth, N. S. Richard, & M. S. Kimber

(Eds.), *Approaches to peace: An intellectual map* (pp. 299–332). United States Institute of Peace.

McDougal, M. S. (1991). Law and peace. In W. S. Thompson, M. J. Kenneth, N. S. Richard, & M. S. Kimber (Eds.), *Approaches to peace: An intellectual map* (pp. 129–170). United States Institute of Peace.

Rosenau, J. N. (1980). *The study of global interdependence: Essays on the transnationalisation of world affairs*. Frances Pinter (Publishers) Ltd.

Sabine, G. H. (1964). *A history of political theory*. Lowe & Brydone (Printers) Ltd.

Stedman, S. J. (2002). Introduction. In S. J. Stedman, D. Rothchild, & E. M. Cousens (Eds.), *Ending civil wars: The implementation of peace agreements* (pp. 1–40). Lynne Rienner Publishers Inc.

Stedman, S. J., & Rothchild, D. (1996). Peace operations: From short-term to long-term commitment. *International Peacekeeping, 3*(2), 17–35.

Stedman, S. J., Rothchild, D., & Cousens, E. M. (Eds.). (2002). *Ending civil wars: The implementation of peace agreements*. Lynne Rienner Publishers Inc.

Uppsala Conflict Data Program. (n.d.). *Bangladesh: Chittagong hill tracts*. https://ucdp.uu.se/conflict/322. Accessed 5 September 2020.

Wallensteen, P., & Sollenberg, M. (1997). Armed conflict, conflict termination and peace agreements, 1989–1996. *Journal of Peace Research, 34*(3), 339–358.

Waltz, K. N. (2001). *Man, the state and war: A theoretical analysis*. Columbia University Press.

Waltz, K. N. (2010). *Theory of international politics*. Waveland Press Inc.

CHAPTER 3

From Eruption of the Conflict to Its Management

3.1 Chapter Introduction

This chapter mainly encompasses the root causes of the CHT conflict to answer the research question relating to the background of the conflict. The negotiation process for signing the CHT Peace Agreement in 1997 is also addressed. Although it is challenging to discuss such an elaborate history concisely, the chapter attempts to focus on most of the concerns relating to the causes of the conflict as well as the peace-negotiated initiatives. Even after signing the Agreement, the new dispute is centred on its implementation process. To understand the politics relating to the implementation dispute, it is essential to address the root causes of the conflict, the seeds of which were mostly sown during the British colonial regime. This chapter attempts to clarify the process of marginalisation of the Hill people, which primarily began during the British colonial rule. Even after that era, a very similar approach was followed by the Pakistan regime and successive Bangladesh government, thus alienating the Hill people from their socio-economic and political way of life. To incorporate these aspects, in addition to the introduction and conclusion, the chapter consists of four sections, with some sub-sections, that are briefly mentioned below.

Section 3.2 discusses the pre-colonial period from the beginning of the settling down of various indigenous ethnic communities in the CHT through to the time of the Mughal rulers. Section 3.3 addresses the

© The Author(s), under exclusive license to Springer Nature
Singapore Pte Ltd. 2022
S. Bala, *Politics of Peace Agreement Implementation*,
https://doi.org/10.1007/978-981-16-1944-1_3

British period when CHT were administered in a way different to that in other parts of the Indian subcontinent. In the beginning, the British East India Company's main intention was to gain wealth. However, later, the British colonial rulers captured the whole political economy of the CHT through control over the land and forests of the Hill people. Section 3.4 explains the Pakistan period when marginalisation continued along the same line as during the earlier colonial period. Although various politico-administrative changes in the Constitution of Pakistan and development projects were introduced during this period, the results revealed that most were contrary to the well-being of the Hill communities. Section 3.5 discusses the Bangladesh period in which the Hill people also experienced bitterness as they had with the earlier regimes. Before the enactment of the Constitution of Bangladesh in 1972, the Hill people demanded constitutional autonomy including their own legislature. However, their demand was rejected, and, as shown in the subsequent history, the armed conflict between the insurgents of the CHT and the Bangladesh security forces became embedded, causing massive destruction including thousands of deaths. Both sides agreed that the conflict needed a political solution and following the lengthy negotiation process, the CHT Peace Agreement was signed in 1997. The following sections seek to address the root causes of the conflict and the background of signing the Agreement to explain the situation from the eruption of the conflict down to its management.

3.2 Pre-colonial Period: Beginning of the Erosion of the Hill People's Autonomy

Except for a few documents, no written literature about the CHT during the pre-colonial period was found. The revenue documents of the Mughals gave a first written description of the Hill people, and later on, a detailed description of the same was furnished by the British administration of the region (Mohsin, 2002, p. 11). As in many societies with limited access to reading and writing, the Hill people themselves mainly relied on oral traditions. Emphasising the above three sources as well as social customs, language and facial characteristics, scholars attempted to historicise the CHT Hill people during the pre-colonial period. Although this kind of historiography is often tentative, its importance should not be overlooked as it provides the Hill communities with a sense of history and connection. However, the Kingdom of Arakan ruled the Chittagong hilly region throughout the sixth and seventh centuries. Following the Arakanese dynasty, this region was ruled by different kingdoms until the Mughal conquest. Basically, CHT and Chittagong became a bone of contention between the rulers of the Hill Tripura and Arakan, and it frequently changed hands. According to one account, Bira Raja, the founder of the Hill Tripura Raj Dynasty in 590 A.D., defeated the king of Hill Chittagong and established Rangamati as his capital (Ishaq, 1971, p. 25). In 1340 A.D., Sultan Fakhruddin Mubarak Shah conquered Chittagong (possibly including parts of the Hill Tracts). He was the Sultan of Sonargaon (1338–1349) and established the first dynasty of the Sultanate in Bengal.

In the fifteenth century, some Hill ethnic communities, including the Chakma and Marma (Mughs), moved into the Chittagong region and settled in different parts of this area. A Committee of Revenue report (1874) suggests that most of the Hill people shifted into the territory from what is now known as Myanmar (Burma), and the period of movement was from the fifteenth to mid-nineteenth centuries. The report also stated that the Kukis (one of the Hill ethnic communities) were the earliest settlers in the region followed by the Chakma. Before the Mughal victory, Chittagong had neither an administrative set-up nor any fixed boundaries, and the Hill people remained politically independent. In 1666, Shaista Khan, the Mughal governor of Bengal under Emperor Aurangzeb Alamgir, conquered Chittagong from the Arakanese and the name of Chittagong was changed to Islamabad by order of Emperor Aurangzeb. This marked the beginning of the erosion of the Hill people's political autonomy (Mohsin, 2002, p. 22). Furthermore, Mughal records (Committee of Revenue, 1784) revealed that the Chakma Chief Jallal Khan willingly agreed to pay tax to the Mughals in return for trading rights with the people living on the plains. This tax was paid in cotton: afterwards, this region was known as Kapas Mahal (land of cotton). As most daily necessities, such as salt, dried fish, spices, sugar and kerosene were not available in the CHT, the Chakma Chiefs requested consent from the Mughal administrator of Chittagong to allow Bengali merchants to trade with these Hill communities. Moreover, the Chiefs employed the Bengalis to work as courtiers and employed Bengali servants. Although resistance was found by the Chakmas against the Mughals in the seventeenth century, it was not sustained due to the countermeasures adopted by the Mughal administration; eventually, people from different ethnic groups agreed to pay tax to the Mughals. However, in 1760, the district of Chittagong and the CHT were ceded to the British East India Company by Mir Qasim Ali Khan, the semi-independent governor under the Mughals.

3.3 British Period (1760–1947): Beginning of the Marginalisation of the Hill People

During the British period, today's CHT were isolated, protected and identified as a tribal area; they were not directly administered as a colony as were other parts of the Indian subcontinent. The British controlled the region at the end of the nineteenth century when their rule in South Asia was extended in general and consolidated for reasons of frontier security. Actually, the East India Company adopted different strategies to govern the CHT people. As economic interest was one of the main intentions, tax was regularly collected in cash or kind by the Company. Although the company's initial aim was to gain wealth, later on, motivated by greed and profit, it opted for a total political and economic control of the area. It should be noted that, due to the policy of segregation, the Hill ethnic communities, and specifically their chiefs, regarded the British as their protectors, thus allowing the British greater ease in ruling the CHT (Mohsin, 2002, p. 27). The British policy vis-à-vis the CHT was basically to ensure the economic, political and security interests of the British; and also to keep at the same time the indigenous ethnic people alienated from the Bengalis. The marginalisation and the alienation process of the Hill people are discussed in the following sub-sections.

3.3.1 *Political and Administrative Developments*

As the British East India Company's main concern was economic benefit, they initially followed a non-interventionist policy in the Chittagong Hill Tracts (CHT). Since 1858 when the British Monarch ruled India directly, the CHT were administered by the British through a number of regulations passed from time to time. Later on, the colonial officers were invested with massive power to control the CHT indigenous people making it sure that the latter lived in isolation with restricted economic and political activity. In fact, the British decreed a special administrative status for the region. The CHT Regulation of 1900 had a significant role in administering the CHT, with some amendments which were established against the regulation's true spirit by successive rules. Moreover, the regulation has played a debatable role in some contemporary issues over the CHT case.

The CHT Regulation of 1900 appeared as a source of rights for the Hill communities and a challenge to the legitimacy of the Bengal settlers' inhabitation in the region (Chittagong Hill Tracts [CHT] Commission, 1991, p. 10). However, the colonial government's documents claim that the tribal people did not initially oppose the Bengali migrants. The Bengalis also came in this region on a quest for agricultural lands for themselves. Moreover, by the 1890s, half of the 3,000 hectares of reclaimed lands were occupied by Bengali migrants (Mey, 1984, p. 22). Many Bengali migrants also settled in the CHT from 1900 to 1947 during the British colonial government (Abedin, 1997, p. 33). In the current debate, the CHT Regulation of 1900 stands for certain rights of the Hill people and as a historic compromise between the Hill people's rights and external political control (CHT Commission, 1991, p. 11). Thus, it is necessary to consider some of the provisions of the Regulation of 1900, which clarify our conception of the administrative system during that time through understanding the root causes of the conflict in the region. The Chittagong Hill Tracts Regulation of 1900 is concisely analysed below.

As a way to protect the Hill people from Bengali migrants and also to keep the region calm as well as segregated from the political turmoil of the anti-British movement, the Chittagong Hill Tracts Regulation, 1900 (Act 1 of 1900), was enacted and came into effect on 1 May 1900 (Mohsin, 2002, p. 32). This Act is, often, known as the CHT Manual amending the Act XXII of 1860. The CHT Manual laid down the detailed rules and regulations for the CHT's administration. For example, under Section 18 of the CHT Manual, rules and regulations applicable in other parts of Bengal were no longer applicable in the context of the Chittagong Hill Tracts (CHT). Article 7 of Chapter III placed the CHT under the administration of the Superintendent, presently known as the Deputy Commissioner (DC). He/she was authorised with special powers by the Governor of Bengal. Article 38.A of Chapter IV stated that the CHT was divided into three major administrative subdivisions, viz. Rangamati, Ramgarh and Bandarban. In each sub-division, a Sub-Divisional Officer (SDO) was employed. Each sub-division was also sub-divided into some Thanas (police station), and each Thana had some villages under its jurisdiction. This structure was, in fact, standard throughout the area of Bengal.

The CHT Manual restricted and controlled the entrance of Bengalis in the region. It stated that:

> no person other than Chakma, Mogh or a member of any hill tribe indigenous to the Chittagong Hill Tracts, the Lushai hills, the Arakan hill or the State of Tripura shall enter or reside within the Chittagong Hill Tracts unless he is in possession of a permit granted by the Deputy Commissioner. (Adopted from Gain, 2000, p. 17)

In fact, restriction of the movement and settlement of Bengali migrants in the CHT was one of the strategies of the British government to keep revolutionaries as well as freedom fighters out of this area. However, it did not totally ban the infiltration and settlement of Bengali migrants in the CHT; instead, it narrowed this down and placed it under the settlement of the Superintendent. The CHT Manual, in fact, absolutely reserved and ensured the authority of the British over the CHT: it was considered as being politically motivated. With this Act, the British arrogated arbitrary power over the CHT, its people and land (Abedin, 1997, p. 26). Although Rule 34 of the CHT Regulation restricted possession of land by outsiders in the CHT, it could not impose a total ban. For example, Rule 34(b), Rule 34(c), Rule 34(d) and Rule 34(e) allowed Bengalis to possess the land in the CHT for plantations on a commercial basis, or for industrial, residential or commercial purposes, respectively. However, under Rule 52, without prior permission from the DC, no non-indigenous person could enter or reside in the Chittagong Hill Tracts (CHT). More importantly, under Rule 51, the Superintendent (better known as the DC) could expel any person from the CHT within 24 hours if he/she was found to be unwanted by the governing authority.

In parallel, another administrative structure was introduced in the Hill Tracts. On 1 September 1881, the Bengal Government divided the CHT into three Circles, with the CHT Manual confirming this division. The three Circles were (are): the Chakma Revenue Circle of 4,294.20 square kilometres (excluding government Reserved Forest of 1,976.16 square kilometres) in Rangamati zone; the Bohmang Revenue Circle of 3,739.94 square kilometres (excluding government Reserved Forest of 1,605.79 square kilometres) in Bandarban zone; and the Mong Revenue Circle of 1,691.26 square kilometres in Ramgarh zone (Shelley, 1992, p. 78). These Circles were again divided into 373 Mouzas (clusters of villages) and each Mouza was split into Paras or individual villages. The government appointed a Chief (in Bengali, better known as a Raja) as the head in each Circle. Each Mouza was placed under a Headman[1] or Dewan, who was appointed by the Chief with the DC's consent, and each Para was placed under a Karbari. The Mouza Headman appointed the Karbari with the Chief's consent. Usually, the offices of the Raja and Headman were hereditary. In fact, through this traditional set-up, the British developed a tier of royalty which was mostly hierarchical.

In this way, in the CHT, two parallel administrative structures were (are) present. Although the CHT Manual maintained the traditional institutions of the Circle Chiefs and Headmen, ultimately all power—executive, judicial and financial—was vested upon the DC of the concerned Circle. The power of the Chiefs was limited to the collection of taxes and the dispensation of justice in the traditional courts. Article 38 of Chapter IV states that the Chiefs were responsible for forming an Advisory Council and assisting the DC in the administration of their respective Circle. Through Article 40 of Chapter IV, the Mouza Headmen were accountable for the collection of taxes and the settlement of disputes within their Mouzas. They passed the tax to the respective Circle Chief who passed it to the DC of the respective Circle. The Karbaris were entrusted with the responsibility of social administration and discipline in their respective villages. In reality, the CHT Manual played no role in developing or changing the fate of the indigenous people of the CHT; instead, it clipped their rights and privileges. As noted by Mohsin (2002), the CHT Regulation of 1900, as a legal document, eroded the Hill communities' sovereignty and provided the background for their alienation from the political system even though it was a system into which they were later integrated (p. 33).

However, various rules under the CHT Regulation of 1900 were at times amended using various regulations, acts and government notifications, mentionable in 1920, 1925, 1933 and 1935 (Shelley, 1992, p. 84). Noteworthy, in 1920, by an amendment to the CHT Manual, the CHT were declared a Backward Tract. It yielded the Governor-General-in-Council the responsibility of administering the CHT as an excluded area. Through the Government of India Act of 1935, the CHT were denominated as a Totally Excluded Area. This was considered as the formal

---

[1] The Headman is also known as Roaja in Mong and Bohmang Circles.

splitting of political links from the province of Bengal; thus, the process of marginalisation continued.

3.3.2 Economic and Socio-Cultural Management

Many of the ethnic conflicts primarily arise from the demand for the recognition of ethnic identity by the marginalised groups. Needless to say, without perceiving the actual political and economic discrimination, the cultural trait might not become an issue. The people of the CHT accustomed their pre-industrial mode of production, that is, *jhum* (slash-and-burn farming or swidden agriculture), as their point of distinc tiveness. The *jhum* cultivation was often considered a primitive method of agriculture (the mode of traditional tribal cultivation), and the common property was characteristic of their economic system. The Hill people had plenty of land for *jhum* cultivation which was their primary and traditional occupation with practically no significant adverse impact on the environment. During the pre-colonial period, no encroachment was made in this domain. To *jhum* cultivation is added a number of secondary occupations to support the life of the Hill people like hunting, food-gathering, trapping and fishing. As mentioned by Chowdhury (2001), the Hill people called themselves 'we' meaning the Jumma nation, as opposed to 'they'—the Bangalees—who used cultivation by plough as their mode of agriculture (p. 94). More explicitly, the term 'Jummas' is used to identify the Hill people, whereas the name 'Bengalis' indicates the people living on the plain lands. The manner of differentiation in this context was primarily cultural, which was substantiated by political as well as economic marginalisation. Moreover, when we observe it closely, we find that the foundation of this type of ethnic boundary was established during the British colonial regime. However, the economic system of the Hill people was different from that of today's market economy, and it was not favourable for the expansion of finished goods imported from Britain. As reported by Mohsin (2002), it was asserted by the British that *jhum* was a 'primitive' method of agriculture as they calculated it wasted resources as long fallow periods were a *jhum* practice. The British, therefore, endeavoured to replace *jhum* by plough cultivation which did not require fallow periods. According to the British, this would provide greater economic gains as well as being regarded as a technologically improved practice (p. 81).

However, for the CHT indigenous people, *jhum* was regarded as a way of life. It was a part of their social and cultural norms and was considered to be more than an activity with economic value. The whole process of *jhum* cultivation and harvesting is based on the concept of collective (common) ownership, exchange and sharing. Conversely, there is a conflicting view that examines the idea that *jhum* is harmful and wasteful and must be abandoned for the benefit of the Hill people who practice it.[2] In fact, the British colonial rulers strongly discouraged it. After 1860, taxes were levied based on land rather than based on individuals. The intention behind this shift was to tether the CHT farmers to a piece of land. Subsequently, the British colonial rulers abolished the pre-existing tradition of debt-bondage which had caused the Hill people to be dependent on the Bengali moneylenders who charged high-interest rates. This arrangement propelled the Hill communities into a capitalist market system, and they found themselves in a new web of dependency.

Combined efforts were initiated to encourage the *jhumias*[3] to obtain plough cultivation from 1868 to 1871. For example, credit advances to the amount of Rs. 38,100 were available to the interested CHT people. By 1872, the total area of the plains leased for plough cultivation was 1,702 hectares, and advance loans in cash amounted to £3,274 in total (Dewan, 1990, p. 152). In fact, the British colonial administrators were looking for the opportunity to increase their revenues from the CHT, and the introduction of plough cultivation was also encouraged as a result. It also facilitated them in terms of consolidating and enhancing their political position through the direct control of the commodification of land. Moreover, for the first time, the Hill people were in touch with a different kind of political economy which prompted changes in their own culture and societal structure. Their society was vastly affected by this new system. In some instances, a breakdown of social structures occurred through contact with the British colonial rulers.

---

[2] Details about this debate are discussed by Agarwal (1988, pp. 134–143).

[3] The Hill people engaged in *jhum* cultivation are collectively known as *jhumias* (farmers).

3.3.3 Acquisition of Land and Forests by the British

In the earlier section, the fact that the Hill people considered the CHT land as their community property was mentioned. Conversely, in 1868, the British colonial rulers claimed ownership of all lands in the Hill Tracts (Mohsin, 2002, p. 87). Although the Chiefs of the CHT resisted the acquisition of land by the state, the British government never recognised the land rights of the Chiefs. The British acquired authoritative power over the land through their increasing social, economic and political control in the area. As the influence of their administration expanded over the CHT, the British introduced civil and traditional institutions where the Chiefs were empowered to collect taxes and rents from the Hill people on behalf of the government. In the CHT, the British introduced two types of land tenures: (i) private rights and (ii) usufruct. From 1868 onwards, private rights were given to the people who agreed to use plough cultivation. With the aim of acquiring this right, a person had to obtain the land registration from the DC's office. He/she paid rent for it either directly to the government official or through the concerned Headman of the village. The term 'usufruct' meant the right to use the land over which the state held ownership rights, and this practice continued about the *jhum* lands. This right pertained to anyone who cleared the forest and occupied it first, and then, obtained it by the registration of the land with the concerned Headman. However, finally, DC was conferred absolute power over the land. Moreover, the CHT indigenous people lost their land, as the land could now be leased to outsiders for commercial purposes.

More than 82% of the total area of the CHT was comprised of forests (Hunter, 1876, p. 29). Traditionally, the Hill communities had used the forest resources for *jhum* cultivation and domestic purposes, and they also regarded the forests as community property. However, in 1865, the Indian Forest Reserve Act was passed, and this Act barred the local people from entering as well as using the resources of the forests of the Hill Tracts.

By February 1871, almost the entire area of the CHT, viz. 5,670 out of 6,882 square miles, was proclaimed to be the Government Reserve Forest (Cowan, 1923, p. 14). The local CHT people were allowed to use forest produce only for domestic needs. Furthermore, in 1875, government-owned forests were divided into two categories: Reserve Forests (RFs) and District Forests (DFs). Presently, DFs are known as Unclassified

State Forests (USFs). The RFs were entirely under the management of the state's forest department, and *jhum* cultivation or any use of forest produce was wholly banned. The DFs were under the direct control of the DC, and *jhum* harvesting, including the use of forest products for domestic purposes, was allowed with certain restrictions that the DC could impose from time to time. On the other hand, the state also allotted high-quality land to European entrepreneurs for plantations. Thus, the British colonial administrators' policy was directed by their profit-making intentions. By these means, the CHT indigenous people were deprived of their community rights over the forest resources, which also resulted in a scarcity of land available for *jhum* cultivation.

3.4 Pakistan Period (1947–1971): Continued Marginalisation

On 14 August 1947, Pakistan was created on the basis of the two-nation theory, but it was certainly not homogeneous. As the two-nation theory was the basis of the partition, it was only reasonable that CHT, a non-Muslim populated area (95% of the population was non-Muslim), would be included within India. The CHT leaders also hoped for and expected such an outcome. The three Circle Chiefs demanded the recognition of each of their Circle as native states from the British, the Congress and the Muslim League leaders. Failing to obtain this recognition, the Hill leaders proposed the formation of a confederation with the Indian states of Tripura, Kuchbihar and Khasia. In contrast, the Marma Chief suggested a union with Burma (presently called Myanmar). In the vortex of partition politics, all these demands were unheeded when the Boundary Commission Chairman, Sir Cyril Radcliffe, awarded the CHT to East Pakistan (now Bangladesh) on 17 August 1947, a few days after the independence of Pakistan (on 14 August) and India (on 15 August).[4] The process of marginalisation continued in the new state of Pakistan as is revealed and discussed in the following sections.

---

[4] For further exposition on this discussion, see Chakma (1986).

3.4.1 Politico-Administrative Changes

During the regime of Pakistan, several changes were incorporated in the existing administrative set-up that had continued from the British colonial legacy. The CHT Regulation of 1900 provided the basis of the administrative structure. In 1955, although the central government of Pakistan attempted to repeal the special status of the CHT, the abolition of the status was postponed owing to strong objections by the Hill people. Moreover, the first Constitution of Pakistan in 1956 retained the special status of the CHT as an Excluded Area. This progress stabilised the CHT for an interval of time, but, within a few years, the old problems reappeared. During Ayub Khan's tenure as the President of Pakistan, the Constitution of 1962 modified the status of the CHT from an Excluded Area to a Tribal Area. On the one hand, the CHT were, in fact, distinguished as a special region that was culturally distinct from the other areas of Bangladesh. On the other hand, administrative distinctiveness of the CHT was no longer retained. As in other regions of Pakistan, the system of Basic Democracies (BD)[5] was introduced in the Chittagong Hill Tracts (CHT). This system undermined the traditional institutions of the CHT, as, under this system, a Basic Democrat (although he/she was a local person) had more power and functions in the villages than a Mouza Headman. For example, all development programmes were carried out by the BD members in collaboration with the government-appointed Circle officers who were consistently chosen from the Bengali community. Besides, by the mid-1960s, the government had transferred all local indigenous Hill employees in the administration to other parts of East Pakistan. The local administration was entirely staffed by Bengalis (Huq, 1992, p. 56).

In 1962, the special status of the CHT was withdrawn through a constitutional amendment which came into effect in 1964 despite strong protests by the Hill local leaders. On 21 October 1971, the Pakistan

---

[5] Basic Democracies were introduced by the Pakistan military regime of Ayub Khan with the aim of hampering political opposition from the parties in East Pakistan and to consolidate West Pakistan's subjugation over East Pakistan. It was a four-tiered pyramidal structure dominated by government officials and the Council Chairman. Except for the lowest tier (Union Council or Union Committee), government officials and nominated members outnumbered the elected members. Thus, Basic Democrats were more likely to be government agents (Jahan, 1972, as cited in Mohsin, 2002, p. 43).

government arranged for some changes to Rule 34 of the CHT Regulation of 1900 through a gazette notification. It gave equal rights and opportunities to both the Hill and non-Hill people. With permission from the Board of Revenue, they would be eligible for terrace cultivation, rubber plantations, the acquisition of lands for industrial purposes and for building houses in this area. However, at the administrative level, the CHT Regulation of 1900 remained the principal basis of regulations and was the means by which the DCs were endowed with all powers. In fact, the CHT Manual had never been repealed. It was violated as well as applied to pursue the interests of the ruling elites. Although some amendments were enacted in the Regulation of 1900, it never addressed the interests of the Hill ethnic communities. Moreover, due to the status conferred in the CHT Manual, the CHT continued to be a non-regulated district, a status that restricted the political activities in the Chittagong Hill Tracts (CHT). Furthermore, the Circle Chiefs did not accept a political platform that would have undermined their position (Mohsin, 2002, p. 47). These reveal that the motives were to keep the Hill people alienated as well as marginalised from political activities against the ruling elites.

3.4.2 *Development Projects: Way of Economic Exploitation*

Various development policies in the CHT adopted by the Pakistan government had led to several controversial debates. On the one hand, these development initiatives mostly exploited the natural resources of this area. On the other hand, the initiatives exhibited little concern regarding the impact on the Hill communities. Broadly, economic policies in the state of Pakistan were adopted in the name of national development and national integration. However, many development plants resulted in uprooting the Hill people from their places of habitual residence. For example, the Karnafuli Paper Mill, the largest paper mill in Asia, set up during Pakistan time in 1953 in the Marma-inhabited area of Chandraghona is located in the Chittagong Hill Tracts (CHT). The raw materials for the mill, that is, bamboo and softwood lumber, were mainly extracted from this area of the Hill Tracts. Although the resources of the area were used for the paper mill, it had employed less than 1% of the Hill people. More importantly, the construction of this paper mill led to the displacement of the Marma community and loss of their land, as the land was acquired by the Pakistan government to build the paper mill. Now, there are no Hill people's settlements near the paper mill, and almost 100% of the population living nearby comprises of Bengalis who migrated to the area after the paper mill was built (Mohsin & Ahmed, 1996, pp. 275–276).

Another example of the displacement of the Hill people was analysed in the construction of the Kaptai Hydro-electric Project that was built on the Karnafuli River in Rangamati district with the financial and technical support of the United States. For this project, a vast lake was built to the north and east of a barrage at Kaptai village between 1957 and 1962, and it submerged an area of 54,000 acres of settled, cultivable land, that is, about 40% and 90% of the total acreage of the CHT and Rangamati subdivision, respectively. As a result of this project, more than 100,000 people were landless and homeless, and within this demographic, more than 90% were of indigenous origin (Chowdhury, 2001, p. 93). Among the displaced persons, around 40,000 people crossed over to India and 20,000 to Myanmar, while many were internally displaced. The affected people were not adequately compensated for their losses, and even the compensation provided to some of the affected persons was not adequate. The Pakistan government had set the initial amount of US$51 million for the rehabilitation of the affected people, but only US$2.6 million was actually spent (Chowdhury, 2012, p. 39). During an interview, T. S. P. Master (personal communication, May 25, 2016), Ex-Chairman of Bandarban Hill District Council (BHDC), expressed his concern regarding this project as follows: after the construction of the Kaptai dam, many of the Chakma indigenous people were bound to migrate to the Bohmang and Mong Circles [now, well known as Bandarban and Khagrachhari districts, respectively]. This generated population density as well as pressure within our Circle. [Besides], now the Bengali settlers [migrants] are more than us. We are suffering in our land. If this continues, we shall be diminished.

Based on the fieldwork conducted in the CHT and a review of the secondary sources, it has been observed that the Kaptai Hydro-electric Project is one of the crucial causal factors for most of the problems in the area. The statement mentioned above endorses this finding. The Kaptai Hydro-electric Project resulted in an immense change in the traditional patterns of life, which is strongly associated with the problem of the scarcity of land. This is one of the crucial issues regarding the implementation and/or non-implementation politics of the CHT Peace Agreement.

According to the 1961 census, the total area of CHT was 13,241.8 square kilometres, of which 11,395.8 square kilometres (85.3%) of the land in the district was forested (Rahman, 2011, p. 84). In 1962, the Pakistan government decided to reserve another (third) class of forests (apart from the two already reserved by the British colonial government) to be known as Protected Forests (PFs). In this PF area, the government also banned *jhum* cultivation, and in its place, the government planned to establish the Softwood Working Circle and Fruit Tree Working Circle (Adnan, 2004, p. 23). This benefited the Bengali businessmen who could now have a monopoly over the trade of this region. The construction of the Kaptai dam had developed the communication facilities in the area. The withdrawal of restrictions (e.g. Rule 34 and Rule 52 of the CHT Manual) together with improved communication only facilitated the increase in the number of the Bengalis migrants. Conversely, the CHT indigenous people were further marginalised by the policies mentioned above. In fact, these development policies made the CHT a profitable area that opened up new opportunities for the Bengali migrants. In this regard, the land was an obvious attraction for the Bengalis, in terms of both the withdrawal of the status of the CHT as a special region and the encouragement of settled cultivation. Table 3.1 shows the increasing percentage of Bengali migrants.

Table 3.1 Demographic account of the Hill people and the Bengali (settlers) inhabited in the Chittagong Hill Tracts (CHT)

Year	Total population	Hill people	%	Bengali (settlers)	%
1872	63,054	61,957	98	1,097	2
1901	124,762	116,000	93	8,762	7
1951	287,688	261,538	91	26,150	9
1981	746,649	441,776	59	304,873	41
1991	974,445	501,144	51	473,301	49
2011 (the most recent Population and Housing Census in Bangladesh)	1,598,231	845,541	52.9	752,690	47.1

Source Developed by author based on Ranjan (2015, p. 143) and Table 1.1

In the next chapter (Sect. 4.4.5), the issue of the Bengali settlers, as it is linked to the implementation and/or non-implementation politics of the CHT Peace Agreement, shall be analysed further. From the discussion above, it is evident that development policies in the CHT not only displaced the Hill ethnic communities but also induced a sense of alienation among them.

3.5 Bangladesh Period (1971–1997)

After the nine month long liberation war, based on Bengali nationalism, Bangladesh attained independence from Pakistan on 16 December 1971. In this new state, the experience of the Hill people was bitter because of their indifference to the cause of Bengali nationalism during the Pakistan regime, and particularly, for their role in the liberation war of Bangladesh. There are different opinions regarding the role of the CHT indigenous people in the freedom movement. It is a matter of regret that the Hill people were branded as being pro-Pakistan, even though some indigenous leaders crossed over to India and joined the independence movement for Bangladesh. The position of the Hill leaders, especially the role of Circle Chiefs, as well as other factors, is responsible for the controversy discussed above. As noted by Mohsin (2002), of the three Circle Chiefs of the CHT, the Mong Raja Mong Prue Chai Chowdhury joined the liberation forces in favour of today's Bangladesh, while Bohmang Raja Mong Shoi Prue Chowdhury remained non-committal. However, the Chakma Raja Tri Dev Roy supported the Pakistan army; thus, they had different views (pp. 55–56). After the independence of Bangladesh, many Headmen and local leaders of the CHT were arrested and persecuted ([*The*] *Daily Star*, 1998, as cited in Chowdhury, 2012, p. 50). Besides, the *muktibahini* (freedom fighters) went on a rampage in the Hill Tracts searching for *razakars*[6] and members of the Pakistani military. Thus, a seed of insecurity was sown in the minds of the Hill people at the rise of independence, and regarding the lives of the Hill ethnic communities in the state of Bangladesh. This caused feelings of apathy and to a certain extent, alienation. In the following sub-sections, the marginalisation of the Hill people will be analysed by addressing the policies adopted by the Bengali ruling authorities.

---

[6] The Bengali collaborators of Pakistani soldiers during the liberation war.

3.5.1 Sheikh Mujibur Rahman's Government (1972–1975): The Beginning of Resistance by the Hill People

The newly independent state of Bangladesh moved ahead with the formation of its constitution. Considering the past experiences of exploitation and deep mistrust on the part of the Bengalis, the CHT indigenous people felt that it was necessary to have constitutional safeguards for their protection as a separate ethnic community (Mohsin, 2002, p. 57). During the process of drafting the constitution, on 15 February 1972, a delegation of Hill people led by Manobendra Narayan (M. N.) Larma (the lone elected Member of Parliament [MP] from the CHT) met the then Prime Minister Sheikh Mujibur Rahman (Mujib) and presented four demands to be included in the constitution:

a) autonomy for the Chittagong Hill Tracts, including its own legislature;
b) retention of the 1900 CHT Manual in the Constitution of Bangladesh;
c) continuation of tribal chiefs' offices;
d) constitutional provisions restricting the amendment of the Regulation of 1900, and imposition of a ban on the influx of the non-tribal people into the CHT. (Haq & Haque, 1990, pp. 44–46)

However, the Prime Minister rejected the demands and asked the Hill leaders to forget about their separate identity and adopt Bengali nationalism. This was unacceptable to Larma (along with other indigenous leaders) who by then had come forward as the champion of the Hill people's cause. On 7 March 1972, Larma consequently formed a regional political organisation, the PCJSS. An armed wing of the PCJSS known as Shanti Bahini[7] (SB, Peace Force) was added on 7 January 1973. The PCJSS claimed the Jumma nationalism of the Hill ethnic people as a distinctive identity, and henceforth, the PCJSS emerged as the leading spokesman for the Hill people's cause.

---

[7] While the GoB estimated that Shanti Bahini (SB) guerrillas numbered only 200, SB claimed that it had as many as 1,500 members. Moreover, reserve forces of about 50,000 trained youth were organised into militia activities (Chowdhury, 2012, p. 47). The Uppsala Conflict Data Program [UCDP] (n.d.) revealed that around 5,000 lightly armed guerrilla fighters from among the CHT indigenous people were estimated to have been organised as SB fighters.

On 4 November 1972, the Constitution of Bangladesh was adopted by the Parliament, and Article 1 of Part 1 declared Bangladesh to be a unitary state. Through Article 3 of Part 1, Bengali was adopted as the state language, and Article 6 of Part 1 pronounced that the citizens of Bangladesh were to be known as Bengalis. It assumed that the constitution was the reflection of the ideals of Bengali nationalism. In the National Assembly, Larma pointed out, through a sustained argument, the assimilationist policy of the GoB and stated:

> You cannot impose your national identity on others. I am a Chakma not a Bengali. I am a citizen of Bangladesh, Bangladeshi. You are also Bangladeshi but your national identity is Bengali ... they (Hill people) can never become Bengali. (Parliamentary Debates, 1972, as cited in Mohsin, 2002, p. 62)

Amid these politics, on 23 January 1974, the National Parliament passed a Bill declaring Bangladesh as a uni-cultural and uni-lingual nation-state. However, Sheikh Mujib was assassinated in a military coup on 15 August 1975, and the army officers postponed the Constitution of Bangladesh. This political change appeared to be a challenge for Larma's project of regional autonomy through constitutional means.

3.5.2   Military and Quasi-Military Regime (1976–1990)

After the assassination of Mujib, the military took over the state power, and Major General Ziaur Rahman (Zia) emerged as the chief martial law administrator, and later, the President of Bangladesh. On the other hand, M. N. Larma crossed over to India, and hereafter, the PCJSS was to operate from its Tripura[8] base in India. Initially, the GoB viewed the CHT problem in terms of economic as well as security concerns and initiated several policies to counter these issues during this period. For example, the Chittagong Hill Tracts Development Board (CHTDB) was established in January 1976 with funding from the GoB and the Asian Development Bank (ADB). Although the composition of the Board was altered with different regimes, its head remained a government official. The head (Chairman) is the chief executive of the Board, and he advises the GoB on all policy matters affecting the CHT issue. However, the

---

[8] Tripura is the bordering state (province) of India.

Board's activities revealed the underlying motive of providing benefits to the Bengali settlers in the CHT (Mohsin, 2002, pp. 123–124). In July 1977, another initiative was undertaken through the construction of a forum called the Tribal Convention, the stated objective of which was to open up a channel of communication with the PCJSS leaders (Chakma, 2012, p. 127). Between July 1977 and December 1978, the convention held four rounds of dialogue with representatives of the PCJSS before the process came to an end.

During this period, along with the militarisation of the region, approximately 150,000 Bengalis were settled in the CHT and were provided with land, cash and rations (Chowdhury, 2012, pp. 54–55). The Hill people considered the government-sponsored migration policy of Bengalis living on the plain land relocating to the CHT as being ethnic cleansing and a move to reduce the Hill ethnic people into a minority community. In the midst of various situations of turmoil, in 1977, SB attacked a convoy of the Bangladesh army in the CHT; this is regarded as the beginning of the armed rebellion (Chowdhury, 2001, p. 94). To counter this insurgency in the mid-1980s, the 24th division, which formed about one-third of Bangladesh's entire army, was deployed in the CHT (UCDP, n.d.). On the other hand, the army often committed an excess amount of personnel, amounting to a violation of human rights, in counterinsurgency operations (Chowdhury, 2012, p. 54). Subsequently, at the request of the Ministry of Home Affairs, the Minister of Defence took charge and remained active from 1977 to the final conclusion of the CHT Peace Agreement in 1997. The army has four Brigade Headquarters in the CHT: Rangamati, Khagrachhari, Dighinala and Bandarban. As per the information collected from the army's sources, the CHT Commission (1991) divulged that more than 230 army camps, over 100 Bangladesh Rifles (BDR) and more than 80 Police camps were set up in the CHT (p. 34). Although the CHT commission claimed that there was one member of the security force for every 20 Hill persons (Chittagong Hill Tracts [CHT] Commission, 1992, p. 8), the ruling authorities did not reveal the exact number of security forces deployed in this area.

Following the May 1981 assassination of Major General Zia, General Hussain Muhammad (H. M.) Ershad assumed state power through a bloodless coup in March 1982. Along with other demands, most importantly, the PCJSS's demand for autonomy with its own legislature was rejected by the Ershad regime on the grounds that such autonomy was not provided for in the framework of the Constitution of Bangladesh.

Instead, through the enactment of a Parliament Act on 28 March 1989, the government had established three Local Government Councils (LGCs) for the districts of Rangamati, Khagrachhari and Bandarban. During Ershad's period, only 3 out of the 22 subjects were handed over to the LGCs (in short, District Councils), namely (i) agriculture, (ii) health and family planning, and (iii) primary education (CHT Commission, 1992, p. 10). Although two-thirds of the members were indigenous leaders (each Council is headed by one indigenous Chairman), the District Councils had been rejected by the PCJSS as well as by the CHT indigenous people. The most important objections by them were as follows:

- The Act has no constitutional basis and it can be repealed and changed at any time.
- The presence of Bengali settlers is legalised in this area.
- Land rights of the indigenous communities are not safeguarded and there is no provision of return of land acquired by Bengalis. In fact, only 10% of the total area of the [C]HT is under the jurisdiction of the Councils.
- De-facto power does not lie with the District Councils, but with the military. (CHT Commission, 1992, pp. 11–12)

Furthermore, these District Councils were dependent on the government's financial support to undertake any development projects and for their annual budget. In the case of civil administration, the Deputy Commissioners are still exercising power and privileges conferred to them by the CHT Manual of 1900. However, as noted by Chowdhury (2012), although the CHT Regulation of 1900 was suspended in 1989, it was never annulled (p. 40).

3.5.3 *Land, Forests and the Issue of the Bengali Settlers*

Land, forests and the issue of the Bengali settlers are the crux of the problem in the CHT, all of which are primarily interrelated. In 1979, the government did away with the restrictions against the settlement of lands by non-Hill people through an amendment to Rule 34 of the CHT Regulation of 1900. Besides the military measures, successive administrators undertook a Bengali settlement programme as a counterinsurgency strategy. According to one estimate, around 400,000 Bengalis in total were said to have been settled in the CHT by 1984 (*The Guardian*, 1984, as cited in Mohsin, 2002, p. 113). As a result of this settlement policy, approximately 100,000 CHT indigenous people became homeless. About half of these people became refugees in the states of Tripura and Mizoram in India, and the rest were internally displaced. The government argued that the Bengalis had been settled on *khas*[9] land, so there had been no intrusion of the Hill people's private property. However, differences exist between the Hill people and the Bengali ruling elites regarding the concept of *khas* land. As mentioned by Mohsin (2002), the traditional *jhum* land and forest land indispensable to the CHT indigenous people were regarded by the government as *khas* land (p. 118).

On the other hand, the Bengali ruling class blames the *jhum* cultivators and *jhum* cultivation for soil degradation as well as deforestation. *Jhum* had been prohibited in half of the total area of the CHT for more than a century to maintain the RFs (Mohsin, 2002, p. 135). Moreover, in 1992, the GoB decided to declare 37,387.5 acres of land in Khagrachhari, 76,000 acres in Rangamati and 7,389.2 acres in Bandarban as RFs (Sangbed, 1992, as cited in Mohsin, 2002, p. 135). Thus, the Hill people's displacement and alienation from land and forests increased each day, which was intensified by the Bengali settlement programme.

3.5.4 Moving Towards Signing of the CHT Peace Agreement (1991–1997)

In 1991, after the restoration of parliamentary forms of democracy in Bangladesh, the Bangladesh Nationalist Party (BNP) formed the government. Under the leadership of the then Prime Minister Begum Khaleda Zia, the new prospect of solving the conflict unfolded. Although foreign aid was to be secured by the country, the international pressure intensified pushing for the introduction of reforms and good governance. By that time, it had become explicit that the CHT issue had to be settled politically, not militarily. On 10 July 1992, the government constituted a nine-member multi-party parliamentary committee to conduct a direct negotiation with the PCJSS. The PCJSS also responded positively and announced a unilateral ceasefire from 1 August 1992, which was extended routinely every three months (about thirty-five times) until December

---

[9] The state authority claims that it is unused land owned by the Government of Bangladesh (GoB).

1997 (Mohsin, 2003, pp. 40–41). In December 1992, the PCJSS put forward the following modified demands:

(1) regional autonomy for the CHT with regional council [RC] recognized by Bangladesh constitution;
(2) restoration of land rights of the tribal people with a ban on the allocation of land to the Bengalis from the plains;
(3) withdrawal of security forces from the CHT;
(4) constitutional recognition of ethnic minorities and a guarantee that their rights would not be altered without their consent; and
(5) withdrawal of Bengalis settled from the CHT those who entered after 17 August 1947. (Adopted from Chakma, 2012, p. 128)

The government refused to consider the demands, but the negotiation continued from both sides with an attitude of compromise. By 1995, an agreement was almost conducted, but two major issues remained unresolved: the point of autonomy and the subject of Bengali settlements. Although significant developments occurred in several matters, the two sides did not arrive at a conclusion.

However, the Awami League (AL) formed the government in 1996 through the National Parliamentary elections, and the government led by Prime Minister Sheikh Hasina had shown some readiness regarding a settlement of the CHT conflict. The government constituted a twelve-member National Committee on Chittagong Hill Tracts (NCCHT), headed by Abul Hasanat Abdullah, the chief whip of the government in the National Parliament, within a few weeks of taking the oath. Notably, neither of these committees—the multi-party parliamentary committee nor the NCCHT—was formed by the Parliament of Bangladesh (Chowdhury, 2012, pp. 57–58). Again, the PCJSS revised its demands and submitted them to the then AL-led government in the first round of meetings held in December 1996, which are mentioned below.

1. Constitutional recognition of ethnic minorities in the [C]HT
2. Formation of RC comprising the three hill districts with greater autonomy
3. Strengthening the existing LGCs
4. Withdrawal of security forces from [C]HT
5. Withdrawal of Bengali settlers. (Hasan, 1997, as cited in Chowdhury, 2012, p. 58)

This conflict spanning two decades cost the lives of more than 8,500 rebels, soldiers and civilians, of which 2,500 were civilians. Besides, over 50,000 Hill people were forced to flee to the Indian state of Tripura (Chowdhury, 2012, p. 5). Furthermore, another book revealed that at least 25,000 people were killed in the conflict between 1977 and 1997 (*The Daily Star*, 2003, as cited in Chakma, 2012, p. 126). Also, unofficial sources claimed that the actual number was more than the number revealed by official channels. The AL-led government and the PCJSS recognised the fact that such conflict cannot be solved militarily, and instead, a political solution would be fruitful in terms of ending the armed conflict. After seven rounds of closed-door negotiations, Abul Hasanat Abdullah, on behalf of the GoB, and Jyotirindra Bodhipriya Larma, on behalf of the inhabitants of the CHT, signed the historic CHT Peace Agreement on 2 December 1997 in Dhaka. It was hoped that the Agreement would put an end to the conflict. However, new challenges appeared concerning its implementation of politics.

3.6 Chapter Conclusion

From the initial historical review, it is evident that the Hill people were largely politically independent during the pre-colonial period. However, when the Mughal ruler conquered Chittagong, it marked the beginning of the erosion of the Hill communities' political autonomy. Moreover, Mughal records reveal that the Chakma Chief agreed to pay taxes to the Mughals in return for trading rights with those living on the plain lands. As mentioned previously, the process of the marginalisation of the Hill people mainly took place during the British colonial government era, as the British captured the political economy of the entire region to gain wealth. In doing so, they promulgated several initiatives from time to time. Most importantly, at the administrative level, through the introduction of the CHT Regulation of 1900, the British established power and authority over the CHT, its people and their lands. Although the British introduced civil and traditional institutions, the Chiefs (Rajas) were only empowered to collect taxes from the Hill ethnic communities on behalf of the government. In fact, all powers—executive, judicial and financial—were vested in the government-appointed district Superintendent. However, the Hill people regarded *jhum* cultivation as a way of life that was a part of their socio-cultural and economic background, but this form of cultivation was strongly discouraged by the British. With the British declaring RFs and banning *jhum* cultivation in this area, the Hill people were deprived of their community rights over the forest resources, with this also resulting in the scarcity of available land. These are the crux of the CHT Peace Agreement's implementation and/or non-implementation.

The behaviour of the state's domination shifted during the Pakistan era, where the CHT Manual provided the basic structure at the administrative level with some amendments. The government, along with donor agencies, also introduced some development projects which mostly exploited the natural resources of this area. For example, the Kaptai Hydro-electric project is one of the noticeable casual factors for many of the problems in the area, as it submerged vast areas of cultivable land in the total acreage of the Chittagong Hill Tracts (CHT). Because of this project, many people migrated to India while many others were internally displaced. On the other hand, the withdrawal of some restrictions from the CHT Manual facilitated the Bengali migrants in settling in the area, which intensified the scarcity of cultivable land.

However, in the new state of Bangladesh, considering their earlier experience of marginalisation, the Hill people demanded constitutional autonomy with their own legislature on the verge of the formation of the Constitution of Bangladesh. The state authority deemed it a question of national integrity and rejected their demands, and furthermore, adopted the constitution which declared Bangladesh as a unitary state. Afterwards, by forming a regional political organisation, the PCJSS continued their demand for autonomy. During the military and quasi-military rulers' period, the CHT issue was regarded as an economic and security concern. After the restoration of parliamentary forms of democracy in Bangladesh, a new hope was fostered as the government resumed initiatives for dialogue with the PCJSS leadership, believing that the problem should be solved politically. After several negotiation meetings during different government's regime, in 1997, the CHT Peace Agreement was signed. Conversely, as the Agreement has not yet been fully implemented, current politics are centred on the dispute of its implementation status as claimed by the GoB and the PCJSS leaders. This issue is addressed in the next chapter.

References

Abedin, Z. (1997). *CHT that sheds blood*. Ramon Publisher.
Adnan, S. (2004). *Migration land alienation and ethnic conflict: Causes of poverty in the Chittagong Hill Tracts of Bangladesh*. Research & Advisory Services.
Agarwal, A. K. (1988). *North-eastern economy: Problems and prospects*. Mittal Publications.
Chakma, B. (2012). Bound to be failed?: The 1997 Chittagong Hill Tracts 'peace accord'. In N. Uddin (Ed.), *Politics of peace: A case of the Chittagong Hill Tracts in Bangladesh* (pp. 121–142). Institute of Culture & Development Research.
Chakma, S. (1986). *Prasanga: Parbattya Chattagram* (Context: The Chittagong Hill Tracts). Nath Brothers.
Chowdhury, N. J. (2012). *Chittagong Hill tracts peace accord implementation: Promise and performance*. A H Development Publishing House.
Chowdhury, Z. H. (2001). Is the ethnic problem intractable? Prospects for success of the CHT peace treaty. *Social Science Review, 18*(2), 87–108.
Cowan, J. M. (1923). *Working plan for the forests of Chittagong Hill Tracts division*. Bengal Government Press.
Dewan, A. K. (1990). *Class and ethnicity in the hills of Bangladesh* (Unpublished doctoral dissertation). McGill University.
Gain, P. (Ed.). (2000). *The Chittagong Hill Tracts: Life and nature at risk*. Society for Environment and Human Development.
Haq, S., & Haque, E. (1990). *Disintegration process in action: The case of South Asia*. Bangladesh Institute of Law and International Affairs.
Hunter, W. W. (1876). *A statistical account of Bengal. Vol. VI. Chittagong Hill Tracts, Chittagong, Noakhali, Tipperah, Hill Tipperah*. Trubner & Co.
Huq, M. M. (1992). Changing nature of dominant social forces and interventions in the Chittagong Hill Tracts. *The Journal of Social Studies, 56*, 67–92.
Ishaq, M. (Ed.). (1971). *Bangladesh district gazetteers: Chittagong Hill-Tracts*. Establishment Division, Ministry of Cabinet Affairs, Government of Bangladesh.
Mey, W. (1984). *Genocide in the Chittagong Hill Tracts, Bangladesh* (IWGIA Document No. 51). International Work Group for Indigenous Affairs.
Mohsin, A. (2002). *The politics of nationalism: The case of the Chittagong Hill Tracts, Bangladesh*. The University Press Ltd.
Mohsin, A. (2003). *The Chittagong Hill Tracts, Bangladesh: On the difficult road to peace*. Lynne Rienner.

Mohsin, A., & Ahmed, I. (1996). Modernity, alienation and the environment: The experience of the hill people. *Journal of the Asiatic Society of Bangladesh, 41*(2), 265–286.

Rahman, M. M. (2011). *Struggling against exclusion—Adibasi in Chittagong Hill Tracts, Bangladesh*. Media-Tryck, Lund University.

Ranjan, S. P. (2015). *Practicing peace in the indigenous context: A study on three villages of the Chittagong Hill Tracts (CHT) in Bangladesh* (Doctoral dissertation). Hiroshima University.

Shelley, M. R. (Ed.). (1992). *The Chittagong Hill Tracts of Bangladesh: The untold story*. Centre For Development Research.

(The) Chittagong Hill Tracts Commission. (1991). *Life is not ours: Land and human rights in the Chittagong Hill Tracts, Bangladesh*. https://www.iwgia.org/images/publications//0129_Life_is_not_ours_1-108.pdf. Accessed 2 October 2020.

(The) Chittagong Hill Tracts Commission. (1992). *Life is not ours: Land and human rights in the Chittagong Hill Tracts, Bangladesh: An update of the May 1991 report*. https://www.iwgia.org/images/publications//0129_Life_is_not_ours_-_an_UPDATE.pdf. Accessed 2 October 2020.

Uppsala Conflict Data Program. (n.d.). *Bangladesh: Chittagong Hill Tracts*. https://ucdp.uu.se/conflict/322. Accessed 5 September 2020.

CHAPTER 4

Assessment of the Implementation Status of the CHT Peace Agreement

4.1 Chapter Introduction

In this chapter, an attempt has been made to highlight the implementation status of the CHT Peace Agreement. On the one hand, currently, the GoB claims that it has implemented the Agreement to a significant extent. On the contrary, the PCJSS's recognition of the situation differs from the government's claim (this dispute will be addressed in detail later in this chapter). However, it is not wrong to say that the Agreement inherently contained many ambiguities, especially relating to its implementation status. Before scrutinising this dispute, it would be pertinent to address two other important topics: the factors that contributed to the enactment of the CHT Peace Agreement in 1997 and its key features. However, in addition to the introduction and conclusion, this chapter deals with three interrelated matters that are addressed into three sections. Section 4.2 explores that certain underlying factors played a significant role in signing the CHT Peace Agreement in 1997. Although the GoB and the PCJSS were the primary parties in its negotiation, there were many visible (or invisible) motivations, for example, the PCJSS's fatigue caused by prolonged conflict, the realisation of the GoB regarding its political solution, the restoration of parliamentary forms of government in Bangladesh in the 1990s, India's changing strategy towards the CHT case, the activities of the diaspora, human rights forums, Western donor governments, NGOs, etc. These factors are discussed briefly in this section.

Section 4.3 has focused on the subject matter (or content) of the CHT Peace Agreement, in brief. The Agreement is comprised of four major parts, including its 72 sections (provisions/clauses). It has the function of upholding the political, socio-cultural and economic rights of all citizens of the Chittagong Hill Tracts (CHT). All the Agreement's subjects are included in Appendix 4. Section 4.4 deals with the dispute regarding the implementation status claimed by the two primary signatory parties, namely, the GoB and the PCJSS leadership. This section endeavours to incorporate a comparative discussion regarding the respective implementation status as argued by the GoB and the PCJSS. In doing so, the section has mostly relied on the book edited by Tripura (2016), published by the Ministry of Chittagong Hill Tracts Affairs (MoCHTA) and the report on the implementation status published by the PCJSS (2017a), with these sources relevant for an analysis of the number of implemented/non-implemented sections of the CHT Peace Agreement. To understand the real situation regarding the politics that affect the Agreement's implementation, this book throws light on the following gaps and relationships that form the crucial issues. These include maintaining the tribal-inhabited characteristics in the CHT, the settlement of lands by tribal families, transfer of all the subjects (including land management) to the Hill District Council (HDC), the supervisory functions of the CHTRC, the rehabilitation of tribal refugees including internally displaced people, the withdrawal of temporary army camps from the CHT, etc. as per specific sections of the Agreement.

4.2 Factors Underlying Signing of the CHT Peace Agreement

Many researchers have attempted to examine the factors that contributed to introducing the CHT Peace Agreement in 1997, while previous attempts to bring the Agreement into existence could not reach a beneficial solution. To be concise, the following issues are established to have a contributory role in concluding the negotiations and getting the CHT Peace Agreement in 1997.

War fatigue wore both the PCJSS and the GoB (notably, the state's security forces) down, and both parties comprehended the futility of the military approach to the solution of the conflict. By the 1980s, the exhaustion was becoming evident in the ranks of the SB; hence, the opinion in favour of a negotiated settlement gained ground within the PCJSS leadership. Furthermore, the government also became conscious that the CHT case was fundamentally political in nature and that it could not be resolved by military means. From the late 1980s onwards, this consciousness was the leading thought for various government agencies as well as policymakers. The restoration of parliamentary forms of government in Bangladesh in the 1990s and India's changing strategy (its role is further elaborated upon in Chapter 7) regarding the CHT case were the most influential factors in terms of signing the CHT Peace Agreement in 1997 (Chakma, 2012, p. 129; Mohsin, 2003, p. 90).

The international actors and the diaspora from the CHT played an important role in connecting with international human rights organisations to promote international awareness to improve the human rights situation in the CHT and bring it to greater attention. Moreover, donors and Western government also commenced providing economic assistance to improve the human rights situation of the Hill people, as the GoB sought aid from the donors. Also, the CHT indigenous people sought international attention as human rights violations occurred in the CHT available on the websites with the support of information and communication technology. Thus, the GoB confronted pressure from international human rights forums, Western donor governments, international organisations, NGOs, etc., with this providing the impetus to solve the problem. The factor of financial aid as well as international human rights organisations have played an influential role in Dhaka's decision to move towards a political settlement of the conflict through effective negotiations with the PCJSS leadership from the 1990s onward and the signing of the CHT Peace Agreement in 1997 (Chakma, 2012, p. 129). The international actors' involvement in the CHT case is analysed in detail in Chapter 7, and the domestic background of the signing of the Agreement is discussed mostly in Chapter 3 as well as in Chapter 5.

4.3 Key Features of the CHT Peace Agreement and Its Major Subjects

In this section, an attempt has been made to address the subject matter of the CHT Peace Agreement and provide a brief overview of the same, to proceed with its analytical arguments in the subsequent sections. After long years of dialogue and negotiation, when the GoB (more explicitly, the NCCHT) and the PCJSS signed the Agreement, it seemingly put an end to the decades-old ethnic conflict and was also widely hailed in the national and international communities. As mentioned in Chapter 1, the CHT Peace Agreement has four parts and 72 sections (for details, see the CHT Peace Agreement in Appendix 4). The headings of the four parts are (Ka) General, (Kha) Hill District Local Government Council/Hill District Council, (Ga) Chittagong Hill Tracts Regional Council (CHTRC) and (Gha) Rehabilitation, general amnesty and other matters. The document of this Agreement is composed in the Bengali language (with the Bengali word *chukti*, meaning agreement, being used), and the words Ka, Kha, Ga and Gha are the first four consonants of Bangla language, respectively. Briefly, the following are the synthesised points of the CHT Peace Agreement which have been broadly separated as per the four parts: A, B, C and D (*Translated English Version of Agreement Between*, n.d.).

A. The first part named (Ka) General, with four sections, considers the CHT as a tribal-inhabited region and recognises the need for protecting the characteristics as well as attaining overall development in the region. This part also clarifies the responsibility of the two parties to make, alter, amend as well as add laws and procedures for the governance of this area. Besides, this part confirms the provision of a mechanism to observe the progress, stating the formation of an Implementation Committee that will monitor the implementation process of the CHT Peace Agreement. As per Section A.3 of the Agreement, the Implementation Committee will consist of three members: (a) Convenor (a member nominated by the Prime Minister), (b) Member (Chairman of the Task Force that is formed under the purview of the Agreement) and (c) Member (President of PCJSS).

B. The second part (Kha) with 35 sections deals with amending, incorporating, or writing the existing Parbatya Zilla Sthanio Sarkar Parishad Ayin, 1989 (Hill District Local Government Council Act of 1989), Rangamati Parbatya Zilla Sthanio Sarkar Parishad Ayin, 1989 (Rangamati Hill District Local Government Council Act 1989), Bandarban Parbatya Zilla Sthanio Sarkar Parishad Ayin, 1989 (Bandarban Hill District Local Government Council Act 1989) and Khagrachhari Parbatya Zilla Sthanio Sarkar Parishad Ayin, 1989 (Khagrachhari Hill District Local Government Council

Act 1989), including their different sections, and furthermore, states that the name shall be changed to Parbatya Zilla Parishad (Hill District Council) of the concerned three Hill districts. The sections of this part incorporate the detailed provisions on proposed amendments to the District Council laws to strengthen the existing power of the Councils and to extend their jurisdiction to include new subjects. The members, including the tribal Chairman of the District Councils, are to be directly elected by the CHT people, and their tenure in the Council shall be five years instead of three years. This part also provides details regarding the functions and responsibilities of the HDCs:

a) Land and land management;
b) Police (local);
c) Tribal law and social justice;
d) Youth welfare;
e) Environmental protection and development;
f) Local tourism;
g) Improvement [of] trust and other institutions concerning local administration, other than Municipality and Union Council;
h) Issuing license for local commerce and industries;
i) Proper utilization of rivers and streams, canals and Beels and irrigational system other than water resources of the Kaptai Lake;
j) Maintaining of the statistics of birth and death;
k) Wholesale business;
l) Jum cultivation. (*Translated English Version of Agreement Between*, n.d., Section B.34)

C. The third part (Ga) with 14 sections introduces the Chittagong Hill Tracts Regional Council (CHTRC) and lays down the composition, power and functions of this new body. The CHTRC is responsible for coordinating all the development activities carried out by the three HDCs and will also superintend as well as harmonise all the affairs administered by the District Councils. Besides, under the CHT Peace Agreement, if any incompatibility or lack of harmony is found in performing the responsibilities assigned to the three HDCs, the decision of the CHTRC shall be final (*Translated English Version of Agreement Between*, n.d., Section C.9.a). While making any law concerning the CHT, the government will enact such a law in consultation with and as per the advice of the

CHTRC. In the case of the amendment of any law that bears an adverse effect on the development of this region and the welfare of the tribal people, the CHTRC will be asked with applying or submitting a recommendation to the government. In general, as an apex body in the CHT, the CHTRC is also to be in charge of supervising the general administration, development activities and law and order of the region, whereas in reality, it is not always agreed that the CHTRC could exercise such power as a superior body. This part also organises the structure of CHTRC, which consists of 22 members, including its tribal Chairman. Among them, twelve are to be male tribal members, two are to be female tribal members, six are to be male non-tribal members and one is to be a female non-tribal member. Members of the CHTRC and its Chairperson (who enjoys the status of a State Minister) are to be elected by the elected members of the District Councils. Furthermore, the Chairman of the three HDCs will be the ex officio members of the CHTRC, and they shall have the rights to exercise voting power. The tenure of the CHTRC will be five years. As per the provisions of the CHT Peace Agreement, in the case of both the CHTRC and the HDCs, the Chairpersons as well as two-thirds of the seats are to be reserved for the CHT indigenous people, intending to ensure their representation and authority regarding the CHT cause.

D. The fourth part (Gha) with 19 sections deals with a wide range of issues regarding the rehabilitation of the refugees—both returnees from India and internally displaced Hill people, granting general amnesty to the PCJSS's guerrilla fighters and other people involved in the armed struggle, etc. This part of the Agreement also stipulates that a land survey in the CHT following the rehabilitation of the refugees will be conducted and that the land ownership of tribal people is to be recorded and ensured after proper verification. Moreover, it states that the government will provide two acres of land to each landless family. A Commission (Land Commission) headed by a retired justice is to be constituted to settle land disputes. Other members of the Commission are the concerned Circle Chief, Chairman of the CHTRC or representative, Divisional Commissioner/Additional Commissioner and the concerned HDC Chairman. This part of the Agreement also specifies that all the temporary camps of the army will be dismantled, and the soldiers of the dismantled camps will be sent back to the permanent cantonments in phases. A full-fledged ministry dealing with the CHT's affairs, headed by a Minister from among the tribal community, will be established. It is to have a twelve-member Advisory Committee to lend support to its functions.

4.4 Implementation Status: A Dispute

The post-Agreement CHT situation is strongly linked to the implementation concern of the CHT Peace Agreement. As long as the implementation process is not finalised, the real intention of the GoB in implementing the CHT Peace Agreement will be questioned. After signing the Agreement, recent politics have evolved in terms of the dispute concerning the implementation status claimed by the GoB and by the PCJSS. These factors are briefly analysed in the following sub-sections.

4.4.1 Implementation Status Claimed by the Government of Bangladesh (GoB)

On 10 February 2016, in reply to a starred question raised by the independent lawmaker Ushatun Talukder from the Rangamati constituency, Prime Minister Sheikh Hasina informed the National Parliament of Bangladesh of the implementation status of the CHT Peace Agreement that is presented in Table 4.1.

Table 4.1 Data of implementation status claimed by the Government of Bangladesh (GoB)

Part: Sections (provisions/clauses)	Implementation status	Total
A: 1, 2, 3, 4 B: 1, 2, 3, 5, 6, 7, 8, 10, 11, 12, 13, 14, 15, 16, 17, 18, 20, 21, 22, 23, 25, 28, 30, 31, 32, 33 C: 1, 7, 8, 9, 10, 12, 14 D: 1, 5, 8, 10, 11, 12, 13, 14, 15, 16,19	Fully implemented	48 Sections
B: 4.D, 9, 19, 24, 27, 34 C: 2, 3, 4, 5, 6 D: 4, 6, 17, 18	Partially implemented	15 Sections
B: 26, 29, 35 C: 11, 13 D: 2, 3, 7, 9	Under the process of implementation	9 Sections

Source Developed by author based on Tripura (2016, p. 35)

On 21 January 2018, Prime Minister Sheikh Hasina again mentioned that most parts of the CHT Peace Agreement had already been implemented and the rest would certainly be implemented ("CHT People", 2018). After Prime Minister Hasina's speeches in the National Parliament on 2 December 2019, marking the 22nd anniversary of the CHT Peace Agreement, Qadir (2019) noted that 48 of the 72 sections of the Agreement had at that point been fully implemented, while 15 sections were partially implemented and 9 sections were undergoing an implementation process.

4.4.2 Implementation Status Claimed by the Parbatya Chattagram Jana Samhati Samiti (PCJSS)

On 16 February 2016, in reaction to the Prime Minister's speech in Parliament, the PCJSS published and circulated an open letter, explaining many of the nonconformities; for example, the PCJSS, including CHT inhabitants and civil society, claimed that two-thirds of the CHT Peace Agreement, with its crucial provisions, were not yet implemented (Parbatya Chattagram Jana Samhati Samiti, 2016, p. 2). Along the same lines, in a report published in an English newspaper on 3 December 2021, marking the 24th anniversary of the Agreement, PCJSS claimed that 25 clauses of the CHT Peace Agreement had been implemented, with 18 partially implemented and the remaining 29 unimplemented ("Conspiracy on", 2021). Jyotirindra Bodhipriya Larma (i.e. Santu Larma), President of the PCJSS, once mentioned that this was not merely a claim and that they were regularly publishing reports indicating many sections of the Agreement that had not been implemented. The implementation status claimed by the PCJSS is shown in Table 4.2.

Table 4.2 Data of implementation status claimed by the PCJSS

Main issues/provisions	Full impl.	Partial impl.	Un-impl.
A. General			
A.1: Preservation of Tribal-inhabited Feature of CHT Region			√
A.2: Enactment and Amendment of Various Laws			√[a]
A.3: CHT Accord Implementation Monitoring Committee		√	
B. Hill District Local Government Council/Hill District Council			
B.3: Identification of "Non-Tribal Permanent Residents" of the Region			√
B.4(d): Issuance of Certificate to the non-tribal People		√	
B.9: Qualification of a Voter and Voter List			√
B.13 and 14: Appointment of Officers and Employees of the Council	√		
B.19: Development Planning			√
B.24 and 25: District Police			√
B.26: Special Provision relating to Land			√
B.27: Collection of Land Development Tax			√
B.28, 29 and 32: Special Prerogatives of the HDCs			√
B.34 Subjects under Jurisdiction of HDC and their Transfers		√	
C. Chittagong Hill Tracts Regional Council			
C.1: Formation of Regional Council	√		
C.9(a): Supervision and Coordination of HDC functions			√
C.9(b): Supervision and Coordination of Local Councils including the Municipalities			√
C.9(c): Supervision and Coordination of General Administration, Law & Order and Development			√
C.9(d): Coordination of Disaster Management and Relief Program including NGO Activities			√
C.9(e): Coordination and Supervision of Tribal Customary Laws and Community Adjudication			√
C.9(f): Issuance of Licenses for Heavy Industries			√
C.10: General and Overall Supervision over CHT Development Board			√

(continued)

Table 4.2 (continued)

Main issues/provisions	Full impl.	Partial impl.	Un-impl.
C.11: Removal of Inconsistencies of CHT Regulation of 1900 and other related Acts			√
C.13: Prerogatives of CHT Regional Council in Making Law			√
D. Rehabilitation, General Amnesty and Other Matters			
D.1: Rehabilitation of India-returnee Refugees		√	
D.1 and 2: Rehabilitation of the Internally Displaced People			√[a]
D.3: Settlement of Lands with the Landless			√
D.4, 5 and 6: Land Commission and Land Dispute Resolution			√[a]
D.8: Cancellation of Leases on Lands allotted for Rubber and other Plantation			√
D.9: Allocation of Funds and Encouragement on Tourism		√	
D.10: Preservation of Quota and providing Stipend		√	
D.11: Distinctness of Tribal Customs & Culture			√
D.13: Deposit of Arms and Ammunitions by the Members of the PCJSS	√		
D.14 and 16(b): General Amnesty and Withdrawal of Cases		√	
D.16(d)(e)(f): Loan Exemption, Reinstatement in Service and Rehabilitation of Members of the PCJSS		√	
D.17: Withdrawal of Temporary Camps and Transfer of Abandoned Lands			√[a]
D.18: Appointment of Permanent Residents in all kinds of Services on Priority Basis		√	
D.19: Ministry of CHT Affairs	√		
Main Issues: 37	4	9	24

[a]Few initiatives have been taken to implement these fundamental issues. However, essential functions have not yet been started

Source Developed by author based on Parbatya Chattagram Jana Samhati Samiti [PCJSS] (2017a, pp. 41–42) and Parbatya Chattagram Jana Samhati Samiti [PCJSS] (2017b, pp. 45–46)

4.4.3 Dispute Regarding Implementation Status as Argued by the GoB and the PCJSS

Real peace would be much closer if the complete implementation of all the provisions of the CHT Peace Agreement were carried out. Here, an attempt has been made for a comparative analysis of the implementation status claimed by the two primary signatory parties (the GoB and the PCJSS) of the Agreement. Here, some crucial sections of the Agreement have been addressed, that is, A.1 (tribal-inhabited characteristics of CHT), B.26 (land management), B.34 (jurisdiction of HDCs), C.9.a (supervision of the CHTRC), C.13 (prerogatives of the CHTRC), D.1 (rehabilitation of tribal refugees), D.3 (settlement of lands), D.4 (land dispute resolution) and D.17 (withdrawal of temporary army camps). In going through the subject matter of these selected sections (also described in the following tables), it is clear that many are interrelated with the land issue. They are of frequent occurrence. For example, almost all the people at the governmental and non-governmental level assumed the following: if the dispute of land is solved, 80% of the CHT problem will be solved (*"Parbatya Chattagramer"*, 2017). This analysis was similar to that of the Uppsala Conflict Data Program [UCDP] (n.d.): although many of the fundamental legal and administrative aspects of the CHT Peace Agreement had been implemented, some crucial questions remained unresolved, for example, the withdrawal of the military from the CHT and the reclamation of land by returning Hill indigenous people. The content of these sections, as mentioned above, is mostly what has provided me with the logical motivation to adopt them as crucial provisions for the study's subsequent analysis. For comparative discussion, the two sources relied upon are: (1) the Ministry of Chittagong Hill Tracts Affairs (MoCHTA)'s book, edited by Tripura (2016, pp. 49–103), indicating the implementation status of the Agreement claimed by the GoB, and (2) a brief report published by the PCJSS (2017a, pp. 8–31) arguing that many sections of the Agreement have not yet been implemented. These two sources have been selected for the following reasons: MoCHTA's book (Tripura, 2016) presents the most recent readily available organised data about the implementation status claimed by the GoB, while the PCJSS's report of 2017 relevantly contests MoCHTA's book published in 2016 (Tripura, 2016). Moreover, the dispute about the number of implemented sections/provisions of the CHT Peace Agreement is almost the same, even after more than two decades have passed.

In presenting the analysis here, this section incorporates nine tables, and each of the tables contains four rows. The first row consists of the subject matter of the original provisions written in the CHT Peace Agreement (all the provisions/sections are enclosed in Appendix 4). The second row reveals GoB's statement regarding the implementation status of the Agreement and the explanation for their claim based on Tripura (2016), the book mentioned above. The third row incorporates PCJSS's arguments regarding the implementation status, which mostly oppose the government's claim as per the report. Among many of PCJSS's elaborate explanations, here, a few sentences have been cited within the quotation mark. In the fourth row, an attempt has been made to present an analysis based on the previous three rows and other documents that have been studied. The title of the tables, including the section number, indicates the summary of the subject matter of the respective original provision/section of the CHT Peace Agreement.

Table 4.3 A.1 (keeping up tribal-inhabited characteristics of the CHT)

Subject matters	"Both the parties, having considered the Chittagong Hill Tracts region as a tribal-inhabited region, recognized the need of preserving the characteristics of this region and attaining the overall development thereof" (*Translated English Version of Agreement Between*, n.d., Section A.1)
GoB's statement	"Implemented
	Outline of planning has been given for the preservation of the characteristics and overall development of the region in Vision 2021 of the government and 6th Five Year Plan. By inserting sub-section 23(A) in the Constitution of Bangladesh through the 15th amendment, the preservation and development of language and culture of the Tribal and Ethnic minorities of Bangladesh has been ensured" (Tripura, 2016, p. 49)
PCJSS's Argument	"Unimplemented
	The statement pronounced by the government claiming that the issue of development and preservation of language and culture of the tribes, minor races, ethnic sects and communities has been ensured through inclusion in Article 23(a) under the 15th Amendment to the constitution is not appropriate. In order to preserve the tribal pre-dominated characteristics of the region, on part of the government, it is urgent (1) to introduce a statutory measure to the constitution stating that CHT is a region pre-dominated by multi-lingual hill/tribal people; (2) to incorporate the words 'or the hill people of Chittagong Hill Tracts' immediately after the words "in favour of women or children or the backward sections of citizens" in Article 28(4) of the constitution and (3) to adopt and implement a plan for rehabilitation of settlers settled in decades of 1980s in the plain districts" (PCJSS, 2017a, p. 9)
Analysis	Analysing some crucial matters that deserve early resolution according to the Agreement, the PCJSS disagreed with the government's statement about this section. Article 23A states the following: "[t]he State shall take steps to protect and develop the unique local culture and tradition of the tribes, minor races, ethnic sects and communities" (Government of Bangladesh, 2014, p. 7). The PCJSS explicitly urged that three issues be resolved to implement this section. According to the PCJSS, no measure has been undertaken yet to do the same. While the government enacted Article 23A addressing the different sects of people all over the country, the PCJSS demands the constitutional recognition of the tribal people of the CHT and the initiatives in this regard

Source Developed by author from references mentioned above

Table 4.4 B.26 (special provision relating to the land management regarding HDCs' permission)

Subject matters	"Section 64 shall be amended and enacted as follows: a) Notwithstanding anything contained in any other law for the time being in force, no land and premises, including the leasable *Khas* lands, within the territorial limits of the Hill Districts shall be transferable by *Ijara*, settlement, purchase or sale except with the prior permission of the Council; Provided that this provision shall not be applicable in respect of the area of Reserved Forest, Kaptai Hydro-electric Project, Betbunia Satellite Station, State-owned in the industries and factories and the lands recorded in the name of the Government b) Notwithstanding anything contained in any other law for the time being in force, [n]o land, hill or forest under the controlled and within the jurisdiction of the Council shall be acquired or transferred by the Government without consultation with or the consent of the Council c) The Parishad may supervise and control the works of the Headmen, Chainmen, *Amins*, Surveyors, *Kanungos* and Assistant Commissioner (land) d) The reclaimed fringe lands of Kaptai Lake shall be leased out on priority basis to the original owners" (*Translated English Version of Agreement Between*, n.d., Section B.26)
GoB's statement	a) "Under Process HDC Act has been amended in 1998. Settlement, purchase, sale and transfer of Land are done with prior permission of Hill District Council. Allotment of land without special cases (educational institutions, religious institutions, place of cremation, graveyard, governmental office, Scout Building, Freedom fighter's complex and Local Tourism under the management of Hill District Council) remains suspended through MoCHTA (Pa-1)-Pa: District/ Miscellaneous/85/2000-280, Dated 23/10/01 b) Under Process HDC Act has been amended in 1998. Settlement, purchase, sale and transfer of Land are done with prior permission of Hill District Council c) Under Process d) Under Process" (Tripura, 2016, pp. 66–67)
PCJSS's argument	"As per this provision, though opinion is given on part of government to the affect that lands in settlement, purchase, selling, transfer and acquisition is done having prior approval of the HDC is not of jurisprudence. As per Section 34(a) under Part B of the Accord, the subject 'Land and Land Management' is a subject within jurisdiction of HDC. But since the subject has not been transferred to the HDC yet, it is not possible to formulate regulation relating to this provision to deal with it. On the other hand, the Deputy Commissioners have been practicing the process of mutation, acquisition, lease and settlement following the Chittagong Hill Tracts Regulation 1900" (PCJSS, 2017a, pp. 16–17)

(continued)

Table 4.4 (continued)

Analysis	About seeking (and granting) prior permission from the HDCs, the PCJSS disagreed with the government's statement. Chapter 3 addresses the Hill people's alienation in terms of their land and forests. Similar to the preceding regimes (British and Pakistan), the GoB maintains most of the forests and lands of CHT as the state's Reserve Forests (RFs). Therefore, the land becomes the crux of the conflict in this area. Provision B.26.a indicates that this section does not apply to the RFs along with other subjects. Therefore, most of the lands remain out of the HDCs' jurisdiction. The government also agrees that Section B.26 and its sub-sections are under the process/progress of implementation. It is a matter of regret that it is still under process even though more than two decades have passed since the signing of the Agreement

Source Developed by author from references mentioned above

Table 4.5 B.34 (transferred subjects under the jurisdiction of HDCs)

Subject matters	"The following subjects shall be included in the functions and the responsibilities of the Hill District Council: a) Land and land management; b) Police (local); c) Tribal law and social justice; d) Youth welfare; e) Environmental protection and development; f) Local tourism; g) Improvement [of] trust and other institutions concerning local administration, other than Municipality and Union Council; h) Issuing license for local commerce and industries; i) Proper utilization of rivers and streams, canals and Beels and irrigation system other than water resources of the Kaptai Lake; j) Maintaining of the statistics of birth and deaths; k) Wholesale business; l) Jum cultivation" (*Translated English Version of Agreement Between*, n.d., Section B.34)
GoB's statement	"Partially Implemented. … So far 30 subjects/department have been transferred to RHDC [Rangamati Hill District Council] & KHDC [Khagrachhari Hill District Council] and 28 subjects/department have been transferred to BHDC. Remaining subjects/departments are in the process of transfer" (Tripura, 2016, pp. 72–75)
PCJSS's argument	"The subjects mentioned in Section B.34 of the Accord have been incorporated under Schedule 1 of the HDC Act. From among these, the subjects mentioned in serials (g), (h), (j), (l) and (p) have been transferred to HDC through executive order. The rest of the subjects have not been transferred" (PCJSS, 2017a, p. 18)
Analysis	The total subjects under the HDCs are 33, according to the Agreement. The GoB and the PCJSS hold different views regarding the number of subjects/offices that have been transferred to the Councils. As long as all the subjects, including the crucial subject (as mentioned by the PCJSS's statement), are not totally implemented, the HDCs would not adequately be empowered

Source Developed by author from references mentioned above

Table 4.6 C.9.a (supervision and coordination of HDCs' functions through CHTRC)

Subject matters	"The Council shall coordinate all the development activities carried out by the three Hill District Councils, and shall also superintend and harmonize all the affairs of and assigned to the three Hill District Councils. Besides, in the event of lack of harmony or any inconsistency being found in the discharge of responsibilities given to the three Hill District Councils, the decision of the Regional Council shall be final" (*Translated English Version of Agreement Between*, n.d., Section C.9.a)
GoB's statement	"Implemented CHTRC as an apex body can supervise and coordinate all the development activities carried out by the three Hill District Council as per CHTRC Act" (Tripura, 2016, pp. 81–82)
PCJSS's argument	"Till now, it is due to non-cooperation of three HDCs and the Ministry of CHT Affairs, the supervision and coordination of all subjects including the development programs of the three HDCs could not be carried out by CHT Regional Council" (PCJSS, 2017a, p. 19)
Analysis	The CHT Peace Agreement was signed with the spirit of self-governance through the three HDCs and the CHTRC (an apex body in the CHT). If CHTRC is not adequately empowered with its rules as well as policy formulation (or new laws concerning the CHT), the main aim of achieving peace would be difficult. This is considered as a deviation from the Agreement

Source Developed by author from references mentioned above

Table 4.7 C.13 (prerogatives of CHTRC in formulating and amending law)

Subject matters	"In making any law in connection with Chittagong Hill Tracts, the Government shall enact such law in consultation with and as per advice of the Regional Council. If it becomes necessary to amend any law which bears an adverse effect on the development of the three hill districts and welfare of the tribal people or to enact new law, the Council shall be competent to apply or submit recommendations to the Government" (*Translated English Version of Agreement Between*, n.d., Section C.13)
GoB's statement	"Under Process" (Tripura, 2016, p. 84)
PCJSS's argument	"The provision of the Accord has not been implemented. The CHT Regional Council so far, has provided advices in alternation or bringing amendment to such provisions of laws that may make adverse effects to CHT Accord, laws of CHT region and development of hill district and to the path towards welfare of the tribal peoples. But in most cases, either advice from CHT Regional Council was not sought or advice of CHT Regional Council was not accepted" (PCJSS, 2017a, p. 23)
Analysis	In the report, PCJSS (2017a) mentioned many subjects where an opinion from the CHTRC was not sought, or where the government did not accept advice from the CHTRC in amending or formulating new laws concerning the Chittagong Hill Tracts (CHT). This is also considered as a deviation from the CHT Peace Agreement

Source Developed by author from references mentioned above

Table 4.8 D.1 (rehabilitation of India-returnee tribal refugees and Internally Displaced Peoples)

Subject matters	"With a view to bringing the tribal refugees staying in the Tripura State of India back to the country, an agreement was signed on the 9th day of March, '97 at Agartala of Tripura State between the Government and the Leaders of tribal refugees. In pursuance of that Agreement, the tribal refugees started coming back to the country since 28th day of March, '97. This process shall remain un-hindered and to that end all possible cooperation shall be given from the end of the Jana Samhati Samiti. After ascertaining the identity of the Internally Displaced Persons of the three hill districts, rehabilitation measures shall be undertaken through a Task Force" (*Translated English Version of Agreement Between*, n.d., Section D.1)
GoB's statement	"Implemented Mr. Jatindra Lal Tripura is currently serving as the Chairman of the Task Force. 6th meeting of Task Force was held on 26.02.2015. It was mentioned in the meeting, that amount of the 12,223 families of India returned refugees have been rehabilitated. But still many families have not got back their lands" (Tripura, 2016, p. 86)
PCJSS's argument	"Most of the economic facilities as per the Agreement were provided to most of the refugees numbering 64,609 of 12,222 families through the Task Force. But 9,780 Jumma families are yet to get back their lands; 890 families are yet to get cash against pairs of bullocks; … A decision was resolved in the Task Force meeting held on 13-09-2014 to provide the ration and other financial facilities to the internally displaced tribal families and minutes of the meeting including the decision was approved in the Task Force meeting held on 28-02-2015. But the decision has not yet been implemented" (PCJSS, 2017a, p. 24)
Analysis	The GoB defined the number of refugees who had returned from India. On the other hand, the PCJSS identified some issues relating to rehabilitation, for example, land, cash, bank loan, jobs, etc. have not yet been solved. The GoB authority also agreed with the PCJSS regarding the fact that many families have not got their lands back. Even now, the Task Force has not finalised the number of Internally Displaced Peoples (IDPs). According to a source of the Task Force, the IDP families probably number more than 50,000 (Chakma & Barua, 2017)

Source Developed by author from references mentioned above

Table 4.9 D.3 (settlement of lands to the landless tribal families)

Subject matters	"In order to ensure the land-ownership of tribal families having no land or lands below 2 (two) acres, the Government shall, subject to availability of land in the locality, ensure settling 2 (two) acres of land per family. In the event of non-availability of required land, grove-lands shall be tapped" (*Translated English Version of Agreement Between*, n.d., Section D.3)
GoB's statement	"Under Process Due to prevailing situation in CHT apart from some special land cases allotment remains suspended in three hill districts since October 23, 2001 Vide memo no Pachbim(P-1)-Pa: District/Miscellaneous/85/2000-280 dated 23/10/2001. With the functioning of Land Commission [,] it will be possible to allocate necessary lands in this regard" (Tripura, 2016, p. 88)
PCJSS's argument	"This provision of the Accord has not yet been implemented" (PCJSS, 2017a, p. 25)
Analysis	As the landless (or those with lands less than two acres) tribal families have not yet received lands according to this provision, the intention of the government in implementing the Agreement has been questioned

Source Developed by author from references mentioned above

Table 4.10 D.4 (land dispute resolution through Land Commission)

Subject matters	"A Commission (Land Commission) shall be constituted under the leadership of a retired Justice for settlement of disputes regarding lands and premises. This Commission shall, in addition to early disposal of land disputes of the rehabilitated refugees, have full authority to annul the rights of ownership of those hills and lands which have been illegally settled and in respect of which illegal dispossession has taken place. No appeal shall be maintainable against the judgment of this Commission and the decision of this Commission shall be deemed to be final. This provision shall be applicable in case of Fringe-lands" (*Translated English Version of Agreement Between*, n.d., Section D.4)
GoB's statement	"Partially Implemented On 27 May 2013[,] the Land Ministry placed a draft amendment bill titled "CHT Land Disputes Resolution Commission Act (Amendment) Bill" before the Cabinet and accordingly on 3 June 2013 the Cabinet approved this amendment Bill. Again, on 16 June 2013[,] the amendment Bill 2013 was introduced in the Parliament for adoption. The Parliament sent it to the Parliamentary Standing Committee on the Land Ministry seeking its opinion. The bill will be placed soon before the Parliament for final approval" (Tripura, 2016, pp. 88–89)
PCJSS's argument	"The contradictory sections of the CHT Land Dispute Resolution Commission Act 2001 had been amended through passing the CHT Land Dispute Resolution Commission Act (Amendment) 2016 in the parliament of 6 October 2016. After amendment of the law, having the Draft Regulation of the Land Commission formulated, the CHTRC submitted the draft to the Ministry of Lands on 1 January 2017 for approval. But the government has not yet finalized the regulation. As a result, the work for resolution of land dispute has not yet been started to this day" (PCJSS, 2017a, p. 25)
Analysis	After the amendment, on 8 September 2016, the Land Commission called on applications from the aggrieved persons. Although the first deadline expired on 24 October 2016, according to the decision of the Commission, submissions of applications would remain open for an indefinite period (Kormokar & Dewan, 2017). The Commission Chairman, Justice Anwar-ul Haque (who was re-appointed on 11 December 2017), informed that, so far, 22,000 applications have been received for the settlement of the land dispute ("CHT Body", 2018). Conversely, the Commission is not to play a significant role as the rules and regulations have not yet been enacted

Source Developed by author from references mentioned above

Table 4.11 D.17 (withdrawal of temporary camps and handover of abandoned lands)

Subject matters	"a) After the signing and execution of the Agreement between the Government and the Jana Samhati Samiti and immediately after return of the members of Jana Samhati Samiti to normal life, all the temporary camps of the army, the Ansars [auxiliary forces] and the Village Defence Party (VDP), excepting the Border Security Force (BDR) and permanent army establishment (being those three at the three district headquarters and those at Alikadam, Ruma and Dighinala), shall be taken back by phases from Chittagong Hill Tracts to permanent cantonments and the time-limit shall be fixed for its purpose. In case of deterioration of the law and order situation, in time of normal calamities and for similar other purposes, Army Forces may be deployed under the authority of the civil administration in adherence to Law and Rules as are applicable to all the other parts of the country. In this respect, the Regional Council may, in order to get the required or timely help make requests to the appropriate authority b) The lands and premises abandoned by the cantonments, the camps of the military and para-military forces shall be made over to their real owners or to the Hill District Councils" (*Translated English Version of Agreement Between*, n.d., Section D.17)
GoB's statement	a) "Under process" (Tripura, 2016, p. 99) b) "Implemented" (Tripura, 2016, p. 101)
PCJSS's argument	a) "After signing the Accord, it has been learnt that from among more than 500 camps, it was only 70 temporary camps were withdrawn in 1997–1999 and 35 temporary camps in 2009–2013 were withdrawn. But many of the withdrawn camps have been re-established back. … It is to be mentioned that in place of 'Operation Dabanol' (Operation Wildfire), 'Operation Uttoran' (Operation Upliftment) was unilaterally decided and promulgated by the government in CHT. By merit of the 'Operation Uttoron', the army has been playing the decision-making role in all the affairs including the general administration, law & order and development sectors and has been doing its best to hinder the implementation process of the CHT Accord by various means and ways" (PCJSS, 2017a, p. 30) b) "This provision of the Accord is partially implemented. But some cases, though the authorities of the withdrawn camps abandoned the lands, transferring the lands to the original owners has not been done" (PCJSS, 2017a, p. 30)

(continued)

Table 4.11 (continued)

Analysis	a) According to the statement by Prime Minister Sheikh Hasina in the Bangladesh National Parliament on 10 February 2016, 232 temporary army camps were in place during the signing of the CHT Peace Agreement: of these, more than half had been withdrawn phase by phase in the previous 17 years (Tripura, 2016, p. 42). On 21 January 2018, Prime Minister Sheikh Hasina again noted that the government had signed the Agreement and were implementing it: they have withdrawn 250 army camps from the CHT ("CHT People", 2018). The former Secretary of the MoCHTA, Nurul Amin, added that, at that point, the authorities had withdrawn 240 army camps from the region (Ullah, 2018). From these data, as mentioned above, the total number of army camps deployed in the CHT and the number of camps withdrawn remain unclear. However, the PCJSS and the government have not got a consensus regarding the actual number of temporary military camps. Also, the PCJSS expressed their deep concern about the existing temporary camps and their (armies') interference in civil administration. The PCJSS also highlighted the fact that the timeline for withdrawal (return) of the temporary camps to their respective permanent Cantonments had not been fixed yet b) Regarding this provision, PCJSS argued that it had been partially implemented

Source Developed by author from references mentioned above

4.4.4 Summary of Discussion Regarding the Implementation Dispute (Tables 4.3, 4.4, 4.5, 4.6, 4.7, 4.8, 4.9, 4.10, and 4.11)

Almost all researchers who have worked on the CHT case have agreed about the importance of the full implementation of all sections of the CHT Peace Agreement. When the Agreement was signed, its beneficiaries (here, mainly the Hill people and surely the PCJSS) were expecting its complete implementation for some of their demands to be fulfilled. More than two decades have passed since the Agreement was signed, and although the GoB claims that most of the sections have been implemented, the PCJSS disagrees, as addressed in the discussion above. To address this debate, some crucial sections have been analysed, and among these sections: for example, the land-related problem has not been solved yet. In the earlier sub-sections, the following has been mentioned: if the land dispute was solved, 80% of the CHT problem would be solved. The comparative discussion that has been conducted in the tables mentioned above represents the government's real motive in implementing and/or non-implementing the Agreement. If we critically scrutinise the arguments above, it becomes evident from the tables that the GoB also agreed to the fact that most of these crucial sections of the Agreement are partially implemented or under process. Without implementing the crucial subjects, for example, retaining the tribal-inhabited characteristics of the CHT, land management, subjects transferred to the HDCs, the supervisory functions of the CHTRC, the rehabilitation of IDPs, the settlement of lands in terms of the tribal families, the withdrawal of temporary army camps and tribal refugees who have returned from India, it is far from overcoming the challenges of implementation. And this brings into question, the real motives of the government. However, different stakeholders, for example, the government, opposition political parties, CHT indigenous people's groups, Bengali settlers and international actors all hold different views regarding the CHT Peace Agreement and its implementation strategy. It is commonly agreed that divergent views relating to the Agreement have evolved because of the different views existing during the formulation of the Agreement as well as concerning its implementation process. Thus, it is not an exaggeration to say that politics underlie the issue of the CHT Peace Agreement's implementation.

4.4.5 Issue of the Bengali Settlers

From the discussion above, the fixation of land ownership is still the crux of the CHT Peace Agreement's implementation that is further made more complex in terms of the issue of the Bengali settlers. This issue emerged as a central concern of the Hill people after the GoB adopted the transmigration policy of Bengali settlement in the CHT from the 1970s. Its ramifications are widespread as it affects many other important issues, such as the tribal identity of the CHT and the land rights of the Hill people. On the other hand, this issue was not addressed in the CHT Peace Agreement, and without addressing this issue, it is unlikely that complete implementation of the Agreement or enduring peace can be attained in the region. The PCJSS leaders have claimed that there was an unwritten settlement between the two parties regarding the repatriation of Bengali settlers from the CHT, but the GoB rejected the claim (Chakma, 2012, p. 136). Although the question of land rights has been addressed in the Agreement, it is quite tough to solve it without addressing the point of the Bengali settlers as the settlers have already occupied many of the lands. Without proper management of the land problem, once the land has been handed to others, particularly after the Bengali settlers' land grabbing, it remained far from being returned to the CHT indigenous people. Therefore, to facilitate the settlement of land disputes in terms of returning lands to the CHT indigenous people, solving the issue of the Bengali settlers is a prerequisite.

4.5 Chapter Conclusion

With the preceding study of this chapter, an analysis has been attempted to consider the extent to which the CHT Peace Agreement has been implemented or not. Moreover, this chapter tried to address two interrelated issues, that is, the contributory factors of the background of formulation of the Agreement and its key features, which are concisely discussed. The implementation of the provisions of the Agreement is also influenced by a power struggle between mainstream Bengali political parties, indigenous leaders, the bureaucratic and the military elites and other stakeholders related to this case. It has been mentioned in the earlier section of this chapter that many questions have been raised regarding the implementation status and real motive of the government in terms of the CHT Peace Agreement. For example, the process of the fixation of land ownership has not yet been appropriately determined because of the issue of the Bengali settlers' land grabbing in the CHT's land. The withdrawal of temporary military camps is another central concern for the Hill people, as the army and the bureaucracy continue to hold power in this region. The government, including the political parties and bureaucratic elites, are unwilling to hand over power or their interests in the area. Besides, in a realist sense, it is challenging to decentralise power in favour of the local-level institutions when others already exercise such power. Conversely, the Hill ethnic communities, particularly, the PCJSS, have differences with the government regarding the implementation status claimed by the government.

The government is the key actor, as it has exclusive rights in the formulation and definition of laws to implement the CHT Peace Agreement. However, in many cases, the legislative process has not been put into practice at the institutional level. The politicisation of the administration (civil, military and local bodies) at the institutional levels is deep-rooted. For example, CHT-based local institutions continue to be run by the government-nominated and non-elected persons, raising the question of the real motive of the government regarding the implementation of the Agreement. Thus, the implementation strategy of the CHT Peace Agreement has been politicised through the implementing bodies, which is mostly observed at the institutional level. Moreover, the lack of coordination between different institutions, for example, MoCHTA, CHTRC, HDCs and traditional institutions, has continued as part of the difficulties in terms of implementing the Agreement. This concern is discussed in the next chapter.

References

Chakma, B. (2012). Bound to be failed?: The 1997 Chittagong Hill Tracts 'peace accord'. In N. Uddin (Ed.), *Politics of peace: A case of the Chittagong Hill Tracts in Bangladesh* (pp. 121–142). Institute of Culture & Development Research.

Chakma, B., & Barua, P. (2017, December 2). Shoronarthi bishayak task force: Ak bochor savai hoyni [Refugee concerned task force: No meeting held in one year]. *Prothom Alo*, p. 5.

CHT body seeks rules of business: Land Commission chairman tells the first meet after his re-appointment. (2018, February 13). *The Daily Star*. https://www.thedailystar.net/country/cht-body-seeks-rules-business-1533754. Accessed 3 October 2020.

CHT people to enjoy land ownership: PM assures them, calls for maintaining peace, discipline. (2018, January 22). *The Daily Star*. https://www.thedailystar.net/frontpage/cht-people-enjoy-land-ownership-1523221. Accessed 3 October 2020.

Conspiracy on to ruin CHT accord: Says PCJSS chief Santu Larma. (2021, December 3). *The Daily Star*, p. 12.

Kormokar, A., & Dewan, J. (2017, March 14). *Parbatya Chattagramer bhumi birodh nishpotti abar onishwchoatay* [Again, uncertainty in settlement of the land dispute in the CHT]. *Prothom Alo*, p. 20.

Legislative and Parliamentary Affairs Division. (2014). *The constitution of the People's Republic of Bangladesh* [Printed with the latest amendment]. Government of the People's Republic of Bangladesh.

Mohsin, A. (2003). *The Chittagong Hill Tracts, Bangladesh: On the difficult road to peace*. Lynne Rienner.

Parbatya Chattagramer bhumi birodh nishpotti: 16 bochor atke chilo ain songshodhone [Settlement of land dispute in the CHT: 16 years needed to amend the law]. (2017, December 2). *Prothom Alo*, p. 5.

Parbatya Chattagram Jana Samhati Samiti. (2016). *An open letter from the PCJSS to the honorable Prime Minister Sheikh Hasina in context of her speech delivered in reply to a starred question relating to implementation of the CHT accord in the parliament on 10 February 2016*. Information and Publicity Department of the PCJSS.

Parbatya Chattagram Jana Samhati Samiti. (2017a). *A brief report on implementation of the CHT accord: Signed in 1997 between the Government of Bangladesh and the PCJSS*. Information and Publicity Department, Parbatya Chattagram Jana Samhati Samiti (PCJSS).

Parbatya Chattagram Jana Samhati Samiti. (2017b). *Parbatya Chattagram Chukti Bastabayan Prasange \ 2 December 2017* [About the matters of implementation of the Chittagong Hill Tracts agreement \ 2 December 2017]. Information and Publicity Department of Parbatya Chattagram Jana Samhati Samiti (PCJSS).

Qadir, N. (2019, December 2). Welcome peace, abandon violence. *Daily Sun*, p. 7.

Translated English version of agreement between the national committee on Chittagong Hill Tracts constituted by the government and the Parbatya Chattagram Jana Samhati Samiti. (n.d.). http://mochta.portal.gov.bd/sites/default/files/files/mochta.portal.gov.bd/page/8a162c4c_1f3f_4c6e_b3c0_63ad2ef9d2b3/Peace%20Accord%20%28Englidh%29.pdf. Accessed 3 September 2020.

Tripura, N. B. K. (Ed.). (2016). *Chittagong Hill Tracts: Long walk to peace & development*. Ministry of Chittagong Hill Tracts Affairs, Bangladesh Secretariat.

Ullah, A. (2018, December 2). CHT peace accord 48 out of 72 sections implemented Two-thirds of commitments yet to be addressed: PCJSS. *Daily Sun*, pp. 15–16.

Uppsala Conflict Data Program. (n.d.). *Bangladesh: Chittagong Hill Tracts.* https://ucdp.uu.se/conflict/322. Accessed 5 September 2020.

CHAPTER 5

State Actors and Implementation of the CHT Peace Agreement

5.1 Chapter Introduction

The CHT Peace Agreement is typical in terms of the perspective that it is not like any other government policy of Bangladesh. It is an agreement where the state's government (more specifically, the NCCHT) is a signatory party. We have already seen in the earlier chapters that the implementation status is a much-disputed question. Problems are being faced regarding the implementation of all the provisions of the Agreement, and many of the issues must be attributed to political, economic, as well as administrative factors, especially as the Hill people have assumed so, at least. The role of the GoB in implementing all sections of the CHT Peace Agreement is of immense significance as the government has the authoritative power in formulating as well as defining laws regarding the implementation process. Within the state's ambit, the government is the main actor in terms of implementing the Agreement with support from other state institutions, for example, the army, the bureaucracy. In the CHT case, the role of the bureaucracy (civil administration) and the army at the level of policies have profound significance, which strongly affects the implementation of the CHT Peace Agreement.

To address this implementation status at the state level, in addition to the introduction and conclusion, this chapter comprises three sections, that is, governmental response, the army's involvement and the bureaucratic perception of the CHT Peace Agreement. Each section is further

© The Author(s), under exclusive license to Springer Nature Singapore Pte Ltd. 2022
S. Bala, *Politics of Peace Agreement Implementation*,
https://doi.org/10.1007/978-981-16-1944-1_5

divided into sub-sections to explicate the manner in which these three institutions are related to the CHT case, and here, these institutions are relevant, especially regarding the implementation of the Agreement. This discussion is mainly substantiated with narratives collected from direct interviews. By going through the short profile (or professional background) of the interviewees (concisely, this is attached in Appendix 2 in a tabular form), it is easy to understand their involvement in the CHT case and the importance of their experiences. In conducting these interviews to ensure representation from all stakeholders, the interviews have purposively been undertaken to include people from different professional, ethnic and religious backgrounds. This method of conducting interviews was discussed in detail in Chapter 1.

5.2 Response at the Governmental Level

The motives of the government (GoB) in terms of the implementation policy necessitate analysis from the perspective of the mainstream Bengali political parties that formed the government in Bangladesh. To understand the relevance of the politics involved in implementing the CHT Peace Agreement, it is necessary to scrutinise the political parties' actual motives regarding the Agreement and its implementation process. To explore the implementation status of the Agreement with respect to the dispute, it is relevant to address the interplay of politics, commitments and strategies of the ruling political party as well as those of the opposition political parties. To discuss this factor concisely, the study has focused primarily on the two mainstream Bengali ruling political parties—AL and BNP—during the period from June 1996 to March 2022. During this period, except for the BNP-led government (during 2001–2006), the AL has mostly been the ruling party in Bangladesh. Moreover, examples of leftist, rightist and Islamic religion-based parties are also incorporated in this analysis.

5.2.1 Awami League (AL) as a Ruling Political Party

After signing the CHT Peace Agreement, the AL vaunted the Agreement as a landmark achievement, saying that it would not only fetch peaceful national integration but also undeniably open the door to the abundant natural resources of the region and speed up the economic growth of the CHT and other regions of Bangladesh (Rashiduzzaman,

1998, p. 654). The AL, along with leftist political parties, including the Communist Party of Bangladesh, the Workers Party of Bangladesh, Jatiya Samajtantrik Dal and the like, as well as the centre-left parties, such as the National Awami League, Gono Forum and Gonotantry Party, greeted the CHT Peace Agreement. In supporting the Agreement, a group of constitutional experts, lawyers, economists and educators disagreed with the opposition parties' claim. They found that the CHT Peace Agreement was consistent with the basic ideas of the Constitution of Bangladesh. Although the BNP-led opposition had vowed to struggle against the Agreement, the AL-led government had continued to carry on. The Jatiya Party (JP) Chairman, H. M. Ershad, maintained his opposition to the Agreement, but his political party did not take part in the street protests (Rashiduzzaman, 1998, p. 655).

Although the AL-led government has taken several measures to implement the Agreement, the initiatives are not beyond criticism, as many of its crucial sections have not yet been implemented even though more than two decades have passed. As discussed in Chapter 4, the gap between the implementation of the important sections of the Agreement and the outcome supposed to be caused by the degree of commitment towards its implementation exhibits the willingness and/or unwillingness of the AL-led government and its real motive in implementing the Agreement. Conversely, the critics of the CHT Peace Agreement did not find a viable alternative to the Agreement executed by the AL-led government. During an interview, M. S. Hussain (personal communication, June 5, 2016), a retired top-ranking army officer who had served in the CHT, opined that: there was a weakness when the Agreement was formulated—fixation of the ownership of land was the primary (first) impediment. What will be the future of the Bengali settlers? Nothing is written in the Agreement about them. Then there is the second generation of settlers. If any political government puts pressure on or requests the settlers to come back to the plain land [other parts of Bangladesh], maybe they will boldly reject that. No political party would take this risk considering their [Bengali settlers'] voting power.

We have already observed that the AL-led government signed the CHT Peace Agreement with the aspiration to end the decades-old armed conflict and that they have formed government four terms (in total, about two decades in government) during and after the signing of the Agreement. The original content of the Agreement reveals that they had supported the devolution packages for the Hill people. However, more than 24 years have passed since the signing of the Agreement, and the AL could not implement some crucial provisions that were analysed in Chapter 4. Questions may be raised as to why AL signed the Agreement in a hurry without conducting elaborate research and without engaging civil society activists and the national public debate on such a sensitive issue. In the writings of Chowdhury (2012a), criticism has arisen that it was just a political policy of the then government to neutralise the insurgent groups by giving them some sort of nominal power to administer CHT (p. 98). An interview conducted with J. B. Larma (personal communication, May 18, 2016), President of the PCJSS and Chairman of the CHTRC, commented the following: the AL-led government formulated the CHT Peace Agreement. If the various successive governments were willing to implement the Agreement, it would have been possible. We are continuing the non-cooperation movement to pressurise the government. If the GoB implements the Agreement, then there is no rationale behind this non-cooperation movement. The government's reluctance and the undemocratic attitude towards the Agreement are responsible for its partial implementation.

Although it was stated that the CHTRC and the HDCs were being established with sufficient power and authority, the government did not intend to empower these institutions later. The violation of the CHT Peace Agreement's provisions occurred as a result. For example, no full Cabinet Minister has been appointed for the MoCHTA since 2001; instead, the appointment of a State Minister or even a Deputy Minister has been made (Chakma, 2014, p. 133), with the single exception being the appointment of a full Cabinet Minister in 2019. This is regarded as a ruse using any means possible to bring the Hill indigenous leaders to the table for dialogue by engaging them in these institutions but without conferring executive powers upon them (Chowdhury, 2012a, p. 99). Many of the Hill leaders are openly alleging that this is the government's real motive for the non-implementation of the Agreement. S. P. Tripura (personal communication, May 17, 2016), the Organising Secretary of the PCJSS, opined the followings: the government's reluctance is the main impediment to implementing the CHT Peace Agreement. Besides, it includes the lack of a democratic environment or a democratic mindset. Then, the bureaucracy and the military's non-cooperation are other reasons for the non-implementation of the Agreement, but it is broadly under the prerogative of the government's reluctance.

In the same context, P. R. Chakma (personal communication, May 18, 2016), the retired top-ranking bureaucrat and the President of Bangladesh Indigenous Peoples' Forum (BIPF) (CHT wing), opined the following: mainly, the GoB was not willing to give rights to the Hill people. International pressure or lobbying was less significant in this case.

They also revealed that lack of political willingness and promise on the part of the government is responsible for weak implementation of the CHT Peace Agreement. Now, the Hill people not only distrust the promise made by the government, but they also demand the roadmap for the implementation of the Agreement. Thus, the implementation status faces various problems, which is also intensified by the lack of political willingness and commitment by the government. This factor, in particular, is claimed by the PCJSS leadership. In contrast, B. K. Chakma (personal communication, May 18, 2016), Chairman of RHDC, commented the following: the fixation of land rights through the Land Commission is one of the most challenging impediments to implementing the CHT Peace Agreement. The government led by Prime Minister Sheikh Hasina signed the Agreement, and she was very eager to get it implemented but indicated that this would need time.

On 10 February 2016, the independent lawmaker, Shri Ushatan Talukder raised a supplementary question to Prime Minister Sheikh Hasina regarding the recent update on the implementation of the CHT Peace Agreement. In response to this question, Sheikh Hasina mentioned about many of developments regarding the implementation. However, in an interview S. U. Talukder (personal communication, May 20, 2016) opined the following: Prime Minister Sheikh Hasina mostly relied on written speeches, and she does not know the real details about many of the concerns. But Hasina's role is praiseworthy for the inauguration of the newly constructed CHT complex at Baily Road [in Dhaka] in May 2016. In this inauguration, she reaffirmed the withdrawal of temporary army camps from the Chittagong Hill Tracts (CHT). Because of her announcement, the army probably was not pleased.

On the other hand, R. A. M. O. M. Chowdhury (personal communication, June 9, 2016), the AL-backed MP, opined the following: we [indicating the GoB] have formed the Land Commission according to the CHT Peace Agreement. We are optimistic about the Land Commission, which will resolve land-related problems. We positively own the Agreement. I have discussed with Prime Minister Sheikh Hasina about the willingness for the implementation of the Agreement.

Likewise, in the same vein, N. B. K. Tripura (personal communication, June 15, 2016), the top-ranking bureaucrat of MoCHTA, commented the following in an interview: there is no impediment in implementing the Agreement. The government is sincere in implementing it, and this is a continuous process.

5.2.2 Political Motives of the Banglades h Nationalist Party (BNP), Jamaat-e-Islami (JI) and the Jatiya Party (JP) Towards the CHT Peace Agreement

The then main opposition political party, the BNP, along with other right-wing parties, vehemently opposed the deal. Nearly all of the rightist and Islamic fundamentalist national political parties reacted against the CHT Peace Agreement. The then opposition party, specifically the BNP, had expressed its opposition to the Agreement even before signing the Agreement. It is notable that the BNP delegates had refrained from attending the meetings of the National Committee on CHT matters. The Uppsala Conflict Data Program [UCDP] (n.d.) revealed that the BNP rejected the Agreement saying it contradicted the unitary Constitution of Bangladesh and the interest of the Bengali settlers in the Chittagong Hill Tracts (CHT). Furthermore, the BNP marked the Agreement as an exclusion to the unitary government and a sell-out to the 'terrorists' (DS [*The Daily Star*], 1997, as cited in Chowdhury, 2001, p. 98). Also, the party announced a series of agitation programmes against the CHT Peace Agreement. The BNP chairperson, Begum Khaleda Zia, claimed that the Agreement would set up a parallel government in the country and urged to Prime Minister Sheikh Hasina to omit it (Bangladesh Observer, 1998, as cited in Rashiduzzaman, 1998, p. 655). In a rhetorical criticism of the issue, Barrister Nazmul Huda, a former BNP parliamentary, alleged that the Agreement was contrary to the constitutional provisions and could be classified as a total abduction of the authority of the GoB (Independent, 1997, as cited in Rashiduzzaman, 1998, p. 655). The BNP condemned the Agreement as a 'black pact' and alleged that the AL-led government violated the country's sovereignty and the unitary character of the constitution (Dinkal, 1998, as cited in Rashiduzzaman, 1998, p. 655).

The motive of the BNP-led government in terms of the CHT Peace Agreement was not less differential from the past, as has been found in the previous policies of its founder and predecessor Major-General Ziaur Rahman, who pursued a flawed policy to solve the CHT problem that was being caused by the insurgency of the Bengali settlers. The party, while being a part of the opposition, vehemently opposed the Agreement and declared the amendment of some of the provisions of the Agreement after assuming state power ([*The*] *Daily Star*, 1998, as cited in Chowdhury, 2012a, p. 100). The BNP and its right-wing political allies alleged that the Hill rebel leaders' loyalty was more inclined towards India than Bangladesh. The BNP-led government concluded that with the conceded powers, the CHT-based institutions (e.g. HDCs and the CHTRC) would be used to serve the interests of India. The goal of the current BNP-led government, in terms of the Agreement's implementation, was viewed by Santu Larma as following the path of AL's strategy and 'dilly-dallying' in the implementation ([*The*] *Daily Star*, 2002, as cited in Chowdhury, 2012a, p. 100).

On many occasions, the PCJSS leaders complained that the BNP-led government collaborated with and patronised the anti-Agreement group, the UPDF, and posting those officials who were against the CHT Peace Agreement in the CHT (Chowdhury, 2012a, p. 99). During the BNP regime (after 2001), Moni Swapan Dewan, Deputy Minister for the MoCHTA, could not carry out his functions properly due to non-cooperation from the government (Chakma, 2014, p. 136). The BNP-led government has been accused, as in the case of its predecessors, of violating many provisions of the Agreement, for example, providing permanent resident status to 26,000 Bengali families (this is more than 0.1 million people) living in the cluster villages of the Chittagong Hill Tracts (CHT). This indicates the lack of governmental support towards implementing the Agreement ([*The*] *Daily Star*, 2003, as cited in Chowdhury, 2012a, p. 102). Later, although the BNP-backed Prime Minister turned down a plan to review the Agreement, she emphasised on the necessity of treating the Hill people and the Bengali migrants based on equal rights (*Daily Ittefaq*, 2003, as cited in Chowdhury, 2012a, p. 102). These contrasting speeches by the GoB initiated doubt regarding their positive motive in implementing the CHT Peace Agreement and, at the same time, also manifested their apathy towards the implementation process. All these decisions of the BNP-led government eventually seemed to reflect their previous motives of impeding the implementation of the Agreement. R. K. Menon (personal communication, June 6, 2016), the Minister of AL-led government (also, Chairman of Workers Party of Bangladesh), commented as follows: after signing the Agreement, the BNP-led government spent five years in power but did not undertake initiatives for its implementation. Although the AL-led government signed the CHT Peace Agreement, many in the AL leadership are not supportive of its implementation. In this sense, there is governmental reluctance.

In the same tone, as noted by Chowdhury (2012a), both AL and BNP have an absence of political willingness and lack of positive attitude towards the CHT Peace Agreement. Regardless of who signed or opposed the Agreement, in terms of implementation, both governments have turned it into a paper agreement. They have both adopted the same dawdling strategy to narrow its implementation (p. 102).

Likewise, the pro-Islamic JI, and other right-wing political parties, similar to the BNP, claimed that by signing the CHT Peace Agreement, the AL-led government had virtually sold the CHT, the area vital to national security and the economic development of Bangladesh (Rashiduzzaman, 1998, p. 655). The JI rejected the Agreement, as it was signed with Hill indigenous leaders. Moreover, they announced parallel demonstration programmes in a fashion similar to that of the BNP's programmes. Another leading political party, the JP, adopted a policy of checking the Agreement through parliamentary processes (examples are incorporated in the following sub-section).

5.2.3 Constitutional Debate and the Issue of State Sovereignty

Many people concluded that the newly established CHT institutions would lead to the region gravitating towards secession and independence (Inquilab, 1997, as cited in Rashiduzzaman, 1998, p. 655). As the Jatiya Sangshad (National Parliament of Bangladesh) requires the consent of the CHTRC in the case of amending the existing laws affecting the CHT Hill people and to make new laws, parliamentary supremacy under the unitary constitution has also been compromised, according to the BNP's contention both before and after the passage of the Bill (Inquilab, 1998, as cited in Rashiduzzaman, 1998, p. 655). The then opposition party, BNP, challenged the four Bills introduced into the Jatiya Sangshad in April 1998 to implement the CHT Peace Agreement and proposed some 4,000 amendments to the proposal (Rashiduzzaman, 1998, p. 655). When the Speaker of the National Parliament discarded the discussion of the proposed amendments (many of which were assumed to be empty in nature), BNP parliamentarians walked out of the parliamentary session. As a result, a parliamentary debate on this severe case was missed out. M.

A. Rashid (personal communication, June 2, 2016), retired top-ranking army officer who had served in the CHT, commented the following: the mainstream Bengali population [the common people of Bangladesh] generally did not desire this Agreement (or its implementation). The Constitution of Bangladesh ensures a unitary form of government and the common people do not wish to have this power-sharing. Some provisions of the CHT Peace Agreement are contradictory to the Constitution of Bangladesh. In reality, its implementation is challenging.

During the regime of the AL-led government, the Jatiya Sangsad passed the Rangamati Hill District Local Government Council (Amendment) Bill on 3 May 1998, despite the BNP and JI MPs' protest and walkout; afterwords, the Khagrachhari Hill District Bill and Bandarban Hill District Bill were passed on 4 May and 5 May, respectively (Bala, 2018, p. 31). The JP voted against all the Bills in a parliamentary manner. Again, the much-disputed Bill, the Chittagong Hill Tracts Regional Council Bill was passed on 6 May 1998 in the absence of the BNP and JI parliamentary lawmakers, while the JP legislators played the same role as with the preceding legislation (Bala, 2018, p. 31). Besides, a faction of the Bengali ruling elite regarded the CHT Peace Agreement as contrary to the provisions of the Constitution of Bangladesh. Giving a verdict on the writ petition, the High Court judgement of 12–13 April 2010 found that the CHTRC Act violated some articles of the Constitution of Bangladesh, resulting in rendering the Agreement dysfunctional. However, the Agreement survives under the Appellate Division's[1] stay order issued in March 2011 ("Implementation of CHT", 2013).

While the opposition political parties complained that the CHT Peace Agreement had paved the way for the Hill people to have access to about 13,344.28 square kilometres of resource-rich territory, the fact also remains that the AL-led government did not agree to offer the CHT complete autonomy nor did it sacrifice the sovereignty of the state. For example, no government accepted the Hill leaders' long-standing demand that Bengali settlers be repatriated from the Chittagong Hill Tracts (CHT). The dilemma in the post-Agreement Bangladesh, no matter who signed the Agreement or who runs the government, is that the government is unyielding and that every government is uncompromised regarding the question of state sovereignty and the constitutional

---

[1] The highest court of law in Bangladesh, the Supreme Court of Bangladesh, is composed of the High Court Division and the Appellate Division.

integrity of Bangladesh, through which they have assumed authoritative power and are pursuing their own interests in terms of realism.

5.2.4 Politics of Assuming Power Through Winning National Parliamentary Elections

After the signing of the CHT Peace Agreement, the PCJSS and other mainstream Bengali political parties (mainly, AL and BNP) are now rivals for parliamentary seats in the CHT, which were previously dominated by Bengali political parties. The political situation in the CHT has been complicated by the question of how to draft the national electoral voters' list (electoral roll) and the voter list for Hill District Councils (HDCs). According to the CHT Peace Agreement, an individual is entitled to vote for the HDCs' election if "[a] person shall be entitled to be considered as legally eligible for enlistment in the Voters' List if he is (1) a citizen of Bangladesh, (2) not below 18 years of age, (3) not declared by any competent court to be of unsoundly mind, (4) a permanent resident of the hill district" (*Translated English Version of Agreement Between*, n.d., Section B.9). The conditions—(1), (2) and (3)—are comparatively convenient to attain, but the complexity arises in terms of condition (4). According to the CHT Peace Agreement, "[n]on-tribal Permanent Resident shall mean a person who is not a tribal and who has lands of lawful entitlement in the hill districts and who generally lives in the hill districts at a specific address" (*Translated English Version of Agreement Between*, n.d., Section B.3). The dispute regarding permanent residency has not been solved yet, as the issue of settlement of land has not been settled yet. Because of this complexity, the elections of the HDCs and CHTRC have not to be held until date.

The demand of the PCJSS for creating the voters' list by listing only the permanent residents of the CHT and conducting the HDCs as well as national elections with this list had complicated the process of conducting the October 2001 national elections. However, the GoB refused to entertain such a demand on the grounds that only the HDCs' election is to be accomplished by the voters' list formulated according to Section B.9 of the CHT Peace Agreement. Also, the denial is based on Article 122 of the Constitution of Bangladesh which declared that a person is to be registered as a voter from a constituency if he or she is a resident of the area. The PCJSS's claim is based on the argument that if all the residents of the CHT are incorporated in the voters' list, the Bengali settlers would be legalised as residents of the CHT periphery. During an interview with M. A. Rashid (personal communication, June 2, 2016), again, commented the following: the government (or its political party) does not entertain the risk of repatriating Bengali settlers to the plain land [the other parts of Bangladesh] because it targets the Bengalis for their voting support. The main problem with the CHT cause is the fixation on the ownership of land, which includes the issue of the Bengali settlers.

The PCJSS and the Hill people, in general, were also aware that the demographic composition would alter if the Bengali settlers, the military and the bureaucrats were included in the voters' list, as the Bengalis would outnumber the Hill people. If this occurs (and in fact, this is occurring), the possibility of candidates nominated by the mainstream Bengali political parties winning would increase manifold. On the other hand, the PCJSS would regard this as a setback to its intention for political power and the political autonomy for the Hill indigenous people. S. Kamal (personal communication, June 7, 2016), prominent civil society activist and the Co-Chairman of the international Chittagong Hill Tracts Commission, opined the following in an interview: the fixation on the ownership of land is the main problem for the implementation of the CHT Peace Agreement. The Land Commission is not working properly. If a cadastral survey is conducted, then most of the Bengali settlers who have papers and possessions will easily get their land rights. Demographic changes have already happened in the CHT, and the water has flowed along the stream. Now, Bengalis are the majority. If there are elections to the CHTRC and HDCs, Bengali settlers could win the polls. So, Santu Larma desires to protect against this. When we [e.g. Sultana Kamal and Megna Guhathakurata] met with Prime Minister Sheikh Hasina, we found a bit more of a negative impression about implementing the Agreement than before. Maybe, she [Prime Minister Hasina] was convinced by advice from others.

However, consequently, the PCJSS called upon the CHT indigenous people to resist the national elections of 2001 and boycotted the general elections as well. BNP won two seats, while AL won one out of the three constituencies in the CHT (Mohsin, 2003, p. 67). For this reason, the mainstream Bengali political parties' aim of winning National Parliamentary seats in the CHT was attained. Conversely, if PCJSS won the seats, they could highlight the cause of the CHT in the National Parliament (or implementation of the CHT Peace Agreement). In the 10th parliamentary elections held on 5 January 2014, Bir Bahadur Ushwe Sing and

Kujendra Lal Tripura were elected from the Bandarban and Khagrachhari constituencies, respectively, under the banner of AL nomination. Ushatan Talukder, Vice President of the PCJSS Central Committee, was elected from the Rangamati constituency as an independent lawmaker. However, none of the PCJSS-backed members was elected in the 11th parliamentary elections held on 30 December 2018. The AL-backed candidates—Bir Bahadur Ushwe Sing, Kujendra Lal Tripura and Dipankar Talukdar—were elected from the Bandarban, Khagrachhari and Rangamati constituencies, respectively, in this elections. Thus, the mainstream Bengali political parties' intention of assuming power through winning the parliamentary elections is continuing.

5.2.5 Selection, Instead of Election, in the CHT-Based Local Bodies

The CHT Peace Agreement provided an expectation for the resumption of democratic practices in the CHT as three HDCs are meant to be elected, which in turn are supposed to elect the CHTRC members. However, no elections in terms of these HDCs have been held to date. Instead, all governments have appointed the Chairs based on political considerations despite the protests of the Hill people. As noted by Chowdhury (2012b), the chairmen perform as agents to promote the interests of the ruling party-led government in the Chittagong Hill Tracts (CHT). In reality, these organisations lack popular legitimacy, democratic participation and people's confidence (p. 211). On the other hand, regarding the CHTRC, the institution remains strongly politically dominated by the PCJSS-backed Chairman and government-nominated members. It becomes evident from the discussion above that the government is assuming power by controlling the CHT-based local institutions.

5.3 Role of the Army in the CHT's Affairs

It is imperative to mention that the army's involvement was and is now one of the most notable dominant factors in the overall issue of the CHT case. Even after the signing of the CHT Peace Agreement, the army's involvement remains almost the same except for the withdrawal of some temporary camps according to the provisions of the Agreement. The accusation here is that the excessive presence of the army personnel along with other security forces sometimes does not adhere to military professionalism, and the presence of the army interferes in different areas of administrative, political and financial interests. As mentioned by Mohsin (2002):

> Apart from being physically present, the military is also in total control of the administration of CHT. It believes that in order to have an effective counter-insurgency strategy i.e. to fight the SB guerrillas successfully, it has to have an active role in the political and economic life of CHT. (p. 173)

Besides the border security or counterinsurgency in the CHT, the deployment of the army requires analyses from the perspective of their respective interests, which are attempted to be addressed in the following sub-sections.

5.3.1 Army Deployment and Economic Expenses

According to Major-General Syed Mohammad Ibrahim, the number of security forces deployed in the CHT was around 23,000 (Ibrahim, 2001, as cited in Chowdhury, 2012a, p. 114). Military officers (during 1993–1994) who had served in CHT told Mohsin that Bangladesh had deployed one-third of its army in this area, and this information suggested that the figure was around 30,000 (Mohsin, 2002, p. 172). Table 5.1 that deals with the military strength in Bangladesh will provide further clarity regarding the same.

An accusation is that the Bangladesh army has benefitted from the CHT case in several ways. The army's activities in the CHT were projected as nation-building endeavours and were exposed to uphold the quick increases of compiled reports in the Bangladesh army regarding

Table 5.1 Strengths of military forces in Bangladesh

Bangladesh Army	80,000 personnel
Bangladesh Rifles	25,000
Armed Police	10,000
Ansar (auxiliary force)	8,000
Navy	1,500
Training Centre	800
Total	125,300

Source CHTC Report, as cited in Chowdhury (2012a, p. 114)

personnel and revenue receipts. It has been mentioned earlier that a large number of army personnel comparing with the total number were deployed in the Chittagong Hill Tracts (CHT). To maintain the cost of this military deployment in the CHT, the state spent an amount of US$125 million annually (Mohsin, 2002, p. 172). The Bangladesh military once took up 22% of the total cash current expenses, the most extensive single kind of cash current expenses in total terms (Chowdhury, 2012a, p. 116). Furthermore, this expenditure did not cover the food and subsidies that are a part of defence spending. The state, here, the GoB, justified the costs above in the name of national security (Mohsin, 2002, p. 173).

5.3.2 Administrative Control to Gain Economic Benefit

The Hill ethnic communities do not support the presence of the army in the CHT, and they have never done so (Chowdhury, 2012a, p. 115). Therefore, it is understandable that they expect the army's withdrawal from this area as soon as possible. Although the CHT Peace Agreement stated that all the temporary army camps, Ansars and the Village Defence Party (VDP) would be withdrawn, no time limit was fixed. Though more than two decades have passed after the signing of the Agreement, many of the temporary army camps have not been withdrawn. Even, consensus regarding total number of army camps settled in the CHT during insurgency, and the number of camps that has already been withdrawn is an ambiguous matter between the GoB and the PCJSS. This debate was addressed in detail in Chapter 4 under Section D.17 in tabular form (see Table 4.11). Even after the signing of the Agreement, the maintenance of law and order, including some administrative level activities in the CHT, is still largely under the army's control. The army, entrusted with powers through an administrative order, continued Operation Uttoron (Operation Upliftment) in place of Operation Dabanol (Operation Wildfire) that was imposed in the 1970s, and it still holds control over civil administration existing in the Chittagong Hill Tracts (CHT). T. S. P. Master (personal interview, May 25, 2016), Ex-Chairman and Ex-Councillor of BHDC, narrated the following: the army camp acquired 14 acres of my land. If I had possession of this land, I could have lived my life more comfortably. Actually, we are suffering from the scarcity of land. Now, we are living in comparatively better conditions than under the BNP regime. During the BNP-led government, we had to build up army camps with our wood, bamboo, etc. During patrolling, they even took our goat without giving us money. Sometimes, they [the army] bought Adivasi products without paying the actual price.

The army monitored the economic activities of the CHT through its control of the Chittagong Hill Tracts Development Board (CHTDB). The General Officer Commanding (GOC) of the Chittagong Division was the Chairman of the Board (the current Chairman is Nikhil Kumar Chakma). All development actions of the CHT were channelled through this Board. Because of this control, the Hill ethnic communities believed that the developmental activities in the CHT were executed to fulfil the needs of Bengali settlers and army personnel posted in this region. They maintained that the infrastructural projects, for example, construction of roads, electricity, education, health, etc., all served the interests of the Bengali people and the army personnel who inhabited this region. For the CHT indigenous people, development in the CHT entails the development of the Bengalis living in this area. The army also actively supports and aids the civil administration in the case of the Bengali settlement projects (Mohsin, 2002, p. 174).

The international donor agencies have granted a large amount of development aid for the Chittagong Hill Tracts (CHT). However, in reality, many of these funds have been spent on the Bangladeshi army. For example, while the Western donor consortium entirely aided the first five-year term of the CHTDB, the PCJSS claimed that 80% of the total expenditure was spent on infrastructure projects, for example, electricity, telecommunications, all-weather roads and bridges that were especially beneficial to the defence force (Levene, 1999, as cited in Chowdhury, 2012a, p. 116). Even in today's CHT, many of the infrastructural development projects are also channelled by the army. After signing the CHT Peace Agreement, the overall expectation is that the CHT-based local institutions (e.g. HDCs, CHTRC) should endow these development projects.

In some cases, the army is involved in income-generating business, for example, establishing restaurants in certain places where they earn a handsome amount, with this evident during the author's stay in Rangamati for the fieldwork. The CHT indigenous people claimed that some army personnel are occupied with activities other than their professional responsibilities in the Chittagong Hill Tracts (CHT). Besides the legitimate sources of income, some of the army personnel are (were) involved in generating income from unethical sources. Many Hill people alleged that some army personnel receive bribes from the timber and bamboo traders at the Kaptai Lake and also provided a contract to the traders in the forest in return for a percentage of their earnings (Chowdhury, 2012a, p. 116). The amounts of rations distributed by the army to the Bengali settlers living in the cluster villages of Bandarban and Khagrachhari are not above being questioned. In an interview, R. K. Menon (personal communication, June 6, 2016), Minister in the 10th Parliament of Bangladesh, opined the following: army deployment is considered as an income-generating factor. They are engaged in the timber business and are using forest resources. Most of the high-ranking army officers built their Dhaka-based home furniture with this timber. Moreover, they are not eager about the implementation of the CHT Peace Agreement.

Again, M. S. Hussain (personal communication, June 5, 2016), who was also posted in the CHT, commented the following in an interview: 20% extra Hill allowance is given to government employees posted to the Chittagong Hill Tracts (CHT). The army holds a strong position in this area. The army is not willing for the Agreement's implementation. Bureaucracy is a factor for its non-implementation. Thus, the army had [has] benefitted economically, though it is challenging to place the blame on them directly.

5.3.3 *Political Involvement*

As there was no freedom of expression or rights of the association at the political level, the CHT people required the permission of army authorities to organise and hold meetings and get-togethers. Even in terms of arranging religious ceremonies, this kind of permission was required. On the other hand, the army was accused of adopting the colonial means of the divide and rule policy to impose Bengali hegemony in this region (Mohsin, 2002, p. 175). For this purpose, several local indigenous organisations, for example, Chakma Unnayan Sangsad (Chakma Development Council), Marma Unnayan Sangsad (Marma Development Council) and Tripura Unnayan Sangsad (Tripura Development Council), had been set up as per the instruction of the army. The CHT-based local people alleged that these organisations were manned by government-chosen people who proceeded to act as government agents. They further claimed that these organisations had been set up to create communal division among the local Hill people, to counter PCJSS's activities (Mohsin, 2002, p. 175). Besides, the army had helped to set up several organisations of the Bengali settlers' community in the area, that is, Bengali Krishak Sramik Kalyan Parishad (Bengali Farmers and Workers Association), the Parbattya Gano Parishad (PGP, Council of Hill Peoples) and the CHT Peace and Coordination Council. The indigenous people put forth the accusation that these Bengali-led organisations carried out attacks on the Hill people (Mohsin, 2002, p. 175).

5.3.4 Summing-Up of the Army's Role in the Chittagong Hill Tracts (CHT)

It is accepted from the preceding analysis that the army is in both institutionally and economically advantageous position about the case of the CHT conflict. It is presumed that they are willing to continue with their dominance of power regarding the economic and political grounds in the CHT by creating agitation among several anti-Agreement Bengali settlers and indigenous organisations (Chowdhury, 2012a, p. 117). In this background, if the CHTRC is empowered with authority to supervise the CHT's administration, then, in general, the administrative picture would transform in terms of the new control obtained by the CHT-based local institutions (e.g. CHTRC and HDCs); and, the authority of the army would be curtailed immensely (Chowdhury, 2012a, p. 117). As the armed conflict has come to an end through the signing of the CHT Peace Agreement, it is expected that peace and stability will triumph in the Chittagong Hill Tracts (CHT). Consequently, the large number of deployed army personnel will no longer be required except for border security. Subsequently, expenses for this purpose would certainly reduce, but the postings for this large number of army personnel would emerge as a new problem. Thus, a sense of the loss of power, as well as the fear of losing economic benefits, contravenes the professionalism of the army deployed in the CHT (Chowdhury, 2012a, p. 117). Eventually, this Agreement has reduced the political and economic benefit of the army and has been unsuccessful in addressing the issue of the army's support for the Agreement and its implementation process.

During an interview with G. Dewan (personal interview, May 18, 2016), President of the CHT Nagorik (Citizen) Committee expressed the following: the army is playing one of the critical roles in motivating the government's decision. The army is accused of sending a letter to the government not to reform the Land Commission. Prime Minister Sheikh Hasina is sincere in willing to implement the Agreement. However, she alone cannot decide to do this due to the surrounding misguidance from other influential actors. Moreover, the government tries to satisfy the army.

M. B. Tripura (personal communication, May 22, 2016), the Executive Director of a CHT-based local NGO, emphasised the implementation process and commented the following: about implementing the CHT Peace Agreement, AL's willingness is not identical to that of the Government of Bangladesh. This means that state institutions have some other involvement. If the army won this issue, then it would be a good sign. If they played a positive role, then there would be no problem with the Agreement's implementation.

Although the authenticity of these accusations could not be determined, the involvement of the army in some atrocities and human rights violations were reported by some organisations, for example, the international Chittagong Hill Tracts Commission, Amnesty International and the Anti-Slavery Society on many occasions (Chowdhury, 2012a, p. 117). The army, however, denies these accusations.

5.4 Bureaucracy in the CHT-Based Local Administration

Along with the political actors, the role of bureaucrats (administrators) is also significant, as they are the authorities who implement the policy at the local level. At the policy level, the bureaucrats act as both actors and institutions (Howlett & Ramesh, 1995, as cited in Chowdhury, 2012b, p. 215). In reality, politics and administration, instead of being separate areas, are not unrelated. Both objective and subjective in manner, the nature of administration can impact on the political system's policy outcomes (Peters, 1984, as cited in Chowdhury, 2012b, p. 215). Bureaucratic red tape is nothing new in the administrative system in Bangladesh. However, regarding the case of the CHT Peace Agreement's implementation, it is unbearable. The visible assignment of authority to some indigenous-dominated institutions is still perceptible: for example, MoCHTA, CHTRC and HDCs caused unease among the local bureaucracy accustomed to power, privileges, arrogance and public importance (Rashiduzzaman & Chowdhury, 2008, as cited in Chakma, 2014, p. 135). In many ways, these newly introduced institutions are victims, in terms of having to face indignity from the traditional

Hill bureaucratic institutions. This aspect is briefly analysed in the next sub-sections.

5.4.1 Bureaucratic Non-cooperation

Regarding the administrative policy in the CHT, in some cases, the role of administrators is not favourably viewed, as several sections of the CHT Peace Agreement offended the bureaucracy and its interests. For example, according to the Agreement, the CHTRC Chairman with the status of State Minister has the highest administrative and political rank in the entire Chittagong Hill Tracts (CHT). Many officials (bureaucrats) presume that it is uncomfortable to carry out their responsibilities under the supervision of CHTRC authority instead of their traditional system that is the ministerial line of supervision (Chowdhury, 2012b, pp. 215–216). The bureaucrats assume that the Agreement ruins centralisation and promotes faulty decentralisation of power and authority. According to them, parallel systems (faulty decentralisation)—a special arrangement for the CHT and another for the rest of the country—introduce several specific problems.

Another reason for this antagonism is the lack of confidence and trust in the Hill indigenous leaders, who are not believed to have the adequate experience and potential to run the multifaceted administration in the CHT (Chowdhury, 2012b, p. 216). Many of the bureaucrats in the CHT are indifferent to the Chairmanship of Santu Larma because of his role during the insurgency period. The bureaucrats assume that the CHTRC leads to duplication and overlapping while raising the extent of complications in administration as HDCs are conferred with enough power and authority for self-governance. The lack of interest in and the lack of support from the bureaucrats towards the CHTRC affect the situation by causing a delay in formulating rules and regulations, and sending the directive to the concerned institutions paved the path for the denial of the devolution of power and authority to the CHTRC. In an interview, R. K. Menon (personal communication, June 6, 2016) opined the following: the bureaucracy (e.g. DC, SP—Superintendent of Police) desires to assume power with the upper hand. They are not willing to empower HDCs and CHTRC. The fixation on the ownership of land is the fundamental problem in implementing the CHT Peace Agreement.

The accusation has been made that noticeable bureaucratic non-cooperation surfaced owing to the unresolved impediment in its implementation. For example, the State Minister's status as the CHTRC's Chairman appeared to the local traditional institutions, the HDCs and the MoCHTA as a matter of a power struggle. The formation of such a high-ranking post in the local governance system was considered as an indignity to the Bangladesh civil servants, who habitually enjoyed the colonial style of the order of precedence among local bureaucrats and other district-level high-ranking officials. They were perceived to be uncomfortable with the special rank and privileges of Santu Larma, who is placed at the highest rank and position over all the Bangladesh government officials posted in the CHT and adjacent districts (Rashiduzzaman & Chowdhury, 2008, as cited in Chakma, 2014, p. 135). A. Mohsin (personal communication, June 6, 2016), a prominent researcher in the field of the CHT case, opined the following in an interview: the bureaucracy is very eager to exercise power in the CHT and, recently, the army transferred some power to the bureaucracy. The complexity of the ownership of land is one of the main problems in the CHT issue.

5.4.2 Lack of Coordination Between the CHT's Institutions

Lack of coordination and cooperation between the CHT's institutions is one of the critical issues for the non-implementation of the CHT Peace Agreement. For example, the lack of coordination between the MoCHTA and other affiliated institutions, that is, CHTRC, HDCs and traditional institutions also prevailed. This acutely weakens the functioning of the respective institutions. Because of the lack of support from the MoCHTA, the CHTRC (the literal apex body in the CHT) cannot function properly. As noted by Chowdhury (2012b), in reality, the government increased the executive power of MoCHTA instead of that of CHTRC, thus securing government control over the CHT (p. 210). Besides, the demand of the CHTRC to empower through the executive power was bypassed by the past government as well as the present government. In terms of developmental activities, many of the powers and functions of the MoCHTA and the CHTRC have overlapped, which has formed a power struggle between the two institutions over the question of who has control.

Although the MoCHTA was set up to support the CHTRC, it turned out to be the principal executive authority in the CHT, and the CHTRC was compelled to be subordinate to the MoCHTA as a coordinating body. The MoCHTA contacts the Deputy Commissioner (DC) rather than the CHTRC Chairman regarding the CHT affairs, and this action is somewhat embarrassing to the CHTRC as it is neglected (Rashiduzzaman & Chowdhury, 2008, as cited in Chakma, 2014, p. 134). Then, the CHTDB and the three HDCs that are directly under the supervision of MoCHTA often disregard the supervisory and coordinating authority of CHTRC. These trends in administrative behaviour generate frustrations among the office porters and limit their effectiveness in facilitating and supporting development initiatives. Eventually, the CHTRC, which was established to coordinate and resolve the problems of the Hill people (and also the Hill institutions), has been perceived to be ineffective (Chakma, 2014, p. 134).

5.4.3 *Deputy Commissioners' Role in the CHT's Administration*

Another influential administrator in the context of the CHT's administration is the DC of the concerned district. In the CHT Peace Agreement, the role of the DCs in administering three Hill Districts is not determined. This does not touch upon specific questions, that is, who will supervise the functions of the DCs and what the nature of their tasks will be. It is idealistic to expect that the refurbished HDCs and the newly formed CHTRC will recognise the DCs as the pivot of their new administration. According to the provisions of the Agreement, literally, the DCs can assume no more power than a limited coordinating role with the consent of the CHTRC leadership and are endowed with the authority to manage protocol responsibilities that hamper their personal and institutional interests. The CHTRC and each of the HDCs have an executive officer with the corresponding rank of a Joint Secretary and a Deputy Secretary, respectively, in national civil service. This makes the CHTRC Chairman impervious to the customary control of the district or Deputy Commissioner.

5.4.4 *Summary of the Bureaucratic Mindset in the CHT's Administration*

From the discussion above, it becomes understandable that the CHT Peace Agreement's bureaucratic nature indicates the unacceptability of the CHTRC and its leadership to the administrators in the Chittagong Hill

Tracts (CHT). This analysis is relevant to some extent in understanding their skilful denial to accept and disregard the supervisory authority of the CHTRC. This sense of deprivation of the CHTRC's mandate regarding the rank would be mitigated if government officials would consider the special status of the Chairman of CHTRC as a special arrangement to bring political stability to the conflict-prone Chittagong Hill Tracts (CHT). In this regard, B. R. Tripura (personal communication, May 23, 2016), female Vice-chairman of Khagrachhari district, commented the following in an interview: proper message may not have been conveyed to the decision-making authority, that is, to the government of Prime Minister Sheikh Hasina—hopefully, individually, she [Hasina] is optimistic on the indigenous issue; but the bureaucracy and the army are vital factors. Bureaucrats especially are not willing to give equal rights. Moreover, intra-group conflict (e.g. PCJSS vs. UPDF; or within PCJSS) is also responsible for the partial implementation of the Agreement.

Moreover, during an interview, M. Guhathakurta (personal communication, June 8, 2018), Professor (retired) of the University of Dhaka, opined that: there are vested interests from different groups of people, for example, investment in tourism or the timber business where the bureaucracy, the military or even private businessmen have different interests. These interest groups motivate the government's decision.

5.5 Chapter Conclusion

First, it becomes evident from the earlier discussion that political consensus between the mainstream Bengali political parties has not been developed from the inception of the signing of the CHT Peace Agreement. Although the AL-led government had signed the Agreement with the PCJSS leadership, their motive, as a governing party, in implementing the Agreement is not without question. From the beginning, the BNP was not in favour of the Agreement. Regardless of who signed the Agreement or who holds state power, the main concern is that even though more than two decades have passed, many of the crucial provisions have not been implemented yet. The politics of winning the National Parliamentary seats in the CHT by winning political support from the Bengali settlers or political selection of the Chairman of the HDCs, etc. are identical to the unwillingness from the government's side. Moreover, the issue of the voter list is dependent on the subject of permanent residency, which is not solved yet; the fixation on ownership of land remains undetermined.

From the realist perspective, these are mostly related to the intention of continuing one's own interests—either by assuming power through winning the National Parliamentary elections or by apparently protecting the state's integrity. Although many of the interviewees agreed with this view, a few from the government's side disagreed.

Second, it has been discussed that the government (or the ruling political party) is not the sole influential actor regarding the case of CHT; the bureaucracy (civil administration) and the army are also involved in the CHT issue, including its implementation process. In some cases, the army's engagements surpass the ethos of military professionalism; these are mostly related to economic interests. Political and administrative control is one of the ways to ensure interest. However, it is difficult to directly prove the concomitant accusations that arise. Third, the bureaucratic indifference about implementing the CHT Peace Agreement becomes another impediment. The traditional civil service officers feel more comfortable working under the supervision of the ministerial line than the newly introduced CHT-based local institutions. There have been accusations saying that the CHTRC and the HDCs are not empowered enough due to bureaucratic non-cooperation as well as the willingness to exercise power that is placed in their hands. Additionally, lack of coordination between the MoCHTA, the CHTRC, the HDCs and the traditional institutions is also responsible for the partial (or weak) implementation of the Agreement. In summary, this analysis indicates that different groups are involved with varying levels of interests concerning the CHT Peace Agreement.

REFERENCES

Bala, S. (2018). Mapping local factions in the peace accord implementation process: A case study of the Chittagong Hill Tracts peace accord in Bangladesh. *Journal of International Development and Cooperation, 24*(2), 25–33.

Chakma, A. B. (2014). Peacebuilding in the Chittagong Hill Tracts (CHT): An institutionalist approach. *Journal of the Asiatic Society of Bangladesh (Hum), 59*(1), 111–138.

Chowdhury, N. J. (2012a). *Chittagong Hill Tracts peace accord implementation: Promise and performance*. A H Development Publishing House.

Chowdhury, N. J. (2012b). The Chittagong Hill Tracts accord implementation in Bangladesh: Ideals and realities. In N. Uddin (Ed.), *Politics of peace: A case of the Chittagong Hill Tracts in Bangladesh* (pp. 205–221). Institute of Culture & Development Research.

Chowdhury, Z. H. (2001). Is the ethnic problem intractable? Prospects for success of the CHT peace treaty. *Social Science Review, 18*(2), 87–108.

Implementation of CHT peace accord: Remove the bottlenecks. (2013, September 17). *The Daily Star*, p. 6.

Mohsin, A. (2002). *The politics of nationalism: The case of the Chittagong Hill Tracts, Bangladesh*. The University Press Ltd.

Mohsin, A. (2003). *The Chittagong Hill Tracts, Bangladesh: On the difficult road to peace*. Lynne Rienner Publishers Inc.

Rashiduzzaman, M. (1998). Bangladesh's Chittagong Hill Tracts peace accord: Institutional features and strategic concerns. *Asian Survey, 38*(7), 653–670.

Uppsala Conflict Data Program. (n.d.). *Bangladesh: Chittagong Hill Tracts*. https://ucdp.uu.se/conflict/322. Accessed 5 September 2020.

CHAPTER 6

Empirical Study at CHT-Based Local Level

6.1 Chapter Introduction

As argued in Chapters 1 and 2 in the spectrum of literature review, the analysis of connectivity between the state, the CHT-based local people's activities and the international communities' involvement associated with the politics of the CHT Peace Agreement has not been sufficiently attempted: this is worthy of analysis. In a manner identical to the state level (i.e. the national level), other key factors that complicate the problem in implementing the Agreement are the rivalries between the tribal groups as well as between the tribal people and Bengali settlers living in the Chittagong Hill Tracts (CHT). State-level analysis from a theoretical perspective has already been addressed in Chapter 5; now, the role of the CHT-based local level will be analysed in this chapter. The CHT Peace Agreement has been successful insofar as it has at least ended the decades-old armed insurgency in the CHT and was welcomed at home as well as abroad. In contrast, it is not beyond criticism even though it required the build-up of national and local (CHT-based) consensus in the case.

This chapter is an extended version of Bala, S. (2018). Mapping local factions in the peace accord implementation process: A case study of the Chittagong Hill Tracts peace accord in Bangladesh. *Journal of International Development and Cooperation, 24*(2), 25–33.

© The Author(s), under exclusive license to Springer Nature Singapore Pte Ltd. 2022
S. Bala, *Politics of Peace Agreement Implementation*,
https://doi.org/10.1007/978-981-16-1944-1_6

As mentioned earlier, the post-Agreement CHT situation is intrinsically connected with the question regarding the implementation of the Agreement. As long as implementation of all sections of the Agreement is not finalised, the peace initiatives will be questioned.

In the aftermath of the CHT Peace Agreement, a prolonged phase of antagonism started between the CHT-based local group rivalries, therein comprising intra-community (between tribal people) as well as inter-community (tribal people vs. Bengalis) antagonism. Moreover, the Hill leadership was mainly divided over two processes, namely the formulation of the Agreement and the implementation of its provisions. From this perspective, it is imperative to address these group dynamics because they have affected the implementation policy of the Agreement. This chapter aims to address how the implementation of the CHT Peace Agreement relates to local-level group rivalries. In addition to the introduction and conclusion, the chapter consists of four sections. Section 6.2 presents the analysis of the intra-community group dynamics, while Sect. 6.3 addresses the inter-community (Bengali settlers vs. Hill people) relationships affecting the CHT Peace Agreement. Section 6.4 presents the factional rivalries in Fig. 6.1. Section 6.5 summarises these group dynamics (interests) at the CHT-based local level.

6.2 Intra-Community Rivalries

Historically and socio-economically, the Chakma indigenous community of the CHT was (and is) at the top and was expected to receive most of the opportunities from the embodiment of institutions and development activities that were expected to follow in the years following the CHT Peace Agreement. Although the Chakmas were the majority and the dominant indigenous community among both the PCJSS and the SB fighters who were engaged in the armed conflict, the politico-military organisation of the insurgents was not monolithic (Shelley, 1992, p. 116). The ideological, personal and factional rivalries that divided the leadership of the Chakma insurgents eventually led to the formation of the Jana Samhati Samiti (JSS, shortened from PCJSS) under Priti Kumar Chakma (former Major in SB) and the assassination of the founder-leader of the PCJSS, M. N. Larma (brother of Santu Larma), on 10 November 1983 (Mohsin, 2003, p. 67). One astonishing consequence of this violent incident was the surrender of many members of the Priti faction on 29 June 1985; however, he stayed back in India (Shelley, 1992, p. 116). M. Kamal (personal communication, June 1, 2016), a prominent researcher on the CHT case, mentioned the following in an interview: government agencies motivated the rivalry between the groups. A group of RAW [Research and Analysis Wing] intelligence from India supported a section of the PCJSS in the movement seeking independence of the CHT from Bangladesh. This group [well known as the Priti group] urged the rapid liberation of the region. On the other hand, M. N. Larma [from the mainstream group] desired self-autonomy within the state of Bangladesh. This group emphasised regular [slow] movement, but M. N. Larma was assassinated by the other section [the Priti group].

Meanwhile, after the assassination of M. N. Larma, Jyotirindra Bodhipriya Larma (alias, Santu Larma) took over the leadership of the PCJSS. On the other hand, the surrender of the Priti faction (or Priti group) and the events that followed gradually eroded the support of the indigenous communities of Tripura and Marma towards the Chakma insurgents. These two communities had refrained from participating in the insurgency for several years, and many of their leaders had resumed their everyday lives. Bandarban, the domicile of the ethnic communities of Marma and Murong Hill communities, was almost free from insurgent activities in the early 1990s (Shelley, 1992, p. 117). Moreover, the indigenous leadership was divided over the formulation of the CHT Peace Agreement and its implementation processes; and faced problems over some of the other contentious issues.

Though the Agreement was signed to establish peace and promote the rights of the indigenous communities, it could not satisfy some of the smaller indigenous communities (mainly considering their number of population) and the Bengali settlers living in the Chittagong Hill Tracts (CHT). Ethnic interaction seems to have a rigid structure as the representation ratio for each of the different indigenous ethnic communities, the Bengalis in the CHTRC and the three HDCs in the CHT has been predetermined. If the composition of the CHTRC is examined, the reason for the dissatisfaction with the other smaller indigenous communities becomes clear. According to a provision of the Agreement, the Chairman of the CHTRC must be a person who belongs to a tribe. Out of the 12 male tribal members of the CHTRC, the following representation was predetermined (Table 6.1).

The smaller and relatively backward indigenous communities desired more representation within the CHTRC; in fact, some smaller Hill communities aimed to create a proportional representation system.

Table 6.1 Composition of Adivasi representation on CHTRC

Name of the Adivasi communities	Percentage (%) of the CHT population	Representatives (seats)	Literacy rate in percentage (%)
Chakma	31	5	70
Marma	17	3	20
Tripura	7	2	20
Murung and Tanchangya		1	
Lusai, Bowm, Pangkho, Khumi, Chak and Khiang		1	
Two of the female members were elected roles: one from the Chakma tribe and the other from the other tribes			

Source Developed by author based on *Translated English Version of Agreement Between* (n.d., Section C.3) and Chowdhury (2012a, p. 128)

However, as stated beforehand, the Chakmas enjoyed the upper hand as they dominated the SB—the most prominent Hill indigenous leaders of the PCJSS were from the Chakma ethnic community. Immediately after the CHT Peace Agreement was signed, some of the smaller indigenous communities complained that the Agreement was an unfavourable deal for them (Bala, 2018, p. 29). However, the PCJSS succeeded as an important political organisation in comparison with other organisations that were formed during the post-Agreement CHT developments. Santu Larma, the leader of this group who signed the Agreement, ascended as the Chairman of the CHTRC. Thereafter, the PCJSS was expected to emerge as a political party and possibly dominate Bangladeshi politics concerning the CHT; subsequently, it appeared as a regional political party on 2 December 1999 (Mohsin, 2003, p. 66). It was desired that the PCJSS would articulate indigenous grievances as a way of promoting regional matters. However, some smaller Hill ethnic communities perceived the marginalisation engendered by the larger indigenous ethnic community, that is, the Chakmas who dominated the PCJSS. The extent to which the PCJSS could mobilise (or integrate) the smaller Hill communities and other local factions in the CHT still remains unclear. In a nutshell, respected interviewees—M. S. Dewan, B. R. Tripura, S. Kamal, R. S. Partha, N. B. K. Tripura—agreed about the fact that these group rivalries affected the implementation of the Agreement and were connected to their interests.

On the other hand, apart from the aforementioned discussion of the intra Hill communities' rivalries, the CHT Peace Agreement signed by the PCJSS was not accepted by some of the Hill organisations which have been struggling for the autonomy of the CHT, including constitutional recognition. These organisations perceived the Agreement and its provisions as inconsistent with their claim of autonomy, which did not acknowledge their self-identity and other contentious issues, such as their rights over land (Chowdhury, 2012a, p. 124). They argued that the Agreement had no basis as it was not constitutionally adopted and could be amended at any time with just a majority vote in the National Parliament. In connection to this problem, the CHT Peace Agreement created a split within the three major Hill indigenous organisations, that is, the Pahari Gono Parishad (PGP or Hill People's Council), the Pahari Chattra Parishad (PCP or Hill Students' Council) and the Hill Women's Federation (HWF) (Chowdhury, 2001, pp. 98–99). In turn, these three organisations could be broadly classified into two factions—pro-PCJSS and anti-PCJSS. The pro-PCJSS faction naturally supported the Agreement and organised processions, in the Hill Districts, which addressed the Agreement. Hundreds of people, including women from different indigenous ethnic groups, willingly took part in the procession and paraded on the main streets. Some of the other indigenous social organisations, namely the Parbattya Bhikkhu Sangha, the Praja Kalyan Samiti of Kaptai Dam and the Tripura Welfare Association, also hailed the CHT Peace Agreement.

Conversely, the anti-Agreement faction of the Hill ethnic people rejected the CHT Peace Agreement and termed it as an 'agreement of compromise' (Chowdhury, 2001, p. 99). Members belonging to these groups (comprising each of the PGP, the PCP and the HWF) formed the CHT-based political party, the UPDF, on 26 December 1998 (Chittagong Hill Tracts Commission, 2000, p. 21). Members of the UPDF promised to continue the movement for full autonomy of the CHT and the constitutional recognition of the various indigenous identities. As noted by Mohsin (2002), "[a]ccording to Proshit Khisa, convener of the UPDF, full autonomy implies that except for the matters of taxation, currency, foreign policy including defence and heavy industries the rest of the issues in the CHT would remain with the CHT administration" (p. 215). They claimed that by signing the CHT Peace Agreement, the government sought only to strengthen its control over the region. Moreover, the UPDF leadership asserted that by signing the Agreement, the

PCJSS had betrayed the indigenous people and their rights, which only intended to establish their control in the Chittagong Hill Tracts (CHT). Furthermore, they claimed that the PCJSS had signed the Agreement without prior consultation or discussion with the other Hill indigenous groups and pretended to be the guardian of the Hill people. Even though they had promised to continue their struggle for autonomy and constitutional recognition of indigenous identity, the UPDF members stated that the PCJSS leadership had collaborated with the government in exploiting and repressing the common people in the Chittagong Hill Tracts (CHT). They blamed both the PCJSS and the government for the unrest in the CHT and discarded any involvement of either the political leaders or the army. However, in an interview, A. Mohsin (personal communication, June 6, 2016), a Professor of the University of Dhaka, commented that, presently, the UPDF is ready to compromise on their former demand for full autonomy.

R. Chakma (personal communication, May 22, 2016), the District Organiser of the UPDF of Khagrachhari and M. Chakma (personal communication, May 22, 2016), a member of the UPDF of Khagrachhari unit, while being interviewed as representatives of UPDF, opined the following: we [the UPDF] did not sign the CHT Peace Agreement. Currently, we have three demands: land rights, the repatriation of Bengali settlers from the CHT and military withdrawal from the Chittagong Hill Tracts (CHT). The Agreement has fundamental weakness. It cannot be implemented as it has no causal basis. Group conflict (PCJSS vs. UPDF) is not very affectual, but it is one kind of symptom. The third party creates this situation of group conflict. However, this party [the UPDF] was established because of the people's desire, and we work in favour of the common people. For the well-being of the mass people, we receive aid from the local CHT people.

It became apparent to members of the UPDF that the PCJSS disapproved of its political presence to acquire support for themselves. Moreover, the PCJSS leadership claimed that the government itself had motivated the formation of the UPDF and sustained to support them in their efforts to depress and destroy the PCJSS. Additionally, they also supposed that the UPDF was like a 'team B' of the government as it continued to provoke instability within the region and hindered the implementation process of the Agreement (Chowdhury, 2012a, p. 125). On many occasions, the PCJSS leaders complained that certain quarters among the political leaders, army and civil bureaucracy were backing the UPDF. They condemned the latter for the downfall of law and order in the region and demanded strict legal action against them. As a matter of fact, in the recent years, some media resources have been releasing news about the army's action against UPDF members, which could be attributed either to the PCJSS's claim or to the urgency of maintaining law and order in the Chittagong Hill Tracts (CHT). For example, according to news from the Ministry of Defence of Bangladesh, an armed member of the UPDF was killed in a gunfight with a team of joint forces in Khagrachhari Sadar Upazila on 14 October 2016, due to anti-law activity ("Gunfight With", 2016). Besides, factions within the UPDF were revealed when we find the news of the formation of a new party—UPDF (democratic) on 15 November 2017. After its construction, from December 2017 to February 2018, five UPDF members were murdered; including some allegations on others, the UPDF mainly accused its rival UPDF (democratic) for these killings ("UPDF Member", 2018). After that, three activists of the UPDF were shot dead on 28 May 2018 in Rangamati; Sochol Chakma, the organiser of the Rangamati UPDF, blamed the PCJSS (M. N. Larma faction) for these murders ("Three UPDF", 2018).

Moreover, group rivalries are found within the PCJSS. For example, on 2 December 2015, in different places at the Baghaichhari Upazila in Rangamati, the Santu faction of PCJSS, the Manobendra faction of PCJSS and the Border Guard Bangladesh (BGB) celebrated the 18th anniversary of the signing of the CHT Peace Agreement ("*Parbatya Chuktir*", 2015). This news revealed that different factions within the PCJSS celebrated the ceremony in different places. However, in 2010, the M. N. Larma faction was formed in the PCJSS split. The shocking news was that even the top-ranking members were killed; for example, the Vice President of the PCJSS (M. N. Larma faction), Shaktimann Chakma, died in a gun attack on 3 May 2018, with PCJSS activists alleging that the UPDF (Democratic) was responsible for this attack ("Upazila Chairman", 2018). In the same tone, J. B. Larma, popularly known Santu Larma (personal communication, May 18, 2016), the PCJSS's President, opined the following in an interview: after 11 January 2007, [the regime of the military-backed caretaker government in Bangladesh] similar to other political parties, the then GoB tried to form factions within the PCJSS. For this reason, the PCJSS [M. N. Larma] faction was introduced. If the government, including the other agencies, is eager to implement the CHT Peace Agreement, then implementation is realisable.

This remark revealed the existence of another faction within the PCJSS. The more important concern was that the PCJSS's President (also the Chairman of CHTRC) mostly emphasised on the unwillingness of the GoB (including other state institutions) in implementing the Agreement; the analysis in Chapter 5 also reveals the same.

Another critical problem in several factions within the indigenous communities is the struggle for or control of power. The relatively smaller Hill indigenous communities feel unrepresented and, thus, are indifferent to the fact that the PCJSS has the responsibility to implement the CHT Peace Agreement. Accusations assert that the violent conflict between the CHT-based political parties—the PCJSS and the UPDF—has not established favourable conditions for implementing the Agreement; the conflict has resulted in the killing, kidnapping and mutilation of hundreds of CHT people. According to the leading English newspaper of Bangladesh, among the Hill groups/organisations, 600 members belonging to various factions have been killed in factional rivalries since the 1997 signing of the Agreement ("Violence in the Hills", 2018). From December 2017 to the publication date of the newspaper, 86 people have been killed in suspected inter-party conflicts between CHT-based political parties; according to the Bandarban police, activists of the rival ethnic groups have been in clashes as they seek to establish supremacy in the CHT (*"Bandarbane Elopathari"*, 2020). Besides, they have often fought over extortion and supremacy within the Hill region. In a press release, Inter Services Public Relation Directorate (ISPR) of Bangladesh stated that in the Bandarban district of CHT, an army member and three terrorists were killed on 2 February 2022 during an exchange of fire between the two. While the ISPR claimed that the three terrorists were the members of PCJSS involved in various extortion activities, the PCJSS as against the ISPR's claim, mentioned that no member of the regional party of CHT was involved in the stated incident ("Army NCO", 2022). In an interview, B. K. Chakma (personal communication, May 18, 2016), Chairman of the Rangamati Hill District Council, opined that, before signing the Agreement, one group/party collected extortion from the CHT people, now three groups/parties are collecting extortion.

By one group, B. K. Chakma is probably indicating the PCJSS; by three groups, he is indicating the PCJSS (Santu), the UPDF and the

PCJSS (M. N. Larma)/Bengali settler-led factions. However, analysing the subsequent denial of the PCJSS, its motive—while claiming to be the sole representative of the CHT's indigenous people—in its dialogue with the UPDF, excluded the possibility of attaining peace (Jamil & Panday, 2012, p. 181). U. W. M. Jolly (personal communication, May 26, 2016), the Education and Culture Secretary of the PCJSS, opined that, if reciprocal respect [trust and confidence] developed between the Hill groups, then peace would be attained easily.

Still, these group rivalries are aggravating the instability in this region by dividing the people and creating the problematic issue regarding the implementation of the CHT Peace Agreement. Most of the interviewees (particularly those from the CHT local area along with the civil society members from other parts of Bangladesh) agreed to the fact that this intra-group rivalry impeded the implementation of the CHT Peace Agreement. Conversely, they also assumed that this was not the leading cause; instead, they emphasised on the government's reluctance to implement the Agreement. They stated that the government is more influential than the PCJSS (obviously, from the UPDF) and has enough power and authority to implement the Agreement. J. L. Tripura (personal communication, May 22, 2016), the Chairman (State-Minister status) of the Task Force, opined the following: intra-group rivalries are affecting the Agreement's implementation process. However, presently, the UPDF is not the formidable obstruction. The Agreement is not implemented because of some unseen causes. The government (including other state institutions) has enough strength to implement the CHT Peace Agreement. Flatterers are using this opportunity of disunity.

In the same tone, M. Guhathakurta (personal communication, June 8, 2016), the Executive Director of Research Initiatives Bangladesh (retired Professor of the University of Dhaka), mentioned the following in an interview: intra-group conflict (PCJSS vs. UPDF; and within the PCJSS) is not the core cause for the non-implementation of the CHT Peace Agreement. It is an excuse through which the government (including the bureaucracy and the military) is taking the opportunity to slow down the implementation of the Agreement. The army considers this issue a security problem.

6.3 Inter-Community (Bengali Settlers vs. Hill People) Relationships Affecting the CHT Peace Agreement

Both socially and politically, most non-indigenous Hill inhabitants seek to be categorised as Bengalis (mostly the Bengali settlers). It is imperative to carefully develop inter-community (Bengali–tribal) trust, in the earliest stages, for implementing the CHT Peace Agreement. Any prevalence of inter-ethnic rivalry will lead to extensive destabilisation of the CHT and threaten the implementation of the Agreement. During the negotiation process of its formation, the Bengali settlers' group formed the Parbattya All Party United Organisation on 14 March 1997 with the aim of protecting their rights and privileges in the CHT (Inqilab, 1997, as cited in Mohsin, 2002, p. 209). Notably, the Bengali settlers' organisation—Parbattya Gano Parishad (PGP)—denounced the Agreement and almost all of the Bengali settlers hoisted a black flag at their homes in contradiction to the Agreement, especially after its endorsement. The Bengali demonstrators in the three Hill Districts, particularly in Khagrachhari, were reportedly arrested for protesting against the Agreement's implementation (Rashiduzzaman, 1998, p. 662). Although the Bengali settlers were initially organising a resistance movement, it seemed that the situation calmed down with the passage of time.

The Bengalis, who now constitute about 47.1% of the CHT population, were allotted six male representatives and one female representative within the CHTRC. The Bengalis living in the CHT demanded equal rights and status, as envisaged in the CHT Peace Agreement, for the indigenous people along with their proper representation in the CHTRC. Moreover, they demanded that either the position of the Chairman of the CHTRC should be made contestable for all of the ethnic communities living in the CHT, or the Vice-Chairman's position should be introduced for a Bengali to maintain the balance of power between the indigenous and the Bengali ethnic people (Chowdhury, 2012b, p. 217). The denial of their claim has hardened their attitude towards the implementation of the Agreement. F. H. Badsha (personal communication, June 9, 2016), the President of the Parliamentary Caucus on Indigenous Peoples of Bangladesh and the Member of Parliament, expressed the following view in an interview: the CHT-based local Bengalis are not willing for the Agreement's implementation. For this reason, the implementation process is a slow one. Intra-group conflict (PCJSS vs. UPDF and within the PCJSS) is also affecting the implementation process. The fixation of the ownership of land is the main problem. Now, the Bengali settlers are more in number than the CHT Pahari. However, if the government is willing to implement the Agreement, this will be solved.

Accusation has been raised that military-backed organisations, that is, the Bengali Krishak Sramik Kalyan Parishad, the Parbattya Gano Parishad and the CHT Peace and Coordination Council have been set up in order to secure the interests of the Bengalis living in the Chittagong Hill Tracts (CHT). Also, Hill people highlighted the fact that these organisations endeavour to ensure the rights and privileges of only the Bengali settlers; this, in effect, is part of the government's tactics to legitimise the settlement of Bengali settlers in the CHT (Mohsin, 2002, p. 175). Likewise, several Hill leaders have claimed that the government has initiated socio-economic developments that have been accomplished against the interests of the CHT indigenous people, and in favour of the Bengalis living in that region.

Another dimension of inter-community (Bengalis–tribal) rivalries is based on the differences in religious beliefs. The predominantly Muslim Bengali settlers have not been expected to support the PCJSS due to their mostly Buddhist membership (the number and percentage of religious composition in the CHT are reported in Table 6.2).

Table 6.2 Religious composition of the CHT people

Census year	Religious group: Buddhist (in percentage)	Religious group: Muslim (in percentage)
1951	74.8	6.3
1961	71.5	11.7
1974	66.4	18.8
1981	51.2 (Calculated)	35.5 (Calculated)
1991	42.4 (Calculated)	44.8 (Calculated)
2001	43.4 (Calculated)	43.2 (Calculated)
2011 (most recent Census)	42.5 (Calculated)	43.5 (Calculated)

Source Developed by author based on Bangladesh Bureau of Statistics [BBS] (2015a, p. 22; 2015b, p. 22; 2015c, p. 22), and Shanawez (2011, p. 186)

Possibly, most of the settlers leaned towards the then opposition BNP and right-wing Islamic parties that were campaigning for the Bengali settlers' interests (although their real motive is open to debate). From the initial to the transitional phase of implementation of the CHT Peace Agreement, the Bengali settlers presumed a sense of distrust and anxiety that could only be diminished by transparency and openness from all sides. The worried Bengali settlers were known to have been backing the existing opposition party's claim that the Agreement should protect the interests of all Hill dwellers, including the Bengalis. M. A. Rashid (personal communication, June 2, 2016), a retired army officer who had served in the CHT, opined the following: the rivalry between the Bengali migrants and the Paharis [Hill people] has a social cause. The main problem is determining the ownership of land, which is also associated with the settlers' issue. Interestingly, most of the settlers support the BNP, then, the Jamaat-e-Islam. The CHT indigenous people mainly support the Awami League (AL). Not all the Paharis support Santu Larma's leadership. The formation of the UPDF is a case in the point.

It has come to our knowledge that the Bengalis of the CHT have set up a programme of planned protests against the CHT Land Dispute Resolution Commission (Amendment) Act 2016 which was passed in the National Parliament on 6 October 2016. Similarly, five Bengali organisations of CHT called for general strikes in the three Hill districts, on 13 October 2016 and 16 October 2016, against this Act and demanded the release of a Bengali leader who was arrested in Bandarban ("Five Bengali", 2016). This anti-Agreement procession has affected the implementation process (the mainstream Bengali political parties' interest regarding the Bengalis settlers' issue has been addressed in detail in Chapter 5). While the PCJSS leadership has welcomed the amendment, the leaders of Bengali organisations have demanded its repeal, alleging that they would be consequently deprived of land rights in the CHT (Bala, 2018, p. 30).

6.4 Factional Rivalries of the CHT People

Based on the analysis as addressed in the earlier sections, all factional rivalries between/among the CHT people are presented in Fig. 6.1.

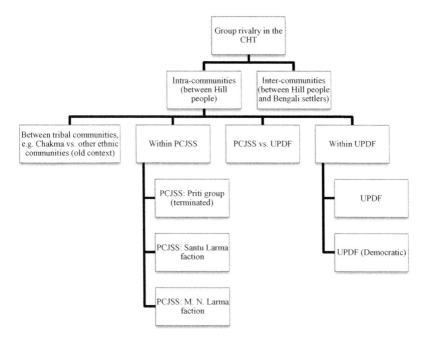

Fig. 6.1 CHT-based local-level group dynamics (*Source* Developed by author based on the earlier discussion)

6.5 Brief Analysis of Group Dynamics in the Chittagong Hill Tracts (CHT)

From the above discussion, it becomes evident that group rivalries (or conflicts) prevail in the CHT, whether it is within intra- and inter-communities (grounded on ethnicity). Based on the primary data that was collected from the interviewees and the secondary sources, it is inferred that these group rivalries are affecting the implementation process of the CHT Peace Agreement. The significant concern is that, on the one hand, the PCJSS is demanding the full implementation of the Agreement as a way to fulfil many of the aspirations of the Hill people. On the other hand, the UPDF has a specific demand that aims at full autonomy of the Hill tribal people. Besides this intra-faction, the Bengali settlers are not cooperative with the Agreement and its implementation initiatives. As stated by the Uppsala Conflict Data Program [UCDP] (n.d.), a constant rivalry continues between pro- and anti-Agreement groups within the tribal community, as well as tension between the tribal people and Bengali settlers. In summary, different groups within the CHT desire to retain their own interests. It is generally agreed that due to lack of unity at the local level, third parties (e.g. state institutions) may take the opportunity to fulfil their interests. Based on the analysis done earlier, at the state level, the government (including other state institutions) might have the possibility of taking the opportunity for the partial (or weak) implementation of the CHT Peace Agreement. However, government officials disagree with this view (this is also analysed, in detail, in Chapter 5). Thus, the local-level disunity provides the third party's opportunity (e.g. state-level institutions) to achieve their interest, which has severely affected the Agreement's implementation.

6.6 Chapter Conclusion

From the earlier analysis of this chapter, it is evident that the implementation of the CHT Peace Agreement is clearly connected with group rivalries based on local-level politics. At the local level, group rivalries within indigenous ethnic communities, between PCJSS and UPDF political parties, and between Hill people and Bengali settlers, are mostly analysed with the aim of finding how these rivalries affect the problem of the Agreement's implementation. Although the Chakmas comprised the majority within the CHT indigenous people, their leadership was not monolithic. For example, even after signing the Agreement, some smaller Hill communities have desired more representation in the CHTRC, where the Chakmas occupy the highest representative seats.

On the one hand, after signing the CHT Peace Agreement, a faction of the Hill people rejected the Agreement and concomitantly formed a CHT-based political party, namely the UPDF, and continued their movement for full autonomy including the constitutional recognition of indigenous identity. This group rivalry entailed a contest for gaining power, which even resulted in the killing of CHT people; thus, it has affected the implementation process of the Agreement, as the third party (e.g. the government, the army and the bureaucracy) can perceive the rivalry as an opportunity to take advantage of this disunity. On the other hand, some Bengali settlers' organisations were formed in order to protect their rights and privileges in the CHT; however, they are accused of not being supportive of the Agreement's implementation. For example, they have demanded more representation in the CHTRC and sought the repeal of the recently passed CHT Land Dispute Resolution Commission (Amendment) Act 2016. Hence, along with other causes, Bengali settlers are not repatriated as they are considered to comprise a vote bank for the mainstream Bengali political parties. Moreover, it is accused that these group rivalries (also consisting of conflicts between communities) become a favourable condition for the slow pace regarding the implementation of the Agreement.

References

Army NCO, 3 others killed in Bandarban gunfight: PCJSS denies involvement. (2022, February 4). *New Age*, p. 2.

Bala, S. (2018). Mapping local factions in the peace accord implementation process: A case study of the Chittagong Hill Tracts peace accord in Bangladesh. *Journal of International Development and Cooperation, 24*(2), 25–33.

Bandarbane elopathari gulite 6 jon nihoto [Six people were dead in Bandarban because of a random shot]. (2020, July 8). *Prothom Alo*, pp. 1–2.

Bangladesh Bureau of Statistics. (2015a). *Population and housing census 2011, zila reports: Bandarban*. Ministry of Planning, Government of the People's Republic of Bangladesh.

Bangladesh Bureau of Statistics. (2015b). *Population and housing census 2011, zila reports: Khagrachhari*. Ministry of Planning, Government of the People's Republic of Bangladesh.

Bangladesh Bureau of Statistics. (2015c). *Population and housing census 2011, zila reports: Rangamati*. Ministry of Planning, Government of the People's Republic of Bangladesh.

Chowdhury, N. J. (2012a). *Chittagong Hill Tracts peace accord implementation: Promise and performance*. A H Development Publishing House.

Chowdhury, N. J. (2012b). The Chittagong Hill Tracts accord implementation in Bangladesh: Ideals and realities. In N. Uddin (Ed.), *Politics of peace: A case of the Chittagong Hill tracts in Bangladesh* (pp. 205–221). Institute of Culture & Development Research.

Chowdhury, Z. H. (2001). Is the ethnic problem intractable? Prospects for success of the CHT peace Treaty. *Social Science Review, 18*(2), 87–108.

Five Bengali orgs call strike for Thursday, Sunday. (2016, October 12). *New Age*. http://www.newagebd.net/article/700/five-bengali-orgs-call-strike-for-thursday-sunday. Accessed 6 October 2020.

Gunfight with joint forces: UPDF member killed in Khagrachhari. (2016, October 15). *The Daily Star*. https://www.thedailystar.net/backpage/gunfight-joint-forces-updf-member-killed-khagrachhari-1299004. Accessed 6 October 2020.

Jamil, I., & Panday, P. K. (2012). The Chittagong Hill Tracts accord implementation in Bangladesh: Ideals and realities. In N. Uddin (Ed.), *Politics of peace: A case of the Chittagong Hill Tracts in Bangladesh* (pp. 163–189). Institute of Culture & Development Research.

Mohsin, A. (2002). *The politics of nationalism: The case of the Chittagong Hill Tracts, Bangladesh*. The University Press Ltd.

Mohsin, A. (2003). *The Chittagong Hill Tracts, Bangladesh: On the difficult road to peace*. Lynne Rienner Publishers Inc.

Parbatya chuktir barshikite baghaichharite nana ayojon [Different arrangements about the anniversary of the CHT Agreement in Baghaichhari]. (2015, December 6). *Prothom Alo*, p. 3.

Rashiduzzaman, M. (1998). Bangladesh's Chittagong Hill Tracts peace accord: Institutional features and strategic concerns. *Asian Survey, 38*(7), 653–670.

Shanawez, H. M. (2011). Mainstreaming human rights in development in Bangladesh: Conflict and peace-building in Chittagong Hill Tracts (CHTs). *Journal of the Graduate School of Asia-Pacific Studies, 21*, 179–200.

Shelley, M. R. (Ed.). (1992). *The Chittagong Hill Tracts of Bangladesh: The untold story*. Centre for Development Research.

Chittagong Hill Tracts Commission (The). (2000). *Life is not ours: Land and human rights in the Chittagong Hill Tracts, Bangladesh: Update 4*. https://www.iwgia.org/images/publications/Life_is_not_ours_UPDATE4.pdf. Accessed 6 October 2020.

Three UPDF men killed in Rangamati. (2018, May 29). *The Daily Star*. https://www.thedailystar.net/backpage/three-updf-men-killed-rangamati-1582966. Accessed 6 October 2020.

Translated English version of agreement between the National Committee on Chittagong Hill Tracts constituted by the government and The Parbatya Chattagram Jana Samhati Samiti. (n.d.). http://mochta.portal.gov.bd/sites/default/files/files/mochta.portal.gov.bd/page/8a162c4c_1f3f_4c6e_b3c0_63ad2ef9d2b3/Peace%20Accord%20%28Englidh%29.pdf. Accessed 3 September 2020.

Upazila chairman shot dead in Rangamati: Criminals kill UP chairman in Narsingdi. (2018, May 4). *The Daily Star*. https://www.thedailystar.net/frontpage/uz-chairman-shot-dead-rangamati-1571245. Accessed 6 October 2020.

UPDF member shot dead in Khagrachhari. (2018, February 22). *The Daily Star*. https://www.thedailystar.net/backpage/updf-member-shot-dead-khagrachhari-1538302. Accessed 6 October 2020.

Uppsala Conflict Data Program. (n.d.). *Bangladesh: Chittagong Hill Tracts*. https://ucdp.uu.se/conflict/322. Accessed 5 September 2020.

Violence in the Hills: Address the moot problem. (2018, May 6). *The Daily Star*, p. 6.

CHAPTER 7

Empirical Study at International Level

7.1 Chapter Introduction

Based on the historical, conceptual and analytical arguments presented in Chapters 1 and 2, many sub-nationalist movements, as in the case of CHT, have an international dimension with both state and non-state actors being involved. Although the CHT Peace Agreement is mostly the outcome of a long negotiation process primarily initiated by the GoB and the PCJSS, the role of the international community in achieving peace cannot be overlooked. For example, the massive refugees who fled from the CHT had been sheltered in India—this immediately attracted international attention through media, human rights organisations, NGOs, the international community, etc. Various members of the international community welcomed the Agreement hoping that it would not only boost the stabilisation of the internal situation in Bangladesh but also contribute to peace and stability in the south-Asian region. This chapter addresses the connections between the CHT case and the international community and identifies examples of international factors involved in the CHT case. To analyse the international actors' connection with the CHT case, the involvement of three actors is incorporated here in the form of case studies comprising one state actor (i.e. India) and two non-state actors (i.e. Chittagong Hill Tracts Commission and the UNDP). These three actors are studied from three different perspectives, that is, India as a state actor, the Chittagong Hill Tracts Commission as an international human rights-based NGO and the UNDP in its role as an international organisation with respect to their importance in the involvement with the CHT case.

In addition to the introduction and conclusion, this chapter comprises five sections. Section 7.2 deals with how the CHT case is related to the international communities. In Sect. 7.3, considering the connection of India's north-eastern states, India's interest is also analysed because the refugees from the CHT were sheltered in India. In Sect. 7.4, the role of the Chittagong Hill Tracts Commission is addressed from an international human rights-based NGO's perspective. In Sect. 7.5, relating to the study's aim of incorporating an international organisation, the role of the UNDP is analysed in the post-Agreement phase. In Sect. 7.6, some examples are viewed as having an undesirable effect on the Hill people.

7.2 Chittagong Hill Tracts (CHT) Case at the International Level

In this section, an attempt is made to identify how the state-level matters and how the CHT peace initiatives are impacted by its connectivity with other international factors and their interests in the designated area. Being considered as a primary international actor in the area, India had sheltered a massive number of refugees from the CHT and previously supported the PCJSS; its involvement in the CHT case should be analysed. Some international human rights organisations, for example, Anti-Slavery International, Amnesty International, Survival International (UK), Organising Committee Chittagong Hill Tracts Campaign (OCCHTC) (Netherlands), International Work Group for Indigenous Affairs (IWGIA) (Denmark), etc., have published regular news regarding the human rights violations of the Hill people and the international Chittagong Hill Tracts [CHT] Commission published annual reports about the CHT situation (Mohsin, 2003, p. 14). These organisations mostly submitted reports to the GoB and released information to Bangladesh's donor consortium countries and regions, such as Japan, the UK, Denmark, France, Germany, Sweden, Switzerland, the United States and the European Commission (EC). By the 1980s, the international donor consortium had a concern about the human rights violation in the CHT and began to place the impetus (or, to some extent, pressure), on the GoB, to reach a political solution. By the 1990s, the curtail of the Cold War brought qualitative changes in international politics by bringing human rights as well as minority security concerns to the fore; thereby, the UN could pay more attention to these problems (Mohsin, 2003, p. 91). For example, in September 2007, the adoption of the UN Declaration on the Rights of Indigenous Peoples, containing a comprehensive international standard on human rights, raised high expectation among the indigenous ethnic groups' movements all over the world (Gerharz, 2014, p. 1).

In an interview, R. D. Roy (personal communication, May 25, 2016), the Chakma Circle Chief, views the issue as follows:

> Human rights principles are universal, and therefore the United Nations has also prescribed inter-governmental and other international fora to discuss and resolve human rights matters, irrespective of the country it concerns. However, if there are national-level remedies, these must first be exhausted before approaching the UN human rights bodies to address the issue. Many aspects of the non-implementation of major provisions of the CHT Accord are within the purview of human rights. Naturally, when they fail to get a remedy at home, people of the CHT speak at the UN. So do the national human rights institutions and human rights NGOs. There is nothing wrong with that. They should not be persecuted for that. It is the norm in today's era of internationalisation. That may exert some pressure on the government, to expedite its role on the concerned issue.

In this regard, the CHTRC Chairman, J. B. Larma (personal communication, May 18, 2016), expressed the following in an interview: we sought support from the international community and connected with them, and they supported us. For example, India sheltered refugees. Like many international (also national) organisations as well as individuals, for example, Amnesty International in Germany, Ramendra [name of a person] in England played or is playing a valuable role for the Hill people.

7.3 India's Role Regarding the CHT Case

Bangladesh has unique geopolitical connectivity with India, its neighbour, through its borders sharing 175.68 kilometers with the Indian state of Tripura and 236.80 kilometers with the Indian state of Mizoram (Rashiduzzaman & Chowdhury, 2012, p. 26). Many sub-nationalist movements seek external support or shelter for political and, more importantly, military support to sustain their struggle. Before 1975, M. N. Larma had sought help from India but, considering the close relations between the Sheikh Mujib government (the AL-led government) and the

Indian government, his request was denied. Following the military coup and Mujib's assassination on 15 August 1975, India revised its policy and extended clandestine support to the PCJSS and its arm wing—the SB insurgents. The underlying factors for this were political as well as strategic. India was dismayed at the overthrow of its perceived ally, the then ruling governing party (AL), by a military coup. The military and quasi-military leaders of Bangladesh were alleged with harbouring anti-Indian sentiments in New Delhi. After the assassination of Mujib and the subsequent political upset, the PCJSS leaders fled to India. After that, the SB headquarters was established in the Indian state of Tripura; furthermore, SB fighters were trained and armed by the Indian military (Mohsin, 2003, p. 34). Besides, India had been the absentee actor as about 75,000 Hill people were living as refugees in Tripura in the early 1990s (Uppsala Conflict Data Program, n.d.); this is discussed in detail in Chapter 3 (sub-Sect. 3.5.3) and Chapter 4 (Table 4.8). The military activities also resulted in the eviction of about 50,000 Hill people as IDPs (Mohsin, 2003, p. 35). Thus, India was a party to the CHT case, caused by escalation and later de-escalation of the conflict: this can be primarily analysed through the realist view, whether through the lens of classical realism or that of neorealism. For example, from the 1970s to 1996, India's involvement in the CHT case was mostly motivated from the perspective of classical realism. However, when on the verge of signing the CHT Peace Agreement (specifically after 1996), India's involvement was primarily analysed through neorealism. This is also illustrated in the following discussion.

Because of the agitated nature and continuing separatist conflicts in the north-eastern states of India, the concern was not only about Bangladesh as a whole but particularly about the CHT, which was then suspected as insurgencies that had shaken the Seven Sister States of India. When India blamed Bangladesh for sheltering its fleeing insurgents, it conveyed a strategic meaning (Rashiduzzaman & Chowdhury, 2012, p. 27). Indian secessionist groups were in proximity with the Chakma-dominated mutiny of CHT, although this connection was mostly tactical. Tripura and Mizoram have indigenous people's groups who are similar, both ethnically and culturally, with the Hill people of the CHT; the emergence of this common sub-national identity yielded India's security concerns. As reported by Mohsin (2003), during the period of Pakistan rule, the Meitei rebels of Manipur, the Mizo National Front and the Tripura rebels established firm holding in the CHT (p. 89). India's support to the PCJSS was derived from its strategic calculation that it was a countermeasure to the then Dhaka's support for insurgent groups in the Seven Sister States of India, during the military and the quasi-military regime in Bangladesh. Moreover, it became a useful means to keep the GoB under pressure for diplomatic as well as political reasons and to dissuade it from supporting India's north-eastern insurgents (Bhaumik, as cited in Mohsin, 2003, p. 35).

However, India has subsequently played a significant role in the signing of the CHT Peace Agreement. After the end of the Cold War, considering India's geopolitical strength in the South Asian region and the restoration of parliamentary forms of government in Bangladesh, India changed her policy towards the PCJSS or the SB fighters again. The negotiation, which had begun from the time of the military regimes, continued into the era of civilian regimes in Bangladesh in 1991 (this has been addressed in Chapter 3). The parliamentary election of 1996 and the formation of the AL-led government changed the political and strategic climate of India, which pressed the PCJSS leadership for a negotiated settlement with Dhaka and issued ultimatums demanding that the refugees be returned to the CHT in Bangladesh. Historically, the AL and the Indian government has had a cordial relationship as Bangladesh achieved its independence under the political leadership of the AL, which India had primarily supported. New Delhi was assured that a friendly AL-led regime in Dhaka would not allow its territories to be used for insurgency purposes against India's north-eastern states. This way, India played a critical role in forcing the PCJSS leadership to come to the negotiation table and even modify its various demands (Chakma, 2012, p. 129). Thus, India has played a significant role in bringing about the signing of the CHT Peace Agreement.

M. S. Dewan (personal communication, May 19, 2016), Ex-Deputy Minister of MoCHTA, opined the following in an interview: international awareness raised because of the refugees sheltered in India, with the demand for a peaceful solution also discussed internationally. With the SB activities, the Indian (e.g. Assam, Tripura) separatist movement was also motivated. India changed her strategy and later on withdrew support for the PCJSS (even for the SB fighters). India supported the democratic government of Bangladesh rather than the military or quasi-military regimes (e.g. General H. M. Ershad's regime). India was ready to offer the credit of the CHT Peace Agreement to the AL-led government as the Indian government and the AL had a cordial relationship from the Liberation War of Bangladesh.

M. Guhathakurta (personal communication, June 8, 2016) viewed those mentioned above as the political perspective of regional power. She expressed the following: this case is the regional power politics in which India had a very influential role. However, India did not directly take part in the peace negotiating process. The refugees from the CHT were sheltered in India, and the SB members obtained arms from India. But India changed her strategy for a geopolitical reason, emphasising its friendly relations with its neighbour state, Bangladesh.

On the other hand, when interviewed, K. S. Hla (personal communication, May 26, 2016), the Chairman of BHDC, mentioned the following: he didn't find Indian involvement. If there was Indian involvement, they would have found their presence in the ceremony of arms surrender after the formulation of the CHT Peace Agreement.

However, in an interview, the Indian professor S. Singh (personal communication, March 3, 2016) viewed it from several perspectives. He stated the following: the issue has a historical correlation. During the period of India and Pakistan's independence in 1947, one of the Circle Chiefs of the CHT hoisted the Indian flag although it was then part of Pakistan. This was done in some other parts of India as well as in Pakistan because of the very scarce knowledge about the boundary (or maps). India had to bear significant problem of the CHT's refugees who were living in refugee camps in the Tripura province of India. India was eager to solve the problem. Moreover, in reality, every country finds its interests. India desired transit and transhipment to supply the necessary goods to her Seven Sister States. The CHT case fuelled the separatist movements of Tripura and Nagaland, and they were being sheltered in the CHT region. So, India sought to pacify (control) her provinces. Besides these points, historically, the then AL-led government had a friendly relationship with the Indian government.

7.4 Role of the International Chittagong Hill Tracts Commission

By the end of 1989, an independent international commission—Chittagong Hill Tracts Commission—was officially formed at the initiative of Denmark-based IWGIA and the Netherlands-based OCCHTC, intending to investigate allegations of human rights violation in the CHT (Chittagong Hill Tracts [CHT] Commission, 2000, p. 58). At the time, the Commission was jointly chaired by Douglas Sanders (Professor of Law,

University of British Columbia) from Canada and Wilfried Telkaemper (Vice President of the European Parliament from July 1989 to January 1992) from Germany; three other members were appointed from three different countries. The aforesaid international community primarily initiated the formation of this Commission; initially, it was composed of the persons who were experienced regarding the indigenous/human rights issue from different countries. However, after getting permission from the Indian and Bangladeshi governments, the Commission visited the refugee camps in Tripura from 21 to 26 November and the CHT from 8 December 1990 to 1 January 1991. During their visit, the CHT Commission members could travel freely and talk to anyone in private. Moreover, they interviewed many persons consisting of different groups of stakeholders and noted their observations (CHT Commission, 2000, p. 58).

On 23 May 1991, the Commission published its 108-page report titled *Life Is Not Ours. Land and Human Rights in the Chittagong Hill Tracts, Bangladesh* in the House of Lords in London (CHT Commission, 1992, p. 5). Among the broad conclusions, some are mentioned below:

- The Chittagong Hill Tracts are under military control …
- In spite of repeated military and governmental statements that incidents will be prevented, attacks by the military and Bengali settlers on hill peoples have continued …
- The settlement of Bengalis from other parts of Bangladesh has occurred with massive violations of property rights of hill people …
- There is a constant denigration of the economic, social and cultural characteristics of the hill people by government, military and settlers …
- There have been massive violations of the human rights of the hill people in the CHT. (CHT Commission, 1992, pp. 5–6)

Immediately after the publication of the report, it was sent to the then Prime Minister (Begum Khaleda Zia) of Bangladesh, the GOC of the Chittagong Division, the opposition political parties of Bangladesh, the government of India, the Hill people's organisations including the European representative of the PCJSS, the UN bodies, the aid-donating countries, the NGOs, etc., along with an attached letter seeking their comments. The CHT Commission also received some official and unofficial comments from the stakeholders mentioned above.

After that, the report of the CHT Commission has acknowledged the substantial consideration of the Western donor community. For example, the Dutch Minister of Development Cooperation wrote the following to the CHT Commission:

> On the basis of the findings ... I will in dialogue with our colleagues of the other donor countries continue to discuss the matter of human rights with the Government of Bangladesh. ... I assure you of my continued attention for the issues of human rights in general and of the people in the Chittagong Hill Tracts in particular. (CHT Commission, 1992, p. 30)

International donor communities, for example, Western donor governments have expressed their concern about the condition of rights in the CHT and have brought this issue to the GoB (CHT Commission, 1992, p. 19). Additionally, questions have been raised in the German Parliament and the European Parliament regarding the CHT case. For example, several donor countries like Denmark and the Netherlands have a policy that relates to development aid in observing human rights issues within the recipient country (CHT Commission, 1992, p. 19). However, the GoB termed it as being "patently biased and flawed" (CHT Commission, 1992, p. 26). In the early stages of January 1992, Sheikh Hasina (the present Prime Minister of Bangladesh), then the leader of the opposition, sent a letter to the Commission stating the following: "[w]e greatly appreciate your most laudable efforts to address this vital issue concerning Chittagong Hill Tracts and our party will continue to extend cooperation to the work of your commission ..." (CHT Commission, 1992, p. 29). This is a notable event as Sheikh Hasina, as leader of the then main opposition party, expressed her concerns about the CHT; however, even though Prime Minister Hasina-led government has ruled Bangladesh about two decades after signing the Agreement, the Agreement has not yet been fully implemented.

More consideration had been conferred to the CHT case in the meetings of the United Nations Working Group on Indigenous Populations (UNWGIP) in July 1991 and the UN Sub-Commission of Prevention of Discrimination and Protection of Minorities in August 1991. Along with other Hill delegates and international organisations, statements have been submitted by Mr Leif Dunfjeld, who was a member of the CHT

Commission. In February 1992, a delegate from the Jumma People's Network in Europe (an example of the diaspora) prepared a statement at the UN Commission for Human Rights in Geneva (CHT Commission, 1992, pp. 18–19). This way, the CHT Commission and other human rights organisations raised their voice at the international forum and put pressure (and motivation) to solve the problem peacefully. This CHT Commission also published four updates in 1992, 1994, 1997 and 2000. In the update on the year 2000, the Commission has concluded that the CHT Peace Agreement did not turn out to be a guarantor of lasting peace in the Hill Tracts region. It has expressed deep concerns about the developments following the Agreement, particularly its slow pace of implementation, the rivalry between the two Hill groups (PCJSS vs. UPDF) and the coercion of actors for whom the Agreement is unacceptable; they also suggested some recommendations like the previous reports (CHT Commission, 2000, pp. 51–56).

After signing the CHT Peace Agreement in 1997, the former international CHT Commission published their last updated report in 2000; later, the Commission became almost inactive hoping that peace would prevail throughout the Agreement's implementation. Although the Agreement was signed in 1997, the implementation is still being delayed. Realising this, civil society members from Bangladesh and Denmark have taken the initiative to reform the Commission and, in 2008, the international Chittagong Hill Tracts Commission has been reestablished with three co-Chairmen and 15 members from Bangladesh as well as from international water. From 2008 to July 2014, the Commission members visited the CHT seven times in order to explore the human rights conditions of the Hill people. Moreover, they took part in the Long March to the Parliament House of Bangladesh, met with Prime Minister Sheikh Hasina to tell her about the situation of CHT and urged her to implement the CHT Peace Agreement fully. This proved to be an optimistic initiative as the Prime Minister assured them about the Agreement's implementation.[1]

---

[1] This paragraph is mainly written based on the narratives of two interviewees—S. Kamal (co-chairman of the CHT Commission) and I. Dewan (ex-General Secretary of HWF)—on 7 June 2016 and 16 June 2016, respectively, in Dhaka.

R. S. Partha (personal communication, June 18, 2016), who completed his doctoral degree on the CHT subject, mentioned the following in an interview: among the international actors, the CHT Commission was one of the most influential for enhancing peace in the Chittagong Hill Tracts (CHT). The EU [European Union] was also a pressure-creating factor. Amnesty International and the UNDP also played their role. The Jumma People's network in Japan had some connection with this issue.

M. Guhathakurta (personal communication, June 8, 2016) further opined that the CHT Commission enhanced the media influence and played a role as a pressure group factor.

Concerned about the human rights violation of the Hill people, (like other international communities), on 16 September 1992, the European Parliament passed a resolution asking the GoB to refute its military involvement in the CHT and to respect the human rights of the Hill people (CHT Commission, 1994, p. 38). On 9 March 1994, the European Parliament again passed a resolution which included many points concerning the CHT problem. For example, it asked the European Commission to persuade the Bangladeshi authorities towards the development of the human rights of the CHT indigenous people (CHT Commission, 1994, pp. 38–39). Regarding the CHT concern, the research paper published by European Union (n.d.) revealed that the involvement of the European Community in the CHT would contribute to the objectives of enhancing human rights and democracy through a comprehensive approach in the Chittagong Hill Tracts (CHT). According to this paper, the aforementioned approach would consist of providing tools to implement the CHT Peace Agreement (e.g. building institutional capacity) while enhancing confidence-building between the different groups through measures aimed at community empowerment and by promoting social and economic development, notably, through education and health programmes (European Union, n.d., p. 18). For example, under the National Indicative Programme (NIP), the EC had emphasised, along with other donors, on supporting the aspects of political governance where there had been commitments promising reform and support towards human rights issues (European Union, n.d., p. 32). The EU also supports some of the recent UNDP's programmes—this is mentioned in the following section.

7.5 Development Initiatives of the CHT and the United Nations Development Programme (UNDP)

The 1997 CHT Peace Agreement has created both space and opportunities to carry out developmental activities for the CHT-based local people. Initially, the GoB had requested that the UNDP to conduct a 'Needs Assessment Commission' not only to facilitate coordination among the donors but also to send a mission. In April 1998, the mission visited the CHT and presented its report to the GoB in mid-May, identifying a medium to engender more prolonged development goals, such as the supply of food and drinking water, health care, primary education, infrastructure and communication, and building confidence and peace between the communities within the CHT (CHT Commission, 2000, p. 46). In promoting sustainable and locally-applicable development within the Hill region, the UNDP has played (and is still playing) a leading role as coordinator and facilitator. In 2003, it responded to the development needs and signed a 5-year programme with the GoB in late 2005. The programme was titled 'Promotion of Development and Confidence Building' in the CHT and its initial budget was fixed at US$50 million. In 2008, the UNDP also undertook a Strategic Review of the programme in order to identify its significant contribution as well as opportunities for future implication. Thereby, because of its positive contribution aimed at peace and development in the CHT, the programme was extended to September 2013 with an increased budget of US$160.5 million.

This programme, through its Chittagong Hill Tracts Development Facility (CHTDF), provided overall development opportunities for all people and especially the ethnic communities inhabiting the Chittagong Hill Tracts (CHT). Its purpose was to support the government and enable the CHT's institutions as well as their constituent communities to explore the measures for sustainable socio-economic development, based on the principles of self-dependence, local participation and decentralised progress. The main objectives of the programme were as follows:

- Capacities of CHT institutions, including MoCHTA, the Regional Council, the three Hill District Councils, and the traditional institutions of the three Circle Chiefs, are enhanced
- Economic opportunities for small local enterprises, women, youth and farmers are improved

- Literacy is increased through improved access to a strengthened education system adapted to the local context
- Health conditions are improved through a strengthened health system supporting community outreach and localized service delivery
- Local communities are empowered and their capacities to manage their own development are enhanced
- Confidence required to find the solutions to long standing problems and encourage sustainable development and peace in the CHT is created. (*Overview of the CHTDF Project*, n.d.)

The Local Trust-Builders Network is one of the examples initiated by the UNDP in partnership with the EU, Sweden, Japan and Denmark to support sustainable development and peace in the Chittagong Hill Tracts (CHT). As is known, even after signing the CHT Peace Agreement, tension still remains between communities on issues like ownership of land, possession of local resources, or other human rights-related matters. Once again, these rivalries turn into communal conflict and sometimes lead to violent attacks between neighbouring villages. The Local Trust-Builders Network is a group of 149 trained volunteers (both women and men) from different ethnic communities across the CHT, which aims to effectively settle the conflict through constructive dialogue and prevention of violence in the Hill Tracts. Here it is worthwhile to mention the words of trust-builder, Shahena Akter. She noted that the conflict situation is being mediated to achieve a win-win outcome for the parties in conflict with no one regarded as the loser. She added that in this approach, the conflict is restrained and community bonds become more vigorous; thus, the achievement of peace is closer (United Nations Development Programme, n.d.).

The UNDP project addresses not only the development perspective for the CHT people but also puts forth conditions that are associated with the full implementation of the 1997 CHT Peace Agreement. For example, on 1 December 2016, in a move that reaffirmed its promise to implement the Agreement fully, the GoB signed a deal with the UNDP (of over US$31 million) for a new development project named 'Strengthening Inclusive Development in the Chittagong Hill Tracts' and focusing on sustainable and inclusive development of the CHT ("$31m Agreement", 2016). In reality, this is the continuation of an effective earlier project implemented in 2003, with successful results in the three districts of the CHT, as claimed by the UNDP's press release on 1 December 2016. The

Bangladesh country director of the UNDP, Sudipto Mukerjee, indicated that this new phase of development would address not only the new development projects but also the tasks remaining from previous projects in the Chittagong Hill Tracts (CHT). Including all communities in the area would be the primary focus, and it would have a more substantial impact on the ecosystem, social development and the development of institutions ("$31m Agreement", 2016).

As an executing agency, the MoCHTA is supposed to receive overall ownership and responsibilities for the project operations and are accountable for the performances. N. B. K. Tripura (personal communication, June 15, 2016), the Secretary of the MoCHTA, narrated the following in an interview: following the CHT Peace Agreement, in 2003, the UNDP began its activities in the CHT and is playing its role in implementing the Agreement. The EU also provided some donations. Likewise, ECOSOC [Economic and Social Council of the UN] and UNFPA [United Nations Population Fund] have some initiatives for achieving peace through supporting the Agreement's implementation.

Moreover, in an interview, B. Chakma (personal communication, May 19, 2016), the Chief of Community Empowerment of CHTDF (a programme of the UNDP), expressed the following: in implementing the CHT Peace Agreement, we have some activities. For example, several times, influential persons like ambassadors of other countries have attended some of the programmes of the UNDP. They also play a meaningful role in motivating government agencies to implement the Agreement. Sometimes, we arrange some programmes where CHT people (leaders) and government officials (sometimes, decision-making authorities) meet each other. Then, this creates some space in which to interact. If the top and grassroots levels are functioning well, then a progressive impact may be achieved. For example, at the policy level, the Parliamentary Caucus on Indigenous Peoples is supported by the UNDP.

The UNDP has played a supportive role in initiating the formation of the Parliamentary Caucus on Indigenous Peoples in Bangladesh. To uphold the interests of the indigenous people in Bangladesh, both inside and outside the National Parliament, the Parliamentary Caucus on Indigenous Peoples began its work in 2010. In the 10th Parliament, 36 Members of Parliament including four Ministers, four State Ministers and six Technocrat Members constitute the Caucus (Kamal, 2014). With many other objectives targeted towards the upliftment of indigenous people's rights all over Bangladesh, facilitating the full implementation of the CHT Peace Agreement is one of the main goals of this Caucus. For example, it has taken initiatives for the constitutional recognition of indigenous people during the 15th amendment of the Constitution in 2011; furthermore, it has arranged high-level policy dialogues for the full implementation of the Agreement. The EU, the International Labour Organization (ILO), the UNDP and the Oxfam came forth in support of the Caucus provided financial aid. In an interview, F. H. Badsha (personal communication, June 9, 2016), the President of the Parliamentary Caucus and the Member of Parliament, commented the following: although this Caucus is not the governmental body or part of the National Parliament, it can exert pressure on (or lobby) the GoB in Parliament to uphold indigenous rights. When some MPs (e.g. five to 15 members) talk in Parliament about the indigenous matter, this can appear as a pressure-enhancing factor.

7.6 Undesirable Examples of International Organisations' Involvement

Some interviewees did not forget to remark on some projects, aided by a few international organisations, which were against the interests of the Hill people. For example, S. U. Talukder (personal communication, May 20, 2016), the independent lawmaker from Rangamati, reported that, as a result of some projects supported by the World Bank or the ADB, natural disaster, deforestation, animals, birds, etc. were also severely affected. In the same tone, M. B. Tripura (personal communication, May 22, 2016), the Executive Director of a CHT-based local NGO, opined that some international organisations, for example, the World Bank and the ADB uphold their interests through granting loans to the national government, where the interests of international organisations and governments are retained.

The interviewees' claim becomes more apparent if we look at the Kaptai Hydro-electric Project that was constructed in the 1960s with foreign aid (details are addressed in Chapter 3).

However, in an interview, R. A. M. O. M. Chowdhury (personal communication, June 9, 2016), the AL-backed Member of Parliament, opined that this peace process was only initiated by the GoB and the Hill people (particularly the PCJSS), with no third-party involvement.

7.7 Chapter Conclusion

In this chapter, the issue of international actors' involvement in the CHT case of Bangladesh has been addressed. It has been previously mentioned that Santu Larma, the President of PCJSS, sought support for the Hill people from the international community. He mentioned some examples ranging from individuals to international human rights organisations, including the neighbouring countries. In today's globalised society, most human rights issues and indigenous issues are matters of worldwide concern. In this regard, some international NGOs, human rights-based organisations, donor consortium countries, UN bodies, states and even individuals are concerned about the CHT case. With the aim of incorporating different viewpoints, India's role as a state actor has been discussed along with the involvement of the CHT Commission (an independent international commission) and the UNDP as non-state actors. The analysis, as mentioned earlier, led to the inference that India, the bordering country of Bangladesh, has revised its support towards the PCJSS in several instances, owing to its own political and strategic interests. Although India had previously supported the PCJSS, subsequently it has played a critical role during the signing of the CHT Peace Agreement by exerting pressure on the PCJSS to come to the negotiation table. India, like other countries, sought its own political and strategic interests.

Then, it has been previously stated that the international Chittagong Hill Tracts Commission visited the refugee camps in Tripura and the CHT of Bangladesh and published a report and sent it to the various stakeholders in Bangladesh as well as the international community. This created media awareness and the problem attracted international attention; the GoB was also motivated (or pressurised, instead) to solve the problem. After signing the CHT Peace Agreement, the newly formed CHT Commission members, along with other initiatives, met with Prime Minister Sheikh Hasina who assured them about the proper implementation of the Agreement. Next, the UNPD became primarily connected with the Agreement by launching a programme targeted towards the development and confidence-building in the Chittagong Hill Tracts (CHT). In the recent projects, the GoB has reaffirmed its promise to implement the Agreement fully. Besides, in National Parliament of Bangladesh, the Parliamentary Caucus on Indigenous Peoples in Bangladesh has been supported by the UNDP. In summary, the CHT Peace Agreement is viewed differently by various stakeholders, all of whom have their own perspective on whether it caters to their interests or upholds indigenous people's rights.

References

$31m agreement signed for CHT dev. (2016, December 2). *The Daily Star*. https://www.thedailystar.net/city/31m-agreement-signed-cht-dev-132 3877. Accessed 7 October 2020.

Chakma, B. (2012). Bound to be failed?: The 1997 Chittagong Hill Tracts 'peace accord.' In N. Uddin (Ed.), *Politics of peace: A case of the Chittagong Hill Tracts in Bangladesh* (pp. 121–142). Institute of Culture & Development Research.

European Union. (n.d.). *Bangladesh–European Community Country Strategy Paper for the Period 2007–2013*. http://eeas.europa.eu/archives/delegations/bangladesh/documents/eu_bangladesh/csp_07_13_en.pdf. Accessed 4 March 2018.

Gerharz, E. (2014). Recognising indigenous people, the Bangladeshi way: The United Nations declaration, transnational activism and the constitutional amendment affair of 2011. *Indigenous Policy Journal, 24*(4), 1–18.

Kamal, M. (Ed.). (2014). *Parliamentary caucus on indigenous peoples: A genesis of parliamentary advocacy in Bangladesh*. Research and Development Collective.

Mohsin, A. (2003). *The Chittagong Hill Tracts, Bangladesh: On the difficult road to peace*. Lynne Rienner Publishers Inc.

Overview of the CHTDF Project. (n.d.). www.chtdf.org/index.php/about-us/chtdf-overview. Accessed 11 December 2016.

Rashiduzzaman, M., & Chowdhury, M. H. (2012). The CHT accord and the "triangular connectivity." In N. Uddin (Ed.), *Politics of peace: A case of the Chittagong Hill Tracts in Bangladesh* (pp. 26–48). Institute of Culture & Development Research.

Chittagong Hill Tracts Commission (The). (1992). *Life Is Not Ours: Land and Human Rights in the Chittagong Hill Tracts, Bangladesh: An Update of The May 1991 Report*. https://www.iwgia.org/images/publications//0129_Life_is_not_ours_-_an_UPDATE.pdf. Accessed 2 October 2020.

Chittagong Hill Tracts Commission (The). (1994). *Life Is Not Ours: Land and Human Rights in the Chittagong Hill Tracts, Bangladesh: Update 2*. https://www.iwgia.org/images/publications//0129_Life_is_not_ours_-_UPDATE_2.pdf. Accessed 7 October 2020.

Chittagong Hill Tracts Commission (The). (2000). *Life Is Not Ours: Land and Human Rights in the Chittagong Hill Tracts, Bangladesh: Update 4*. https://www.iwgia.org/images/publications/Life_is_not_ours_UPDATE4.pdf. Accessed 6 October 2020.

United Nations Development Programme. (n.d.). *Empowering People for Peace in the Chittagong Hill Tracts*. www.undp.org/content/undp/en/home/ourwork/ourstories/empowering-people-for-peace-in-the-chittagong-hill-tracts.html. Accessed 29 January 2016.

Uppsala Conflict Data Program. (n.d.). *Bangladesh: Chittagong Hill Tracts*. https://ucdp.uu.se/conflict/322. Accessed 5 September 2020.

CHAPTER 8

Dynamics of Peace Agreement Implementation: Research Findings

8.1 Chapter Introduction

The CHT Peace Agreement was signed with the hope that it would herald the onset of peace in the CHT through the implementation of all the provisions of the Agreement. However, one of the disappointing concerns is that the two primary signatory parties of the Agreement have not even found consensus on the question of how many sections of the Agreement have been implemented. In fact, the vast differences claimed by the conflicting parties have affected the peace and stability in the Chittagong Hill Tracts (CHT). As Bangladesh is a sovereign state, successive governments have had the authoritative power to enact new laws or to amend existing laws relating to the implementation of the provisions of the CHT Peace Agreement. At the state level, along with the government (the principal actor), the army and the bureaucracy are influential actors in implementing the Agreement. At the CHT-based local level— mainly the PCJSS, the UPDF and the Bengali settlers—different views are held regarding the Agreement's formulation as well as its implementation procedures. In the earlier chapters, analysis has shown not only how the international community (also present as actors) is involved in the CHT case but also how it is serving its interest.

This chapter seeks to comprehensively analyse the reason behind this gap in recognition of the CHT Peace Agreement's implementation, mainly between the GoB and the PCJSS (as explained in Chapters 3

© The Author(s), under exclusive license to Springer Nature Singapore Pte Ltd. 2022
S. Bala, *Politics of Peace Agreement Implementation*, https://doi.org/10.1007/978-981-16-1944-1_8

and 4). The study has undertaken this work through the empirical lens at multiple levels (Chapters 5, 6 and 7), that is, state, CHT-based local and international levels, based on the framework described in Chapters 1 and 2. Based on the earlier chapters, the following analysis substantiated the fact that is owing to wider gaps in interests, different actors hold different views about the Agreement and its implementation process. With the aim of analysing the objectives through the hypotheses, in addition to the introduction and conclusion, this chapter mainly summarises the discussion by organising it into two sections. Section 8.2 deals with the main findings based on the recapitulation of the earlier chapters, while Sect. 8.3 attempts to revisit the research question, the objectives and the hypotheses.

8.2 Findings Through Comprehensive Analysis

To examine the hypotheses that aimed to answer the research objectives, the main empirical study is incorporated within Chapters 5, 6 and 7 based on the secondary and primary sources of data. To analyse the arguments within these chapters, there is a brief but acute need to address the earlier chapters due to the presence of close connectivity between the chapters; this will be substantiated while addressing the following chapter-by-chapter discussion.

After discussing some fundamental matters, for example, the background of the research question, the objectives, the research method, preview of the various chapters, etc. in Chapter 1 (introductory chapter), Chapter 2 attempts to discuss the theoretical and analytical framework. The analysis in Chapter 2 has shown that both the liberal and the realist theoretical approaches are relevant for studying the implementation of the CHT Peace Agreement. Moreover, it has been shown as to how politics and interests are related to the issue of the Agreement's implementation. To analyse this dispute, an analytical framework has been developed based on three levels (in other words, comparable to the independent variables) of analysis, that is: state level (i.e. the GoB, the army and the bureaucracy), the CHT-based local level (i.e. intra-tribal and Bengali–tribal rivalries) and the international level (i.e. state actors, e.g. India, and non-state actors, e.g. the international CHT Commission and the UNDP). Within this analytical framework, there has been a study about how these actors (under the three levels of analysis) are persuaded by their own interests. If we revisit the empirical discussion (presented in

Chapters 5, 6 and 7) based on the primary and secondary sources of data, the latent politics behind the implementation strategy of the CHT Peace Agreement becomes evident. Finally, it concludes that the widening gaps in interests, between the actors, are responsible for divergent views which remain as obstacles for the partial (or weak) implementation of the Agreement.

Chapter 3 discusses issues ranging from conflict eruption to its management in the Chittagong Hill Tracts (CHT). Because of the policies that have been adopted by the state authority, the Hill indigenous people have been alienated from both the socio-economic and the political spheres of life. This was particularly entrenched by the British colonial rulers who also directed Pakistan's as well as Bangladesh state authorities in the name of implementing different measures. Each of the state authorities, during their tenure, sought their own economic and political interests in the guise of administration (or government) of the Hill people. Although in the beginning, the British East India Company's main focus was to gain wealth from the CHT, later the colonial rulers captured the whole political economy of the CHT by acquiring all the lands and forests within the Chittagong Hill Tracts (CHT). Another noteworthy fact is the enactment of the CHT Regulation of 1900, through which the British mostly established their power and authority over the land and the Hill people in the Chittagong Hill Tracts (CHT). Among many other initiatives, the British also banned the *jhum* cultivation, which is not only regarded as their economic mode of production but also associated with their socio-cultural lifeworld.

This kind of domination was also inherited by the Pakistani rulers, for whom the CHT Manual still comprised the basis of administration in the region. During that regime, successive governments (in some cases, with the help of international donors) initiated many projects in the name of development. However, many of those initiatives were against the interests of the Hill people and mainly exploited the CHT's natural resources. Moreover, the Kaptai Hydro-electric Project, which is considered as a remarkable causal event regarding most of the problems in the CHT case, has been discussed in detail including some examples. However, during the period concomitant to the independence of Bangladesh and with the past experience of marginalisation, the Hill ethnic people demanded constitutional autonomy, including its own legislature, during the formulation of the Constitution of Bangladesh. The state authority identified it as a question of sovereignty or integrity (this was mostly political); it was also associated as an economic problem as the CHT were full of natural resources. Consequently, their demands were rejected, and the later history is rife with stances of armed conflict between the SB fighters and the state's security forces. Through the realisation of a political solution, along with many other motivations, representatives of the GoB and the PCJSS leadership continued the negotiation aimed at the settlement of the problem. Finally, they signed the CHT Peace Agreement in 1997. In summary, through this analysis, it becomes evident that the state authorities have each sought their own interests, which have been either political or economic in nature.

Then, the central aim of Chapter 4 is to address the current status of implementation, as it helps to unfold the real motive of the implementing agencies regarding the implementation of the CHT Peace Agreement. As mentioned earlier, on the one hand, the GoB claims that 48 sections of the Agreement have already been implemented; on the other hand, the PCJSS's chief (Santu Larma) has claimed that only 25 sections of the Agreement have been implemented while excluding the crucial sections. In this chapter, a comparative analysis of some of the crucial sections of the Agreement has been incorporated, such as land issue, withdrawal of temporary army camps, the refugee concern, etc., that display disagreement regarding the recognition between the GoB and the PCJSS. Through this comparative discussion, it becomes evident that the GoB also agreed with the statement that the status of most of these provisions are either under process or partially implemented. From this perspective, the consequent argument is that without the implementation of such crucial sections, it is improper to claim that most sections of the CHT Peace Agreement have been implemented. It has been mentioned earlier that the government (including other state institutions, e.g. the bureaucracy and the army) have the authoritative power to formulate new laws as well as defining existing laws related to the implementation of the Agreement. We have already known that most of the complexities within the CHT case are derived from the problem of the fixation on ownership of the land. After its formation, the Land Commission (to solve the land-related issues in the CHT) spent about 16 years to amend this Act on 6 October 2016. Consequently, a question arises as to how and what period of time one has to wait to view the motives behind the formulation of rules and regulations for the CHT Land Commission (see Table 4.10 for details)? Moreover, this raised another question regarding the real motive of state institutions behind the Agreement's implementation.

The issue of the Bengali settlers is another essential concern that was not incorporated in the CHT Peace Agreement. These Bengali migrants were not only responsible for changing the demographic (now they comprise about 47.1% of the CHT population) view but also initiated problems through the acquisition of land. The PCJSS claimed that there was a verbal agreement regarding the repatriation of Bengali migrants from the Chittagong Hill Tracts (CHT). However, the government denies the presence of any unwritten document (or speech). These Bengali settlers are the voters belonging to the three constituencies (for the National Parliamentary seats) which form the CHT; every mainstream national political party seeks their support (as they are considered as a vote bank) to win the National Parliamentary elections. Since the beginning, the Bengali settlers have not been supportive of the Agreement. This has also been unveiled when some Bengali settlers' organisations have called for a general strike against the formation of the CHT Land Dispute Resolution Commission (Amendment) Act 2016. Thus, the implementation policy is affected by the mainstream Bengali political parties' intention of winning the parliamentary elections by attaining political support from Bengali settlers. Finally, this shows the parties' individuated interests in gaining political power at the state level.

Considering the analysis, it becomes evident that without solving such crucial issues, it is unlikely to claim a willingness to implement the CHT Peace Agreement. Like many previous research projects, it has been assumed that only the number of the provisions of the Agreement should not be the primary concern; rather, implementation of the crucial sections should be the first priority. Besides, more than 24 years have passed since the signing of the Agreement; now, it is integral to implement all the provisions of the Agreement within the shortest possible period. Although the government claims its willingness to implement the Agreement, the implementing agencies might have their vested interests which need to be shunned or sacrificed.

Next, in connection with this implementation dispute, the actual politics regarding the implementation of the CHT Peace Agreement, at the state level, are discussed in Chapter 5, with a connection of both secondary and primary sources of data. Within a sovereign state like Bangladesh, as the government has the authoritative power in the Agreement's implementation, it follows that the government must be the principal implementing manager. Moreover, most of the implementation policies depend on the willingness on the part of the concerned government, which is again increasingly connected with the politics of assuming (or controlling) power. As is known, the mainstream Bengali political parties formed the GoB; the lack of consensus between the leading political parties, regarding the formation of the CHT Peace Agreement, surely affected its implementation policies. During the inception of the signing of the Agreement, the then opposition party BNP, along with its allies, directly opposed it and took several activities against it. Although the AL-led government which signed the Agreement is still the ruling party, its real motive in implementing the Agreement is not beyond criticism. Many have accused that signing of the Agreement was a political tactic of the government to deactivate the PCJSS insurgency, by providing them with the nominal power required to administer the CHT-based local-level institutions. Although the CHTRC and the HDCs were set up with great hopes and aspirations—they would handle the local CHT matters—successive governments did not undertake enough initiatives to empower these local institutions. Instead, these governments usually nominated the Chairman of the three HDCs and members of the CHTRC (also the official staff) while ostensibly serving the interests of the Bengali ruling elites.

Thereby, one of the most significant aspects of the ascension of mainstream Bengali political parties into state power is the winning of the parliamentary seats which are assigned for the Chittagong Hill Tracts (CHT). It is comparatively easy to win these three seats by seeking the support of the Bengali settlers, who constitute about 47.1% of the CHT population at present. Considering this background, no government (among those primarily supported by a political party) is prepared to take the risk of repatriating Bengali settlers as they are supposed to comprise a massive vote bank. The issue of permanent residence is not settled yet, as this is related to the settlement of the land-related problems. In the meantime, an accusation has been made asserting that many of the Bengali settlers have received permanent resident status; this complicates the CHT situation further. From this analysis, it is evident that the government's willingness can be identified as a causal factor related to the political interest of assuming state power, no matter who signed the CHT Peace Agreement or who holds state power at present. These arguments are also substantiated by many interviewees whose narratives were elaborated in Chapter 5. Anyway, the government and its fellow institutions (e.g. the bureaucracy) are still claiming their optimistic willingness towards the Agreement's implementation.

Thereafter, a discussion of the army's involvement in the matter is of immense importance as the CHT case was once placed under the direct control of the army until the CHT Peace Agreement was signed. First, the deployment of a large number of army personnel (including the temporary camps) needs an additional amount of the state's expenditure. Even after signing the Agreement, the army has had its direct/indirect control over the civil administration (e.g. in the name of maintaining law and order) in the Chittagong Hill Tracts (CHT). For example, they have been entrusted with an administrative order stating the continuation of Operation Uttoron (Operation Upliftment) in place of Operation Dabanol (Operation Wildfire). Once, all of the development actions of the CHT were conducted through the CHTDB, whose Chairman was the GOC (comprising army personnel) of the Chittagong Division. But still, the army is accused of being involved in income-generating business which, in some cases, is beyond the realm of military professionalism. Moreover, it is also accused of assisting with the setting up of several local indigenous organisations which predominantly serve the government's interests. If the CHT-based local institutions (e.g. the CHTRC and the HDCs) became sufficiently empowered through the implementation of the CHT Peace Agreement, then the economic and administrative control exercised by the army would be very much curtailed. Eventually, this Agreement has lessened the economic interests (this is also related to political and administrative issues) of the sections of the army which have been deployed in the CHT; however, even this does not successfully address their support towards the Agreement's implementation. Along with many interviewees, it has been agreed that the army plays one of the crucial roles in motivating the government's decision about the implementation policies of the CHT Peace Agreement. However, it is difficult to prove these accusations against an institution like the army.

The bureaucratic/administrative role, regarding the CHT case, holds immense significance as they are one of the key actors as well as an institution responsible for implementing the policy at the local level. Many traditional officials have understood that if the newly established local institutions (e.g. the CHTRC and the HDCs) become sufficiently empowered through the Agreement's implementation, then they have to carry out their responsibilities under the supervision of these institutions instead of their traditional system of the ministerial line; this looks like an uncomfortable situation for the traditional bureaucrats. Accusations have been made asserting that proper messages about the CHT situation (e.g. the implementation policies relating to the Agreement) have not been conveyed to the government, owing to bureaucratic indifference about the implementation of the Agreement and, in many cases, the bureaucracy influences the government's decision. Moreover, similar to the opinion of some interviewees (including an expert researcher's narrative), it has been understood that the bureaucracy has their own interest of exercising (or assuming) power in the CHT and are not willing to empower the CHT-based local institutions. In summary, it becomes evident from the above discussion (based on Chapter 5) that at the state level, every actor (or group) seeks their own interests irrespective of whether it is political, economic, or aimed at exercising power.

Chapter 6 analysed the group rivalries between the CHT-based local people who are primarily supposed to be beneficiaries of the CHT Peace Agreement. Although the GoB is the main actor regarding the implementation of the Agreement, the CHT-based group (i.e. community) rivalries have also impeded its implementation. For example, within the Hill ethnic communities, although the Chakmas were (and still are) the majority (and the most advanced) ethnic community (their members also comprise the majority within the PCJSS), their leadership was not monolithic. For example, even after signing the CHT Peace Agreement, some of the smaller Hill ethnic communities desired more representation (or seats) within the CHTRC, where the Chakmas have occupied the highest representation. Besides, there is also a faction within the PCJSS (e.g. PCJSS—M. N. Larma faction). However, the most noteworthy event is that one faction of the Hill ethnic people rejected the Agreement and formed the UPDF, a political party and continued their movement for full autonomy. On the one hand, PCJSS demanded full implementation of all sections of the Agreement. On the other hand, UPDF demanded full autonomy, including the constitutional recognition of indigenous identity. This group rivalry even resulted in mass destruction, including killings of the people living in the Chittagong Hill Tracts (CHT).

Conversely, the cooperation of the Bengali Muslim settlers was not expected by the Hill people, who were mostly Buddhist. From the inception of the signing of the CHT Peace Agreement, the Bengalis formed some organisations aimed at to protecting their rights (or interests) and privileges in the Chittagong Hill Tracts (CHT). For example, they demanded proper representation within the CHTRC—some Bengali organisations even demanded the repeal of the CHT Land Dispute Resolution Commission (Amendment) Act 2016 in order to ensure their land rights. These Bengali settlers are not supportive of the implementation of the Agreement. Although the Hill indigenous people's leaders are continuously demanding the repatriation of Bengali settlers from the CHT, this is ignored in the interest of winning parliamentary seats (among other dimensions) by gaining the support (in the form of votes) of the Bengali settlers by the mainstream Bengali political parties. As opined by some interviewees, it has been examined, in the literature, that these group rivalries (within Hill indigenous groups or communities; and, between Hill communities and Bengali settlers) were, in some cases, supported by government agencies. Like the interviewees, it has been assumed that the GoB has enough strength (in terms of power and authority) compared to the PCJSS (definitely, from the UPDF)—if it is willing, it can implement the CHT Peace Agreement. Moreover, the government (including the bureaucracy and the military) are accused of taking advantage of these group rivalries (consisting of various communities) and slowing down the Agreement's implementation process.

Then, in Chapter 7, like many sub-nationalist movements, the involvement of international actors is addressed. In this chapter, including some examples of international communities, broadly, three international actors have been incorporated (India as a state actor; the international CHT Commission and the UNDP as non-state actors) in connection with the CHT case. We have known that India—the bordering country of Bangladesh—revised its support towards the PCJSS (and concomitantly, towards the GoB) several times, because of its political and strategic interests. Although the PCJSS was not previously supported by India, after the assassination of Sheikh Mujib, in 1975, it sheltered the SB fighters as well as common Hill people as refugees in Tripura (a province of India). On the other hand, India has been highly concerned about the separatist movements in the Seven Sister States, with these suspected of having been fuelled by the agitation in the Hill Tracts. Moreover, India has revised its related policy after the formation of the parliamentary government in Bangladesh, especially, when the AL (historically, the AL and the Indian government have had a friendly relationship) formed government in 1996. India has played a critical role during the signing of the CHT Peace Agreement by pressing the PCJSS to come to the negotiation table.

Thus, India, like other countries, has been aware of its political as well as strategic interests.

Mainly, the Chittagong Hill Tracts Commission (an independent international commission) and the UNDP have been concerned about the CHT case either because of the concern with human rights or because of the impetus of sociological liberalism (and even due to conceptions of institutional liberalism). After visiting the refugee camps in Tripura and the CHT, the Commission published a report (later, they published four updated versions of the report until 2000), in 1991, in the House of Lords in London. They also sent the report to many stakeholders in Bangladesh as well as to the international community (state and non-state actors) and requested their feedback on the case. These gained international attention through the support of the media, and the GoB might have been motivated (or even pressurised) to solve the CHT's problem. Along with other initiatives, the newly formed members of the CHT Commission met with Prime Minister Sheikh Hasina. They urged her to implement the CHT Peace Agreement, the Prime Minister assured them of the same. On the other hand, since 2003, the UNDP has continued some successful projects aimed at the development and building confidence in the Chittagong Hill Tracts (CHT). In recent years, the UNDP has successfully obtained the GoB's promise of implementing all sections of the Agreement. Moreover, it has supported the Parliamentary Caucus on Indigenous Peoples, which was formed to uphold the interests of indigenous people all over Bangladesh. In summary, the problem of CHT is viewed from different perspectives by the international community, whether it is for their interests (e.g. India's involvement) or for upholding the human rights concern of CHT Hill people (e.g. the CHT Commission, the UNDP, etc.).

Herein, the overall findings have been accumulated, concisely based on the discussion mentioned above, and are presented as follows:

- At the state level, wider gaps of interest, whether political, economic or related to the will to control (or assume) power, are mainly responsible for the different views about implementation of the CHT Peace Agreement harboured by the different actors; this indeed affects the Agreement's implementation strategies.
- At the local level, group rivalries (intra-tribal as well as Bengalis–tribal ones) are one of the causal factors which provide opportunities to the GoB (broadly including the bureaucracy and the military) for

slow-down (or, at least partially) of the CHT Peace Agreement's implementation.
- International actors mainly have the motivational power concerning the implementation of the CHT Peace Agreement (in the form of requests); the final decision is derived at the domestic level and mainly depends on the willingness on the part of the national government.

8.3 Revisiting the Hypotheses, Objectives and Research Question

In the first hypothesis stated in Chapter 1, it has been mentioned that gaps in interests between the actors (the state, along with the local and international community) are responsible for the challenges regarding the successful implementation of the CHT Peace Agreement; each actor holds different views about the same. At the state level, the government, the army and the bureaucracy have their own interests, that is, political, economic or regarding the control (or exercise) of power in the CHT; this is mostly analysed from a realist view. These interests are mainly responsible for the Agreement's partial implementation. Moreover, at the CHT-based local level, although PCJSS has been struggling for full implementation of the Agreement, UPDF has been demanding autonomy of the CHT; the Bengali–tribal rivalries are also affecting the Agreement. These intra- as well as inter-ethnic rivalries have provided favourable conditions for the GoB (including the army and the bureaucracy) and align with their interests regarding the implementation (or non-implementation, instead) of the CHT Peace Agreement. At the international level, although India, from a realist perspective, sought its political and strategic interests in this area, it has been found that most of the international communities were supportive of a peaceful solution to the CHT case and concomitantly approached the GoB with the impetus of a liberal view. However, even though the international community can request (or motivate) the GoB to implement the Agreement, they cannot compel the government or intervene in the process: this is mostly addressed in the second hypothesis.

The earlier chapters (also, briefly, the discussion in this chapter) incorporate the analysis of the spectrum of interests of the various actors regarding the implementation of the CHT Peace Agreement, which

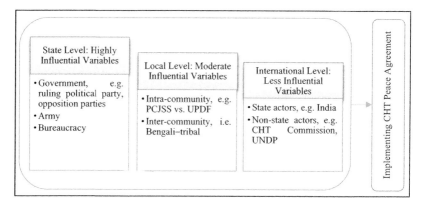

Fig. 8.1 Levels of influence in implementing the CHT peace agreement (*Source* Developed by author based on earlier arguments)

targets the primary objective of this study. Given focus on second research objective throughout this discussion, an analysis of how these multifaceted interests have affected (or even determined) the implementation of the Agreement. Consequently, it has been inferred that varying interests between the actors have led to the partial (or weak) implementation of the Agreement and the different views about the same; this comprises the third objective of this research. By addressing these three core objectives, this study justifies to prove the hypotheses and thus, finally, unravel the research question in order to determine the answer. In other words, if the Agreement's implementation is considered to be a dependent variable, then, at the state level, the government (including the army and the bureaucracy) constitute the highest influential independent variable. At the CHT-based local level, group rivalries (e.g. PCJSS vs. UPDF; Bengali settlers vs. Hill people) is the moderately influential independent variable, while, at the international level, the international actors' involvement is regarded as a less influential independent variable. This relationship is shown in Fig. 8.1.

8.4 Chapter Conclusion

This chapter has a twofold attempt—identifying the main findings of this study through the analysis of the earlier chapters and revealing the interconnections between the research question, the objective and the hypothesis. It is also revealed that these significant findings mainly answer the research question, which is also broadly connected with the research objectives and hypotheses. Primarily, this book has found that at the state level, due to divergent interests among the state actors, the GoB (including other institutions, e.g. the army, the bureaucracy, etc.) are primarily responsible for the partial implementation of the CHT Peace Agreement. It is already known that as a sovereign state, the GoB has the authoritative power regarding the formulation of new laws (or amendment of existing laws) related to the Agreement's implementation. On the other hand, at the CHT-based local level, intra-tribal and Bengali–tribal rivalries have also affected the implementation because a third party (e.g. the GoB, comprising the bureaucracy and the army) might have taken the opportunity of this disunity. Moreover, this book has also revealed that the international community is only connected with the CHT case insofar as they have the motivational role, but they cannot directly pressurise (or intervene within the governance of) a sovereign state like Bangladesh.

This book has also attempted to identify the reason(s) behind the actors holding different views regarding the CHT Peace Agreement and its implementation. In addressing this question, we find that the broader gaps in interests between the actors are mostly responsible for the Agreement's partial implementation; throughout this analysis, the spectrum of interests is also addressed. Furthermore, the varying interests of the actors are revealed as determining factors for the Agreement's implementation process and also as the causes responsible for its consequent partial/slow implementation. Finally, the domestic actors (primarily the aforementioned state-level actors and the CHT-based local actors) are mainly responsible for the problem regarding the Agreement's implementation; again, this is determined by their individuated interests irrespective of whether it is motivated by liberal or realist thought. Thereafter, this study places emphasis on the concluding remark, some of the policy recommendations aimed at solving the problem and its implications, which are addressed in the next chapter—the concluding chapter of this book.

CHAPTER 9

Conclusion

This book addresses to seek state, local and international actors' interests whether it is political, economic, related to power struggle (i.e. centric), or any other kind of interests in implementing the CHT Peace Agreement. In conclusion, the answer to the following research question has been sought throughout the research reported in this book—why do different actors (i.e. the GoB, the Hill people and the international community) hold different views regarding the implementation of the CHT Peace Agreement? In answering this question, a key hypothesis has been developed that the gaps in interests between the various actors, concerning the Agreement's implementation, are responsible for the different views which remain obstacles to its successful implementation. From the inception of its signing, the CHT Peace Agreement has mostly experienced non-identical perception from the state as well as from the CHT-based local-level actors. This, in turn, has narrowed the prospect of its successful implementation. On the one hand, the mainstream Bengali political parties' (which ultimately form the GoB) perception have not been identical to the CHT Peace Agreement. On the other hand, a political consensus has not been developed between the Hill communities at the CHT-based local level. Against this aforementioned backdrop of disunity, this study has been initiated to understand and analyse those interests which are responsible for different views regarding the implementation of the Agreement, which also determine the progress of the implementation policies. Finally, this book sought to note those different views of the relevant actors for implementation of the CHT Peace Agreement, especially in the context of politics within the national affairs and the evolving rivalries between local factions that have impeded resolution of the question of implementation, with international actors exercising less influence on the issue. This will be evident by revisiting the findings. Also, the following section discusses the political stances as analysed primarily throughout Chapters 5–8. It incorporates policy recommendations, the implications, comparative analysis of the CHT Peace Agreement with other peace agreements and avenues for future research.

9.1 Revisiting the Findings: Politics in Actors' Interests

If we note the view that has been derived from the analysis of the earlier chapters, at the state level (in Chapter 5), the political interest of ascending to state power through winning the National Parliamentary elections, which is predominant in the mainstream Bengali political parties, is mainly responsible for the different views regarding the implementation of the CHT Peace Agreement. From the earlier analysis, it is now quite evident that the fixation of land rights for the Hill people is crucial for implementing the Agreement. Again, this becomes complicated as much of these lands have already been grabbed by the Bengali settlers (see Sects. 4.4 of Chapter 4 and 8.2 of Chapter 8 for details). To implement the Agreement, there is an acute need to solve the land-related problem first. If the land rights are returned to the Hill people, many of the Bengali settlers will either be rendered landless or need to be repatriated from the Chittagong Hill Tracts (CHT). No mainstream Bengali political party will take this risk as they receive the voting support of many Bengali settlers that helps them to win the three National Parliamentary seats/constituencies assigned for the three CHT districts—Rangamati, Bandarban and Khagrachhari. It is comparatively easy to win these constituencies (or seats) by gaining their support, as they constitute about 47.1% (as a single ethnic group) of the CHT population (for further study, see sub-Sect. 5.2.4 of Chapter 5). As it concomitantly becomes challenging to make any decision against their interests, the Bengali settlers are thus accused of not being supportive of the Agreement.

On the other hand, like many other issues in Bangladesh, successive governments' decisions about the CHT case are sometimes influenced by the bureaucracy and the army. Among many different interests, the army is mainly indifferent to the implementation of the CHT Peace Agreement because of their willingness to continue adherence to their economic interests. For example, they are accused of being involved in restaurant or timber business, which is not in line with their military professionalism. The bureaucrats are also indifferent to the Agreement, thinking that the newly introduced CHT-based local institutions are merely a duplication of other institutions existing throughout the country. They feel that working under the supervision of these institutions is undignified and uncomfortable in obeying decisions made under the traditional ministerial line. Moreover, they become eager to exercise (or assume) power in the Chittagong Hill Tracts (CHT). At the state level, these different interests—acceding of state power by the mainstream Bengali political parties, the economic interests of the army and the bureaucrats' interest of exercising power—are mainly responsible for the different views regarding the recognition of the CHT Peace Agreement. These remain as obstacles which have impeded the full implementation of the Agreement and they are mostly analysed from realist perspective.

Then, at the CHT-based local level (same in Chapter 6), the beneficiaries of the CHT Peace Agreement—the Hill people (specifically, the PCJSS)—had signed the Agreement to fulfil many of their demands; this also represents one kind of interest, whether it is political or socio-economic in nature. Conversely, the UPDF, another CHT-based political party, was (and still is) against the CHT Peace Agreement and have continued their movement by retaining some of their initial demands, for example, the allocation of land rights to the Hill people, the repatriation of the Bengali settlers and the withdrawal of the army camps from the Chittagong Hill Tracts (CHT). Moreover, the Bengali settlers are not supportive of the Agreement and hold different views regarding the same. Therefore, at the CHT-based local level, different ethnic communities (or groups) have different views that are aligned with their various interests. When there are rivalries between/within the local groups (in this case, at the CHT-based local level), it is typical for the third party (the state-level institutions in this context) to take advantage of this disunity. Moreover, there has been accusation that the CHT-based local-level group (or community) rivalries are fuelled by the state institutions (e.g. the GoB, the mainstream Bengali political parties, the army and the bureaucracy in this context) with the aim of fulfilling their own interests. This has been analysed in the earlier paragraph.

Next, at the international level (as in Chapter 7), the involvement of the international actors, for example, India, the international Chittagong Hill Tracts (CHT) Commission and the UNDP's role, is analysed both from the realist and liberal perspectives. India, being the neighbouring country of Bangladesh, has been primarily associated with the case of CHT as about 75,000 Hill people have lived as refugees in India since the early 1990s. Moreover, India was worried that the CHT case would motivate its north-eastern states to organise their own separatist movements. Therefore, India has revised its support towards the PCJSS (and consequently towards the GoB) several times because of its own interests, for example, to appease/control the north-eastern states' separatist movements or to gain transit/transhipment from Bangladesh—these issues are mostly analysed from the realist point of view. On the other hand, through a primarily liberal (more specifically, neoliberalism) perspective, the international CHT Commission and the UNDP are (as they have been) connected to the CHT case. For example, when the members of the CHT Commission participated in the Long March to the National Parliament of Bangladesh and requested the Prime Minister to implement the CHT Peace Agreement, it created much reportage from media on this case. Thereafter, the UNDP became connected with the CHT case from 2003 by engendering certain development activities, for example, capacity-building of the CHT-based local institutions, confidence-building between the Hill people and the Bengali settlers; the project of 2016, which has been supported by the UNDP, has successfully gained the promise of the GoB regarding the Agreement's full implementation.

Finally, the involvement of international actors in the CHT case is regarded as a motivational role (or, in some cases, as pressure-creating factors) as they cannot intervene in the internal issues of Bangladesh. Such an intervention would have been possible if Bangladesh had been a failed state, so to speak. However, this has not happened. In conclusion, the state's interests reveal its supremacy regarding the implementation of the CHT Peace Agreement—it has been accused of partial (or weak) implementation of the Agreement as well as creating the dispute regarding the selective implementation of its provisions. Moreover, the CHT-based local-level group (or community) conflicts have provided favourable conditions for the state's agencies to fulfil their own interests. Considering the interviewees' narratives and the secondary sources, the multifaceted levels of this analysis ensure a holistic approach toward studying the implementation issue of the CHT Peace Agreement. This is warranted by the uniqueness (or the novelty) of this book.

9.2 Policy Recommendations

From the discussion above, it is revealed that the CHT case has been viewed from different angles by different actors mostly emphasising their political interests, and these have veritably affected the issue of implementation of the CHT Peace Agreement. There might have been some drawbacks during the formulation of the Agreement; at present, however, most of the Hill people (particularly the PCJSS) have been demanding the full implementation of all sections of the Agreement. Like many other researchers, I believe that all the provisions of the Agreement should be implemented as early as possible. Even the GoB and the Hill people could renegotiate some of the unsettled issues (or un-adopted ones, e.g. the issue of the Bengali settlers) which have seriously affected the (non-) implementation of the Agreement. However, the first priority should be given to the implementation of the existing provisions of the CHT Peace Agreement. It has been mentioned earlier that the Agreement has been mainly executed because of the negotiation process between the government's representatives and the PCJSS leadership without the involvement of any visible third party. Likewise, it is expected that the existing incompatibility can be mitigated through the initiatives promulgated by the GoB and the Hill people, particularly by the PCJSS leadership. Within these two primary parties, the GoB (including other state institutions) should initiate the implementation of the Agreement as they have the authoritative power in formulating and defining the related laws.

The CHT Peace Agreement is not like a state policy. Herein, the government's representatives comprise the primary signatory party to the Agreement and are mainly responsible for its implementation. The government claims that it is sincerely committed to the implementation of the rest of the sections of the Agreement. However, during the celebration of the 24th anniversary of the signing of the Agreement, the PCJSS was suspicious about the government's real intention regarding its implementation. Now, the local leaders do not trust the verbal assurance given by government representatives; instead, they have been demanding the roadmap for the Agreement's implementation. In this regard, primarily, there is an acute need for building trust and confidence between the primary parties—the GoB and the PCJSS. The government should announce the roadmap (or at least publish a written document) regarding the implementation measures and take the necessary steps as early as possible. Regarding this issue, not only the government but also other stakeholders, for example, the opposition political parties, the bureaucracy, the military and civil society members should promote a supportive role. As the army and the bureaucracy have considerable influence on the CHT issue, they should change their traditional colonial mindset with respect to ruling the CHT people. These two institutions should consider the special situation of the CHT and put emphasis on their sense of professionalism, and also cooperate with the government's directives regarding the implementation of the CHT Peace Agreement.

At the CHT-based local level, the PCJSS leadership should undertake the necessary attempts to neutralise the local factions, including recognising the UPDF's political acceptance. On the other hand, the UPDF leadership should acknowledge the PCJSS's achievements related to peace initiatives, of which the signing of the CHT Peace Agreement holds the foreground. In consensus with many of the interviewees, my opinion is that if the PCJSS and the UPDF move together in implementing the Agreement, the task will become manageable (or, at least, would help to exert more pressure on the implementing agencies). However, in Chapter 6, the following has been inferred: though the CHT-based local factions are affecting the Agreement's implementation, the GoB still possesses enough strength to implement the Agreement (providing it has the willingness to do so). However, every political party (which is ultimately interested in assuming state power by forming a government) has tried to win the seats assigned for the CHT in the National Parliament, by getting the support of the CHT people. This is because as a single community, the Bengali settlers constitute the majority of the people living in the Chittagong Hill Tracts (CHT). As these Bengali settlers are considered to comprise a vote bank for the mainstream Bengali political parties, many of the implementation policies are also influenced by their presence. Considering this background, it is urgent to find a solution that can not only handle the issue of the Bengali settlers but which will also be favourable for the implementation of the CHT Peace Agreement. Finally, considering the stakeholders' consensus, one suggestion can be there to repatriate the Bengali settlers from CHT to elsewhere in Bangladesh with the financial support of the European Parliament.

Moreover, the CHT indigenous leadership should convince the GoB (including the military and the bureaucracy), the leaders of the various political parties and other stakeholders, assuring them that the Hill people are not in rivalry with the unitary nature of the state or its sovereignty. When the conflicting primary parties find their common ground of interest, it will provide a more favourable condition for implementing the Agreement. For example, the government authorities could utilise the natural resources (e.g. forestry and tourism) which are available in the CHT for the economic growth of Bangladesh, if its socio-political situation becomes more peaceful—this excellent condition could be easily achieved through the implementation of the Agreement. Furthermore, the Hill leadership, especially the PCJSS, should cooperate with the government regarding the implementation of the Agreement to ensure the rights of the Hill people (which are incorporated in the CHT Peace Agreement).

During the negotiation process of the CHT Peace Agreement, no instance of the engagement of civil society members has been identified. The fact that secrecy was retained during the negotiation between the GoB's representatives and the PCJSS leadership led to the common peoples' indifference to the issue. Although some members of civil society have carried out specific constructive initiatives towards implementing the Agreement, their engagement has neither been mentioned nor promoted by the conflicting primary parties. For example, civil society can play a significant role in creating pressure for the Agreement's implementation and can foster nationwide support—therein, their engagement can be integral.

If consensus between the state and local levels could evolve (particularly heralding willingness on the part of the government), it would be comparatively easy to implement the CHT Peace Agreement. As previously mentioned, international actors can motivate or request the sovereign states to act, but not to intervene in the decisions of a strongly governed (or sovereign) state as in Bangladesh. Prime Minister Sheikh Hasina's speech in the National Parliament, along with similar opinions voiced by people belonging to the civil society, has asserted that the problem will be solved nationally. Many of these people have argued that the problem is intrinsic to Bangladesh. If there is international intervention, then external politics will become entangled, these actors might use this case for their own interests. Although some non-state actors have undertaken helpful initiatives aimed at influencing the GoB to implement the CHT Peace Agreement, the final initiative must be taken by the GoB authorities. In this study, it has been revealed that every actor (or stakeholder) tends to serve their own interests. Unless these different views (or the groups' interests) are disavowed or shunned, the mitigation of the conflict remains a challenge. If needed, there should be some sacrifices, regarding some of the provisions of the Agreement, from the government's side as well as from the PCJSS's leadership. Moreover, some sections of the CHT Peace Agreement can be negotiated further to solve some unavoidable critical issues. However, it is my understanding that the implementation of all the existing sections of the Agreement should be given equal priority.

9.3 Implications

This book summarises various actors' interests—whether political, economic, related to a power struggle (from a realist perspective) or aimed at upholding indigenous rights (from a liberal point of view). Actually, these multifaceted interests are responsible for the partial (or weak) implementation of the CHT Peace Agreement. They have raised the dispute about the implementation status of a number of its sections. These multifaceted levels of analysis (state, local and international) provide the holistic approach towards studying the Agreement, especially its implementation dimension that is unique to the Chittagong Hill Tracts (CHT). Therefore, this study unfolds some implications both in theory and regarding the policy recommendations. In the theoretical discourse, one such implication is that both realism and liberalism are relevant for analysing the CHT Peace Agreement and its implementation process. Furthermore, this is an attestation of the views and thoughts of the scholars from the International Society (also known as the English School). They emphasise that there is the concomitant melange of both liberal and realist elements in any discourse with respect to peace agreements or any other means of peace-making. Conversely, we should remember that at the state level, the government (including the military and the bureaucracy) has the ultimate authoritative power which, in most cases, can be exercised in a realist mode.

Another implication at the policy level is that the policymakers may realise the importance of a national-level consensus and its prioritisation regarding the implementation process of the peace agreement. This research will be useful for peace-agreement implementers to assess the values of the interests of different actors (or groups) and find a way to accommodate these interests in the decision-making policies aimed at implementing the peace agreement. This study might be helpful for the policy framers, implementers, peace agreement beneficiaries, practitioners, researchers or other stakeholders to view the problem of implementing a peace agreement from different perspectives (by going beyond the interest-based politics). Moreover, the findings of this study will help to create proper strategies for the formation of new peace agreements and the implementation of the existing peace agreements. It may also raise attention among academics and other researchers with respect to conducting more comprehensive and intensive research regarding the different issues of the CHT Peace Agreement as well as of other peace agreements. Through this study, they will be benefited by finding the source of literature on the CHT case, particularly the different actors' interests that have affected the implementation policies. Thus, this book has a value as secondary source of data.

Finally, this research paves the way for framing the connections between the politics of interest and policies that affect the implementation of peace agreements. States that have signed peace agreements can draw an important message from the CHT case of Bangladesh even regarding post-agreement conditions. Although every conflict has its own uniqueness, a few similarities exist between the peace agreements, if not in structure and composition but at least in aims and goals. The relevant stakeholders of peace agreements, particularly the policymakers, can learn from each other's attempts, successes or failures in implementing peace agreements. This kind of learning will eventually widen the opportunities for peace. The CHT case, like similar cases, has exemplified the state's supremacy in the process of conflict resolution as well as its post-conflict mechanism.

9.4 Comparative Analysis of the CHT Peace Agreement with Other Peace Agreements

In practice, the government holds the supreme authority in signing the peace agreement and the policy formulation regarding its implementation. The situation may be different if the exercise of government's authority is challenged by vested interests involved in the implementation of the peace agreement. The case of the CHT Peace Agreement is no exception. Likewise, some issues of ethnic (or communal) conflict in South Asian countries have consequently led to the experience of state authorities' supremacy. For example, in north-eastern India, although the insurgent groups in Nagaland demanded full independence, it was still declared as a state of the Indian Union in 1963. Although the National Socialist Council of Nagaland has continued its movements for the Greater Nagaland, as of 2015, they have obeyed a ceasefire with the Indian government. The Mizo Peace Agreement of 1986 terminated the main secessionist movement (which demanded autonomy) led by the Mizo National Front in Mizoram, a province of north-eastern India. Another example is the Sri Lankan issue, where the Liberation Tigers of Tamil Eelam (LTTE) continued their movement for a separate homeland—they were militarily defeated by the decision of President Mahindra Rajapaksa-led government in May 2009. Although the issue was once previously mediated by the Norwegian government, the Sri Lankan government finally resolved the problem by exercising its arbitrary power. However, representatives from the Sri Lankan government have come to Bangladesh in order to study the CHT case.

Though the Free Aceh Movement had the goal of making the province of Aceh independent from Indonesia, the armed conflict between the Indonesian military and the indigenous people has been terminated with the signature of a peace agreement in 2005, which included the provision of limited autonomy for the Aceh province. However, presently it is a grey area as the implementation of the autonomous system is not handled as per the desired expectation. These examples reveal the government's supremacy in settling conflicts in powerful sovereign countries. Thus, this study discovers the state agencies' actual motives in the peace process, where the government (or the state authorities) has the supreme authority regarding the implementation of the peace agreements. However, this comprises a lesson for the local-level leaders who become beneficiaries of the peace agreement. They can learn, from the CHT case, that a third party (e.g. government or state institutions) may grab the advantage of the intra-group rivalries at the local level. Thereby, inter-ethnic (or group) rivalries might veritably affect the implementation of the peace agreement, where third-party interests may be promoted. Therefore, the peace agreement beneficiaries should be careful about group rivalries and try to find policies to mitigate the internal feuds.

9.5 Avenues for Further Research

Future research in this field may enrich the knowledge of policymakers regarding as how various other factors have been affecting the full implementation of the CHT Peace Agreement and enable them to scrutinise the viable policies regarding the same issue. The political paradigms that affect the implementation of a peace agreement should be extensively studied before framing the implementation policies. For example, regarding the CHT problem, this research did not much analyse all sections of the CHT Peace Agreement, irrespective of whether the other sections appropriately address the root causes of the conflict. As a beneficiary of the CHT Peace Agreement, presently the PCJSS, on behalf of the Hill people, is demanding full implementation of all sections of the Agreement. The prospects of peace initiatives are now mainly centred around the politics of implementation. I have addressed some crucial sections of the Agreement which have either been implemented or non-implemented and that there is a difference of opinion on the issue between the GoB and PCJSS respectively. A debate as generated by the stated issue is still an ongoing one. Future research should be directed towards the extensive analysis of all sections of the CHT Peace Agreement to determine the root causes of the conflict as well as undertaking a gap analysis to find out the discrepancy between the expectations of the beneficiaries of the Agreement.

Furthermore, this book has analysed the relations between the Bengali settlers and tribal people and the influence of these relations on the implementation of the CHT Peace Agreement. It has marked the essentiality of building trust and confidence between the Bengali and CHT indigenous people to form a favourable condition for implementing the Agreement. It has also discussed how the Bengalis settlers' issue has been considered as a critical causal factor that has complicated land dispute problem. Without solving such crucial matters, it is difficult to achieve peace in the Chittagong Hill Tracts (CHT). There has also been a discussion about how the Bengali settlers' issue is associated with the political interests of the Bengali ruling elite. Like many researchers and interviewees, my question is as follows—why had such an important issue not been incorporated within the written document of the CHT Peace Agreement? Although the interests of the mainstream Bengali ruling political parties partially answer this question, this question remains worthy of extensive future research.

Moreover, as we know that in most conflict-prone societies, women are victimised in various ways, future research must convene to manage this concern.

Appendix 1: Semi-Structured Questionnaire (Checklist)

SL No:	Date:
Name of Respondent:	Age
Occupation:	Gender: M/F
Contract Number:	E-mail:
Identity/nationality: Adivasi/Bengali	Address:

(Free judgement is highly appreciated and multiple answers are accepted).

1. Why has the CHT issue gained (or not gained) considerable attention nationwide and in the international arena as compared to the plain land Adivasi issue?
    a. Due to vast militarised struggle; b. The PCJSS's activities; c. Awareness at the national level; d. International connections/support; e. …
2. What are the main causes which motivated the concerned parties to sign the CHT Peace Agreement in 1997?
    a. War fatigue of the PCJSS; b. Previous governments' continuous initiatives; c. The AL-led government's initiatives; d. International community's networks; e. Alteration of India's strategy; f. End of the Cold War; g. UN initiatives; h. …

3. After signing the Agreement on 2 December 1997, has peace really been attained?
    a. More peaceful than before; b. Less peaceful than before; c. As usual; d. …
4. What is (or are) the main demand(s) of the CHT indigenous people at present?
    a. Full implementation of the Agreement; b. Autonomy (in accordance with the UPDF); c. …
5. What are the impediments to the implementation of the CHT Peace Agreement?
    a. Government's reluctance; b. Dissent from other political parties; c. Intra-group conflicts (PCJSS vs. UPDF and even within the PCJSS); d. International networks; e. The Bengali migrants vs. Paharis issue; f. Non-cooperation by the bureaucracy and the army; g. …
6. We found many casualties, such as deaths, due to the violent conflict between the PCJSS and the UPDF members. Do intra-group rivalries affect the peace initiatives? (What should be the reconciliation process?)
    a. Yes; b. No; c. If yes, please explain; d. …
7. Have there been any international (regional/bilateral) connections regarding the peace efforts in the CHT of Bangladesh?
    a. No; b. Yes (if yes, what networks?); c. United Nations (or the UNDP, or the United Nations Refugee Agency [UNHCR], …); d. International NGOs; e. Local NGOs; f. Prominent individual(s); g. the South Asian Association for Regional Cooperation (SAARC); h. India; i. Pakistan; j. Myanmar; h. …
8. Are international networks successful in upholding the rights of indigenous people?
    a. Yes; b. No; c. Have a motivational power; d. Cannot compel; e. Depends on the conflicting country's nature of governance; f. …
9. Can you please explain the conditions under which international actors enable smaller (considering the number of the population) ethnic groups to achieve their goal?
    a. Presence of a democratic government; b. Ruling parties' positive feedback; c. Presence of a more generous government; d. When international actors put pressure that becomes a motivational force; e. If it is a failed state; f. …

10. Do you think the success of the international community's peace initiatives is determined by the response of the state to the demands of the indigenous people?
   a. Yes; b. No; c. ...
11. For peace in perpetuity in the CHT, what initiatives are required at various levels? —
   a. Local; b. National; c. Regional; d. International; e. Connection of these; f. ...
12. The model of the CHT Peace Agreement can be applied for the resolution of conflicts in other parts of the world. Do you agree?
   a. Yes; b. No; c. ...

Thank you very much for your valuable cooperation by participating in the research.

Appendix 2: List of Interviewees

SL No.	Interviewee[a]	Date and Place	Identity/Nationality	Occupation/Designation[b]
1	A. Mohsin (Amena Mohsin)	6 June 2016, Dhaka	Bengali	Prominent and long-term researcher on the CHT case; Professor of the University of Dhaka
2	B. Chakma (Biplab Chakma)	19 May 2016, Rangamati	Adivasi	Chief of Community Empowerment of CHTDF—a UNDP programme conducted in Bangladesh
3	B. K. Chakma (Brisha Ketu Chakma)	18 May 2016, Rangamati	Adivasi	Chairman of Rangamati Hill District Council (RHDC)
4	B. R. Tripura (Beauty Rani Tripura)	23 May 2016, Khagrachhari	Adivasi	Female Vice Chairman of Sadar Upazila of Khagrachhari
5	F. H. Badsha (Fazle Hossain Badsha)	9 June 2016, National Parliament House, Bangladesh	Bengali	MP of 10th Parliament; General Secretary of Workers Party of Bangladesh; President of Parliamentary Caucus on Indigenous Peoples of Bangladesh

(continued)

(continued)

SL No.	Interviewee[a]	Date and Place	Identity/Nationality	Occupation/Designation[b]
6	G. Dewan (Goutom Dewan)	18 May 2016, Rangamati	Adivasi	President of CHT Nagorik (Citizens') Committee
7	I. Dewan (Ilira Dewan)	16 June 2016, Dhaka	Adivasi	Ex-General Secretary of Hill Women's Federation (Central Committee)
8	J. B. Larma (Jyotirindra Bodhipriya Larma), alias Santu Larma	18 May 2016, Rangamati	Adivasi	President of PCJSS and Chairman of CHTRC
9	J. L. Tripura (Jatindra Lal Tripura)	22 May 2016, Khagrachhari	Adivasi	Chairman (State Minister status) of Task Force for Repatriation & Rehabilitation of Tribal Refugee returned from India & Identification and Rehabilitation of Internally Displaced People; Ex-Chairman of KHDC. Ex-MP (AL-supported) of Khagrachhari (9th Parliament)
10	K. S. Hla (Kyaw Shwe Hla)	26 May 2016, Bandarban	Adivasi	Chairman of BHDC; Ex-Councillor of BHDC
11	M. A. Rashid (Md. Abdur Rashid)	2 June 2016, Dhaka	Bengali	Retired army officer (Major General) who was once posted to the CHT; Executive Director of Institute of Conflict, Law and Development Studies
12	M. B. Tripura (Mathura Bikash Tripura)	22 May 2016, Khagrachhari	Adivasi	Executive Director of a CHT-based local NGO (named, Zabarang Kalyan Samity)
13	M. Chakma (Mithun Chakma)	22 May 2016, Khagrachhari	Adivasi	Member of UPDF, Khagrachhari
14	M. Guhathakurta (Meghna Guhathakurta)	8 June 2016, Dhaka	Bengali	Executive Director of Research Initiatives Bangladesh; former Professor of the University of Dhaka

(continued)

(continued)

SL No.	Interviewee[a]	Date and Place	Identity/Nationality	Occupation/Designation[b]
15	M. Kamal (Mesbah Kamal)	1 June 2016, Dhaka	Bengali	Prominent researcher on the CHT case; Professor of History, University of Dhaka; Coordinator & Technocrat Member of Parliamentary Caucus on Indigenous Peoples; Chairperson of Research and Development Collective
16	M. S. Dewan (Moni Swapan Dewan)	19 May 2016, Rangamati	Adivasi	Ex-Deputy Minister of MoCHTA
17	M. S. Hussain (M. Sakhawat Hussain)	5 June 2016, Dhaka	Bengali	Retired army officer (Brigadier General) who was once posted to the CHT; former (2007–2012) Election Commissioner of Bangladesh
18	N. B. K. Tripura (Naba Bikram Kishore Tripura)	15 June 2016, Bangladesh Secretariat	Adivasi	Secretary of MoCHTA (bureaucrat); Chairman of CHTDB
19	P. R. Chakma (Prakriti Ranjan Chakma)	18 May 2016, Rangamati	Adivasi	Retired Deputy Secretary (bureaucrat); President of Bangladesh Indigenous Peoples Forum, CHT wing
20	R. A. M. O. M. Chowdhury (R. A. M. Obaidul Muktadir Chowdhuri)	9 June 2016, National Parliament House, Bangladesh	Bengali	Chairman of Parliamentary Standing Committee on Ministry of Hill Tracts; AL-backed MP (Brahmanbaria-3) (10th Parliament)
21	R. Chakma (Ricoh Chakma)	22 May 2016, Khagrachhari	Adivasi	District Organiser of UPDF, Khagrachhari

(continued)

(continued)

SL No.	Interviewee[a]	Date and Place	Identity/Nationality	Occupation/Designation[b]
22	R. D. Roy (Raja Devasish Roy)	25 May 2016, Rangamati	Adivasi	Chief of Chakma Circle; Member, UN Permanent Forum on Indigenous Issues; Advocate, Supreme Court; Member (ex-officio), Advisory Committee MoCHTA
23	R. K. Menon (Rashed Khan Menon)	6 June 2016 National Parliament House, Bangladesh	Bengali	Minister in the 10th Parliament; Chairman of Workers Party of Bangladesh
24	R. S. Partha (Ranjan Saha Partha)	18 June 2016, Jahangirnagar University	Bengali	Assistant Professor, Jahangirnagar University, Bangladesh; recently completed PhD on the CHT case
25	S. Kamal (Sultana Kamal)	7 June 2016, Dhaka	Bengali	Co-Chairman of reformed international CHT Commission; former (2006–2008) adviser in the Caretaker Government of Bangladesh; Prominent human rights activist in Bangladesh; Executive Director of Ain o Salish Kendra—a civil rights organisation
26	S. P. Tripura (Shakti Pada Tripura)	17 May 2016, Rangamati	Adivasi	Organising Secretary of PCJSS (Central Committee)
27	S. Singh (Swaran Singh)	3 March 2016, Japan	Indian	Professor, School of International Studies, Jawaharlal Nehru University (India); Professor (Special Appointment), Hiroshima University, Japan
28	S. U. Talukder (Shri Ushatan Talukder)	20 May 2016, Rangamati	Adivasi	Independent MP from Rangamati in the 10th Parliament; Vice President of PCJSS (Central Committee)

(continued)

(continued)

SL No.	Interviewee[a]	Date and Place	Identity/Nationality	Occupation/Designation[b]
29	T. S. P. Master (Thain Saw Prue Master)	25 May 2016, Bandarban	Adivasi	Ex-Chairman (1997–2000) and Councillor (1989–1997) of BHDC
30	U. W. M. Jolly (U-Win-Mong-Jolly)	26 May 2016, Bandarban	Adivasi	Education and Culture Secretary of PCJSS (Central Committee)

[a]Interviewees' names are alphabetically arranged irrespective of their serial number. Their full names are written in parentheses to specify the person with whom the interview was conducted by the author

[b]The current positions (or occupations) at the time of the interview are presented here.

Appendix 3: Map of the Chittagong Hill Tracts (CHT)

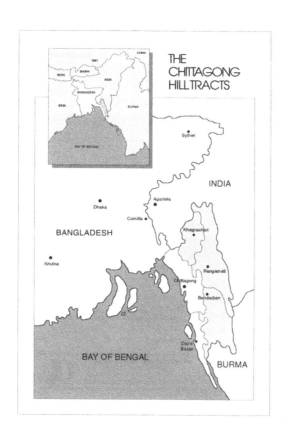

Source The Chittagong Hill Tracts Commission. (2000). *Life is Not Ours: Land and Human Rights in the Chittagong Hill Tracts, Bangladesh: Update 4* (p. 3). https://www.iwgia.org/images/publications/Life_is_not_ours_UPDATE4.pdf. Accessed 6 October 2020.

Appendix 4: Chittagong Hill Tracts Peace Agreement of 1997

Translated English Version of Agreement Between the National Committee on Chittagong Hill Tracts Constituted by the Government and the Parbatya Chattagram Jana Samhati Samiti

Reposing full and unswerving allegiance in the State-sovereignty and territorial integrity of Bangladesh regarding its hill tracts region within the ambit of the Constitution of the People's Republic of Bangladesh, the National Committee on Chittagong Hill Tracts on behalf of the Government of the People's Republic of Bangladesh and the Parbatya Chattagram Jana Samhati Samiti on behalf of the inhabitants of the Chittagong Hill Tracts region have reached the following Agreement, comprised of four Parts (A, B, C, D), with a view to upholding the political, social, cultural, educational and economic rights of all the citizens of the Chittagong Hill Tracts region and expediting their socio-economic development process and preserving and developing the respective rights of all the citizens of Bangladesh:-

(A) General:

1. Both the parties, having considered the Chittagong Hill Tracts region as a tribe-inhabited region, recognized the need of preserving the characteristics of this region and attaining the overall development thereof.
2. Both the parties have agreed to make alter, amend and add to, in consonance with the consensus and responsibilities expressed in the

different sections of this Agreement, the relevant laws, regulations and practices according to law as early as possible.
3. In order to monitor the process of implementation of this Agreement, an Implementation Committee will be formed with the following members:

   a. A member to be nominated by the Prime Minister: Convenor
   b. The Chairman of the Task Force formed with the purview of this Agreement: Member
   c. The President of the Parbatya Chattagram Jana Samhati Samiti: Member

4. The Agreement shall come into force from the date of its signing and execution by both the parties. This Agreement shall remain valid from the date of its effect until all the steps are executed as per this Agreement.

(B) Hill District Local Government Council/Hill District Council:

Both the parties have agreed to alter, amend, add and repeal the Parbatya Zilla Sthanio Sarkar Parishad Ayin, 1989 (Rangamati Parbatya Zilla Sthanio Sarkar Parishad Ayin, 1989, Bandarban Parbatya Zilla Sthanio Sarkar Parishad Ayin, 1989 and Khagrachari Parbatya Zilla Sthanio Sarkar Parishad Ayin, 1989) and its various sections, as may be in force till the date of commencement of this Agreement, in the manner set forth here under:

1. The word "Tribe" used in the various sections of the Council Act shall remain intact.
2. The name of "Parbatya Zilla Sthanio Sarkar Parishad" shall be amended and this Council shall be re-named as "Parbatya Zilla Parishad".
3. "Non-tribal Permanent Resident" shall mean a person who is not a tribal and who has lands of lawful entitlement in the hill districts and who generally lives in the hill districts at a specific address.
4. a. There shall be 3 (three) seats for women in every Hill District Council. One-third (1/3) of these seats shall be for the non-tribals.

b. Sub-section 1, 2, 3 and 4 of Section 4 shall remain in force as per the original Act.
c. The words "Deputy Commissioner" and "Deputy Commissioner's" appearing in the second line of sub-section (5) of Section 4 shall be substituted by the words "Circle Chief" and "Circle Chief's", respectively.
d. The following sub-section shall be added to Section 4: "Whether a person is a non-tribal or not and, if so, which community he is a member of, shall be determined, subject to his producing a certificate from the concerned Mouza Headman/Union Council Chairman/Municipality Chairman, by the concerned Circle Chief and without a certificate in this connection being received from the Circle Chief, no person shall be eligible as a non-tribal to be candidate for the post of a non-tribal member".

5. It is provided in Section 7 that a person elected to the post of Chairman or Member shall, before assumption of office, swear or affirm oath before the Commissioner, Chittagong Division. This shall be amended by provisions to the effect that the Members shall swear or affirm oath before "a Judge of the High Court Division" instead of the "Commissioner, Chittagong Division".
6. The words "to the Commissioner, Chittagong Division" appearing in the fourth line of Section 8 shall be substituted by the words "as per election rules".
7. The words "three years" in the second line of Section 10 shall be substituted by the words "five years".
8. It shall be provided in Section 14 that in the event of the post of Chairman falling vacant for any cause or of his absence, a tribal member elected by other members of the Council shall preside over and discharge other responsibilities.
9. The existing Section 17 shall be substituted by the following sentences: "A person shall be entitled to be considered as legally eligible for enlistment in the Voters' List if he is (1) a citizen of Bangladesh, (2) not below 18 years of age, (3) not declared by any competent court to be of unsoundly mind, (4) a permanent resident of the hill district".
10. The words "delimitation of constituencies" appearing in sub-section 2 of Section 20 shall be distinctly incorporated.
11. There shall be a provision in sub-section 2 of Section 25 to the effect that the Chairman and in his absence, a tribal Member

elected by the other Members shall preside over all the meetings of the Council.

12. Since the entire area of Khagrachari district is not encompassed by the Mong Circle, the words "Khagrachari Mong Chief" appearing in Section 26 of the Act regarding Khagrachari Hill District Council shall be substituted by the words "Mong Circle Chief and Chakma Circle Chief". Similarly, there shall be made a scope for the attendance of the Bohmang Chief in the meetings of Rangamati Hill District Council. In the same manner there shall be provision that the Bohmang Circle Chief, at his will or on being invited, shall be entitled to attend the meetings of Bandarban Hill District Council.

13. It shall be provided in sub-sections (1) and (2) of Section 31 that a Chief Executive Officer of the rank of a Deputy Secretary to the government shall be the Secretary of the Council and the tribal officers shall be given preference for appointment to this post.

14. a. There shall be provision in sub-section (1) of Section 32 that the Council shall be competent, subject to approval by the government, to create posts of officers and employees of different categories for the purpose of smooth completion of the works of the Council.

   b. Sub-section (2) of Section 32 shall be formulated in the following manner "The Council shall, as per Regulations, have competence to appoint Class-III and Class-IV employees and to transfer, suspend, dismiss, remove or otherwise punish them.

   Provided that it shall be the condition attached to such appointments that the tribal residents of the district concerned shall have right of preference".

   c. It shall be provided in sub-section (3) of Section 32 that the Government shall, as per Regulations, have the authority to appoint officers in consultation with the Council and to transfer elsewhere, suspend, dismiss, remove or otherwise punish them.

15. The Words as per Rules shall be inserted in sub-section (3) of Section 33.

16. The words "or in any other way determined by the Government" appearing in the third line of sub-section (1) of Section 36 shall be deleted.

17. a. The provision starting with "Fourthly" in sub-section (1) of Section 37 of the original Act shall remain intact.

b. The phrase "as per as" shall be inserted in clause 'D' of sub-section (2) of Section 37.
18. Sub-section (3) of Section 38 shall be deleted and sub-section (4) shall be formulated as follows: "At any time before the expiry of a financial year, a budget may be prepared and approved, if necessary, for that financial year".
19. The following sub-section shall be added to Section 42: "(4) The Council shall be competent to prepare, undertake and implement, with the help of money receivable from the Government, development projects in respect of the matters transferred to it and all development programs at national level shall be implemented through the Council by the concerned Ministry/Department/Institution".
20. The word "Government" appearing in the second line of sub-section (2) of Section 45 shall be substituted by the word "Council".
21. Sections 50, 51 and 52 shall be repealed and in their stead the following Section shall be enacted: "In order to ensure harmonization of the activities of the Council advice or instructive orders, if necessary, if the Government be convinced on having received such evidence that any activity done or proposed to be done by or on behalf of the Council is inconsistent with law or contrary to public interest, it shall then have the authority to call for in writing from the Council information and explanation about the matter concerned and give advice or directive in that regard".
22. The words, "after the expiry of the period of being defunct" in sub-section (3) of Section 53, shall be deleted and instead thereof the words "Within 90 days of cancellation of the Council" shall be inserted before the words "this Act".
23. The word "Government" will be replaced by word "Ministry" in the third and fourth lines of Section 61.
24. a. Sub-section (1) of Section 62 shall be amended as follows: "Notwithstanding anything contained in any other law for the time being in force, Sub-Inspectors and all members of ranks subordinate thereto of the Hill District Police shall be appointed by the Council as per Regulations and prescribed procedure and the Council shall be competent to transfer them and take punitive action against them in accordance with the procedure prescribed by the Regulations";

Provided that, the tribals of the district shall have preference in case of the said appointment.

b. The words "subject to the provisions of all other laws for the time being in force" as appear in the second line of sub-section (3) of Section 62 shall be repealed and substituted by the words "as per law and rules".

25. The words "to render assistance" in the third line of Section 63 shall remain intact.

26. Section 64 shall be amended and enacted as follows:

a. "Notwithstanding anything contained in any other law for the time being in force, no land and premises, including the leasable Khas lands, within the territorial limits of the Hill Districts shall be transferable by Ijara, settlement, purchase or sale except with the prior permission of the Council;

Provided that this provision shall not be applicable in respect of the area of Reserved Forest, Kaptai Hydro-electric Project, Betbunia Satellite Station, State-owned in the industries and factories and the lands recorded in the name of the Government".

b. "Notwithstanding anything contained in any other law for the time being in force, no land, hill or forest under the controlled and within the jurisdiction of the Council shall be acquired or transferred by the Government without consultation with or the consent of the Council".

c. The Parishad may supervise and control the works of the Headmen, Chainmen, Amins, Surveyors, Kanungos and Assistant Commissioner (land).

d. The reclaimed fringe lands of Kaptai Lake shall be leased out on priority basis to the original owners.

27. Section 65 shall be amended and formulated as follows: "Notwithstanding anything contained in any other law for the time being in force, the responsibility of collecting the Land Development Tax of the district shall rest in the hands of the Council and the collected tax of the district shall be deposited in the fund of the Council".

28. Section 67 shall be amended and formulated as follows: "in the event of necessity for harmonization of the works of the Council and the Governmental authorities, the Government or the Council shall raise proposals on specific subject and the harmonization

of the works shall be effected through mutual communications between the Government and Council".
29. Sub-section (1) of Section 68 shall be amended and formulated as follows: "With a view to carrying out the purposes of this Act, the Government may, upon consultation with the Council, make Rules through Notification in the Government official Gazette and the Council shall have a rights to apply to the Government for review of the said Rules even after they are already made".
30. a. The words "with prior approval of the Government" in the first and second lines of sub-section (1) of Section 69 shall be repealed and after the words "may make" in the third line the following proviso shall be added:
"Provided that if the Government does not agree with any part of the Regulations made, it shall be competent to give advice or directive to the Council towards amendments of the said regulations".
b. The words "conferment of the powers of the Chairman on any officer of the Council" in clause (h) of sub-section (2) of Section 69 shall be deleted.
31. Section 70 shall be deleted.
32. Section 79 shall be amended and formulated as follows:
"If, in the opinion of the council, any law made by the National Parliament or any other authority as applicable to the hill district is one which creates hardship for the said district or is objectionable for the tribals, the Council may, upon stating the cause of hardship or abjection, apply to the Government in writing for amending or relaxing the application of such law and the Government may take remedial measures in accordance with such application".
33. a. The word "discipline" appearing in Item No. 1 under the heading the activities of the Council in the First Schedule shall be substituted by the word "supervision".
b. In Item No. 3 of the Council's activities, the following shall be added: "(1) Vocational education, (2) Primary education through mother tongue, (3) Secondary education".
c. The words "reserved or" appearing in Clause 6(b) of the Council's activities shall be deleted.
34. The following subjects shall be included in the functions and the responsibilities of the Hill District Council:

a. Land and land management;
   b. Police (local);
   c. Tribal law and social justice;
   d. Youth welfare;
   e. Environmental protection and development;
   f. Local tourism;
   g. Improvement of Trust and other institutions concerning local administration, other than Municipality and Union Council;
   h. Issuing license for local commerce and industries;
   i. Proper utilization of rivers and streams, canals and Beels and irrigation system other than water resources of the Kaptai Lake;
   j. Maintaining of the statistics of birth and deaths;
   k. Wholesale business;
   l. Jum cultivation.

35. The following items shall be added to the subjects for imposition of taxes, rates, tolls and fees by the Council as stated in the Second Schedule:

   a. Registration fees of non-mechanical transports;
   b. Tax on buying and selling of commodities;
   c. Holding tax on lands and buildings;
   d. Tax on selling of domestic animals;
   e. Fees for community adjudication;
   f. Holding tax on Government and Non-government industries;
   g. A specified part of the royalty on forest resources;
   h. Supplementary Tax on Cinema, Jatra and Circus;
   i. Part of the royalty received by the Government against granting Licenses or Pattas for the exploitation of mineral resources;
   j. Tax on business;
   k. Tax on lottery;
   I. Tax on catching fish.

(C) Chittagong Hill Tracts Regional Council:

1. Subject to amendment and addition of the various sections in the Parbatya Zilla Sthanio Sarkar Parishad Ayin, 1989 (Act IXX, XX and XXI of 1989) for purpose of making the Hill District Council

more powerful and effective, a Regional Council will be formed comprising the Local Government Councils of three Hill Districts.
2. The elected Members of the Hill District Councils shall, by indirect mode, elect the Chairman of this Council whose status shall be equivalent to that of a State Minister and who shall be a tribal.
3. The Council shall consist of 22 (twenty-two) Members including the Chairman. Two-third of the Members shall be elected from among the tribals. The Council shall determine the modality of its functioning.

The constitution of the Council shall be as follows:

Chairman	1 person
Member (tribal male)	12 persons
Member (tribal female)	2 persons
Member (non-tribal male)	6 persons
Member (non-tribal female)	1 person

Of the male tribal Members, 5 shall be elected from the Chakma tribe, 3 from the Marma tribe, 2 from Tripura tribe, 1 from the Murung and Tanchangya tribes and 1 person from among the Lusai, Bowm, Pangkho, Khumi, Chak and Khiang tribes.

Of the male non-tribal Members, 2 persons shall be elected from each district.

Of the female tribal Members, 1 person shall be elected from the Chakma tribe and another from the rest of the tribes.

4. There shall be reserved 3 (three) seats for the women in the Council and one-third (1/3) thereof shall be for the non-tribals.
5. The Members of the Council shall, by indirect mode, be elected by the elected Members of the three Hill District Councils. The Chairman of the three hill districts shall be ex-officio Members of the Council and they shall have right to vote. The qualification and disqualification of candidature for membership of the Council shall be similar to those of the Members of the Hill District Councils.
6. The tenure of office of the Council shall be 5 (five) years. The procedure and other matters regarding the preparation and approval of the budget of the Council, dissolution of the Council, framing of the Rules of the Council, appointment and control of the officers and employees, etc. shall be similar to the procedure and other matters as are applicable to the Hill District Councils.

7. There shall be the Council, a Chief Executive Officer of the rank equivalent to that of a Joint Secretary to the Government and the tribal candidate shall be given preference for appointment to this post.
8. a. If the post of Chairman of the Council falls vacant, one person from among the other tribal members shall be, by indirect mode, elected Chairman for the interim period by the Members of the three Hill District Councils.
   b. If the post of a Member of the Council falls vacant for any reason, it shall be filled up by by-election.
9. a. The Council shall coordinate all the development activities carried out by the three Hill District Councils and shall also superintend and harmonize all the affairs of and assigned to the three Hill District Councils. Besides, in the event of lack of harmony or any inconsistency being found in the discharge of responsibilities given to the three Hill District Councils, the decision of the Regional Council shall be final.
   b. This Council shall coordinate and supervise the Local Council, including the municipalities.
   c. The Regional Council shall coordinate and supervise the three hill districts in matters of general administration, law and order and development.
   d. The Council shall coordinate the activities of the NGOs in addition to disaster management and carrying out the relief programmes.
   e. Tribal law and community adjudication shall be within the jurisdiction of the Regional Council.
   f. The Council shall be competent to grant License for heavy industries.
10. The Chittagong Hill Tracts Development Board shall discharge the assigned duties under the general and overall supervision of the Council. The Government shall give preference to the eligible tribal candidates in appointing the Chairman of the Development Board.
11. The Chittagong Hill Tracts Regulation of 1900 and other related Acts, Rules and Ordinances being found inconsistent with the Local Government Council Acts of 1989, it shall be removed by law as per advice and recommendations of the Regional Council.

12. Until the formation of the Regional Council through direct and indirect election, the Government shall be competent to constitute an interim Regional Council and to empower it to discharge the responsibilities of assignable to the Council.
13. In making any law in connection with Chittagong Hill Tracts, the Government shall enact such law in consultation with and as per advice of the Regional Council. If it becomes necessary to amend any law which bears an adverse effect on the development of the three hill districts and welfare of the tribal people or to enact new law, the Council shall be competent to apply or submit recommendations to the Government.
14. The sources of the Council Fund shall be as follows:

    a. Money received from the District Council Fund;
    b. Money or profits received from all the properties vested in or managed by the Council;
    c. Loans and grants from the Government and other authorities;
    d. Grants given by any institution or person;
    e. Profits earned from the investments of the Council Fund;
    f. Any money received by the Council;
    g. Money received from other sources provided to the Council as per direction of the Government.

(D) Rehabilitation, General Amnesty and Other Matters:

In order to restore normalcy in the Chittagong Hill Tracts region and, to that end, in respect of the works and matters of rehabilitation, general amnesty and allied issues, both the parties have been arrived at the following consensus and agreed to undertake programs as follows:

1. With a view to bringing the tribal refugees staying in the Tripura State of India back to the country, an agreement was signed on the 9th day of March, '97 at Agartala of Tripura State between the Government and the Leaders of tribal refugees. In pursuance of that Agreement, the tribal refugees started coming back to the country since 28th day of March, '97. This process shall remain un-hindered and to that end all possible cooperation shall be given from the end of the Jana Samhati Samiti. After ascertaining the identity of the Internally Displaced Persons of the three hill

districts, rehabilitation measures shall be undertaken through a Task Force.
2. After the signing the Agreement between the Government and the Jana Samhati Samiti and implementation thereof and rehabilitation of the tribal refugees and internally displaced tribals, the Government shall, as soon as possible, commence, in consultation with the Regional Council be the constituted under this Agreement, the Land Survey in Chittagong Hill Tracts and finally determine the land-ownership of the tribal people through settling the land-disputes on proper verification and shall record theirs land and ensure their rights thereto.
3. In order to ensure the land-ownership of tribal families having no land or lands below 2 (two) acres, the Government shall, subject to availability of land in the locality, ensure settling 2 (two) acres of land per family. In the event of non-availability of required land, grove-lands shall be tapped.
4. A Commission (Land Commission) shall be constituted under the leadership of a retired Justice for settlement of disputes regarding lands and premises. This Commission shall, in addition to early disposal of land disputes of the rehabilitated refugees, have full authority to annul the rights of ownership of those hills and lands which have been illegally settled and in respect of which illegal dispossession has taken place. No appeal shall be maintainable against the judgment of this Commission and the decision of this Commission shall be deemed to be final. This provision shall be applicable in case of Fringe-lands.
5. This Commission shall be constituted with the following Members:
   a. Retired Justice;
   b. Circle Chief (concerned);
   c. Chairman/Representative of the Regional Council;
   d. Divisional Commissioner/Additional Commissioner;
   e. Chairman of the District Council (concerned).
6. a. The tenure of office of the Commission shall be three years. But its tenure shall be extendible in consultation with the Regional Council.
   b. The Commission shall resolve the disputes in consonance with the law, custom and practice in force in the Chittagong Hill Tracts.

7. The loans which were taken by the tribal refugees from Government agencies, but could not be properly utilized on account of the state of belligerency, shall be remitted along with interest.
8. Land allocation for rubber and other plantation: Out of the lands allotted to non-tribal and non-local persons for rubber and other plantations, the lease (allocation) in respect of the lands of those who did not undertake any project during the last ten years or did not properly utilize the lands shall be cancelled.
9. The Government shall allocate additional finance on priority basis for the implementation of increased number of projects towards developments in the Chittagong Hill Tracts. The Government shall implement new Project on priority basis for the construction of required infrastructure for the development of the region and shall allocate necessary finance to this end. Keeping in view the environment of this region, the Government shall encourage the development of tourism facilities for the tourists, indigenous and foreign.
10. Quota reservation and stipend grant: The Government shall maintain the quota system for the tribals in respect of government service and institutions for higher studies until their attainment of parity with other regions of the country. To the aforesaid end, the Government shall grant increased number of stipends for the tribal male and female students in the educational institutions. The Government shall provide necessary scholarships for higher education and research in foreign countries.
11. The Government and the Elected Representatives shall strive to uphold the characteristics of tribal creed and culture. The Government shall patronize and help the cultural activities of the tribes towards their efflorescence at national level.
12. The Jana Samhati Samiti shall, within 45 (forty-five) days of the signing of this Agreement, submit lists of all its members to the Government including the armed ones, and the particulars of arms and ammunitions in its possession and within its control.
13. The Government and the Jana Samhati Samiti shall, within 45 (forty-five) days of the signing of this Agreement, jointly determine the date, time and place for deposit of arms. After the determination of the date and place for deposit of arms and ammunitions of the listed members of Jana Samhati Samiti, all sorts of security shall

be provided for the return of the members of Jana Samhati Samiti as per list also of their family members to normal life.
14. The Government shall declare amnesty for those members who will deposit arms and ammunitions on the scheduled date. The Government shall withdraw all those cases which were lodged against them.
15. In the event of any person's failing to deposit arms within the specified time limit, the Government shall take legal action against such a person.
16. A general amnesty shall be given to all the members of the Jana Samhati Samiti after their return to normal life and a general amnesty shall also be given to all the permanent inhabitants connected with the activities of the Jana Samhati Samiti.

   a. For the purpose of rehabilitating the returning members of the Jana Samhati Samiti, Taka 50,000/00 per family shall be given at a time.
   b. After deposit of arms and return to normal life of all such members, including the armed ones, of the Jana Samhati Samiti against whom cases were filed, warrants of arrest were issued, 'hulias' were published or sentence was given on trial in absentia, as against them all cases shall be withdrawn, warrants of arrest and 'hulias' shall be called back and sentence given in absentia shall be remitted as early as possible. If any member of the Jana Samhati Samiti is in Jail, he too shall be set at liberty.
   c. Similarly, after deposit of arms and return to normal life, no case shall be filed against or punishment be given to or arrest be made of any person merely on account of his/her being a member of the Jana Samhati Samiti.
   d. The loans which were taken by such members of the Jana Samhati Samiti from Government Banks and Establishments, who could not have utilized such loan properly on account of the state of belligerency, shall be remitted with interest.
   e. Those of the returned members of the Jana Samhati Samiti, who were previously in the service of the Government or Government organizations shall be reinstated to their respective posts and the members of the Jana Samhati Samiti and members of their families shall be given employment in accordance with

their qualification. In this respect, government policy regarding relaxation of age-bar for them shall be followed.

f. Priority shall be given to the members of the Jana Samhati Samiti in giving bank loans on simple terms with a view to helping their self-employment generating activities such as cottage industries, horticulture, etc.

g. Education facilities shall be provided to the children of the members of the Jana Samhati Samiti and their certificates obtained from foreign Boards academic Institutions shall be treated as valid.

17. a. After the signing and execution of the Agreement between the Government and the Jana Samhati Samiti and immediately after return of the members of Jana Samhati Samiti to normal life, all the temporary camps of the army, the Ansars and the Village Defence Party (VDP), excepting the Border Security Force (BDR) and permanent army establishment (being those three at the three district headquarters and those at Alikadam, Ruma and Dighinala), shall be taken back by phases from Chittagong Hill Tracts to permanent cantonments and the time-limit shall be fixed for its purpose. In case of deterioration of the law and order situation, in time of normal calamities and for similar other purposes, Army Forces may be deployed under the authority of the civil administration in adherence to Law and Rules as are applicable to all the other parts of the country. In this respect, the Regional Council may, in order to, get the required or timely help make requests to the appropriate authority.

b. The lands and premises abandoned by the cantonments, the camps of the military and para-military forces shall be made over to their real owners or to the Hill District Councils.

18. Against all the posts of officers of all ranks and employees of different classes in government, semi-government, local government and autonomous bodies of the Chittagong Hill Tracts, the permanent dwellers of the Chittagong Hill Tracts shall be appointed, subject to priority being given to the tribals. But, in case of non-availability of a qualified person among the permanent dwellers of Chittagong Hill Tracts for any post, appointment may be made to such post on deputation from the Government or for a definite period.

19. A ministry on Chittagong Hill Tracts shall be established on appointing a Minister from among the tribals. The following Advisory Committee shall be constituted to lend support to this Ministry:

1. The Minister on Chittagong Hill Tracts;
2. The Chairman/Representative, Regional Council;
3. The Chairman/Representative, Rangamati Hill District Council;
4. The Chairman/Representative, Khagrachari Hill District Council;
5. The Chairman/Representative, Bandarban Hill District Council;
6. The Member of the Parliament, Rangamati;
7. The Member of the Parliament, Khagrachari;
8. The Member of the Parliament, Bandarban;
9. The Chakma Raja;
10. The Bohmong Raja;
11. The Mong Raja;
12. Three non-tribal Members nominated by the Government from among the permanent residents of the three hill districts.

This Agreement is prepared in the aforesaid manner in Bengali language and executed and signed in Dhaka on Agrahayan 18, 1404 corresponding to 2 December 1997.

On Behalf of the Government of the People's Republic of Bangladesh
Sd/Illegible
(Abul Hasanat Abdullah)
Convenor,
National Committee on Chittagong Hill Tracts, Government of Bangladesh
B.G.P.-2012/13-2505Com(C-6)—500 Books, 2012

On Behalf of the inhabitants of Chittagong Hill Tracts
Sd/Illegible
(Jyotirindra Bodhipriya Larma)
President,
Parbatya Chattagram Jana Samhati Samiti

Source Translated English Version of Agreement Between the National Committee On Chittagong Hill Tracts Constituted By The Government And The Parbatya Chattagram Jana Samhati Samiti. (n.d.). http://mochta.portal.gov.bd/sites/default/files/files/moc hta.portal.gov.bd/page/8a162c4c_1f3f_4c6e_b3c0_63ad2ef9d2b3/Peace%20Accord%20%28Englidh%29.pdf. Accessed 3 September 2020.

[Some pages are missing from the website, and in consequence, they have been taken from Tripura, N. B. K. (Ed.). (2016). *Chittagong Hill Tracts: Long Walk to Peace &*

Development (pp. 49–103). Ministry of Chittagong Hill Tracts Affairs, Bangladesh Secretariat. Moreover, a few grammatical corrections have been done by the author. And this version of the Agreement (as translated into English from the Bengali language) is almost the same as that of the one as adopted by the PCJSS.]

Index

A
Abul Hasanat Abdullah, 62, 63
Aceh, 174
actor, 9, 21, 35, 37, 38, 92, 95, 117, 135, 136, 138, 149, 151, 158, 159, 161, 172
Adivasi, 2–4, 6, 109, 122, 181–185
administration, 6, 42, 43, 45, 47, 50, 52, 60
administrative control, 108, 117, 157
administrative order, 108, 157
administrative role, 157
administrative status, 44
administrative structure, 6, 46, 52
administrator, 8, 43, 49, 51, 58, 60, 112, 113, 115
Advisory Council, 47
Agreement's implementation, 8–11, 13–16, 19, 21, 34, 36, 38, 64, 68, 90, 91, 101, 110, 112, 127–129, 132, 143, 147, 151, 152, 154, 155, 157, 159–163, 165, 169–171
agriculture, 48, 60

Alamgir, Aurangzeb, 43
alienation, 9, 44, 47, 56, 61, 81
Alikadam, 88, 203
Amnesty International, 112, 136, 137, 144
analytical design, 20, 37
analytical framework, 13, 14, 20, 34, 38, 152
analytical model, 38, 39
ancestral land, 7
Ansars, 88, 108, 203
anti-PCJSS, 123
Anti-Slavery International, 136
Anti-Slavery Society, 112
Appellate Division, 103
applied politics, 24
Arakan, 5
Arakanese dynasty, 43
Arakan hill, 46
arbitrary power, 46, 174
armed conflict, 14, 29, 32, 33, 35, 42, 63, 97, 111, 120, 154, 174
army, 7, 8, 10, 12–15, 33, 35, 38, 58, 59, 72, 88, 89, 92, 95, 97, 103,

106–112, 114, 116, 117, 124, 127, 130, 132, 151, 152, 154, 157, 161–163, 167, 170, 203
Arunachal Pradesh, 6
Asian Development Bank (ADB), 58, 148
Assam, 6, 139
assassination, 58, 59, 120, 121, 138, 159
assimilationist, 58
attack, 59, 111, 125, 141, 146
autonomy, 8, 23, 36, 57–59, 62, 64, 103, 123, 124, 131, 132, 158, 161, 174
Awami League (AL), 35, 62, 63, 96–106, 112, 116, 130, 137–140, 148, 156, 159

B
Bandarban, 3, 5, 45, 46, 54, 59–61, 106, 110, 121, 126, 130, 166, 204
Bandarban Hill District Council (BHDC), 54, 82, 108, 140, 204
Bangladesh army, 15, 59, 107
Bangladesh government, 41, 114
Bangladeshi, 4, 58, 109, 122, 141, 144
Bangladesh military, 108
Bangladesh Nationalist Party (BNP), 61, 96, 97, 100–105, 108, 116, 130, 156
Bangladesh Rifles (BDR), 59
Bangladesh security forces, 14, 42
Bangladesh's donor consortium countries, 136
Basic Democracies (BD), 52
Bawm, 5
Bay of Bengal, 5, 6
beneficiaries, 1, 15, 19, 20, 90, 158, 167, 174, 175
benefit, 32, 49, 59, 173

Bengal, 43, 45, 48
Bengal Government, 46
Bengali, 2, 3, 6, 12, 15, 43, 44, 46–49, 52, 54–62, 70, 103, 105, 109, 110, 120, 121, 128–130, 141, 156, 158, 175, 204
Bengali–tribal, 8, 15, 36, 128, 152, 161, 163
Bengali community, 6, 52
Bengali elites, 2, 6
Bengali ethnic population, 5
Bengali Farmers and Workers Association, 111
Bengali Krishak Sramik Kalyan Parishad, 111, 129
Bengali merchants, 43
Bengali migrants, 45, 46, 55, 64, 101, 130, 155
Bengali nationalism, 56–58
Bengali political parties, 33, 35, 91, 96, 104–106, 116, 130, 133, 155, 156, 159, 165–167, 170
Bengali settlers, 2, 8, 14, 33, 35, 36, 54, 56, 59, 60, 62, 90–92, 97, 100, 101, 103–105, 109–111, 116, 119–121, 124, 128–133, 151, 155, 156, 159, 162, 166–170, 175
Bira Raja, 43
Board of Revenue, 53
Bohmang, 54
Bohmang Raja, 56
Bohmang Revenue Circle, 46
Brigade Headquarters, 59
British, 6, 25, 42, 44–52, 55, 63, 64, 81, 141, 153
British administrator, 5
British colonial regime, 41, 48
British colonial rulers, 14, 42, 49, 50, 153
British East India Company, 42, 44, 153

British Monarch, 44
British period, 42, 44
British policy, 44
Buddhist, 5, 129, 158
bureaucracy, 7, 8, 10, 14, 15, 33, 35, 39, 92, 95, 98, 110, 112–114, 116, 117, 124, 127, 132, 151, 152, 154, 157–163, 167, 170–172
bureaucratic non-cooperation, 113, 114, 117
Bureaucratic red tape, 112
Burma, 43, 51

C
cadastral survey, 105
camps, 59, 72, 88, 89, 106, 108, 140, 141, 149, 157, 160, 167, 203
capacity-building, 168
caretaker government, 125
ceasefire, 61, 174
census, 55
Chak, 5, 197
Chakma, 5, 43, 46, 54, 58, 120–122, 132, 158, 197
Chakma Circle, 12, 137
Chakma Development Council, 110
Chakma Raja, 56, 204
Chakma Revenue Circle, 46
Chakma Unnayan Sangsad, 110
Chandraghona, 53
Chengi, 4
Chief, 43, 44, 47, 50, 51, 57, 58, 62, 63, 137, 140, 145, 154
Children of the Hills, 6
Children of the River, 6
Chittagong, 5, 42–44, 63
Chittagong Hill Tracts (CHT), 2–8, 10–14, 20, 32, 33, 35–37, 39, 41–48, 50–64, 68–74, 77, 79, 83, 84, 86, 88–91, 95–117, 119–132, 135–149, 151, 153–161, 163, 165–167, 170–172, 175, 189, 199–201, 203, 204
Chittagong Hill Tracts Commission (CHT Commission), 37, 45, 59, 60, 105, 112, 123, 135, 136, 140–145, 149, 152, 159, 160, 168
Chittagong Hill Tracts Development Board (CHTDB), 58, 109, 115, 157, 198
Chittagong Hill Tracts Development Facility (CHTDF), 145, 147
Chittagong Hill Tracts Regional Council (CHTRC), 68, 70–72, 77, 83, 84, 87, 90, 92, 98, 101–106, 109, 111–115, 117, 121, 126, 128, 132, 156–159, 196
Chittagong Hill Tracts Regulation of 1900, 45, 198
CHT-based local group dynamics, 10
CHT-based local institutions, 92, 106, 109, 111, 117, 157, 158, 167, 168
CHT-based local level, 15, 33, 36, 38, 120, 151, 152, 161–163, 165, 167, 170
CHT case, 8–13, 15, 32, 33, 37, 45, 67, 69, 90, 95, 96, 106, 107, 114, 121, 135, 136, 138, 140, 142, 149, 151, 153, 154, 157, 159–161, 163, 167–169, 173, 174
CHT ethnic conflict, 6
CHT indigenous people, 2, 32, 44, 49–51, 55–57, 60, 61, 69, 72, 90, 91, 105, 109, 127, 129, 130, 132, 144, 175
CHT Land Dispute Resolution Commission (Amendment) Act 2016, 87, 130, 133, 155, 159

CHT Manual, 45–47, 53, 55, 57, 60, 64, 153
CHT Peace Agreement, 2, 5, 7–16, 19–21, 32–39, 41, 42, 54, 56, 59, 61, 63, 64, 67–74, 77, 78, 83, 84, 89–92, 95–106, 108–117, 119–128, 130–132, 135, 138–140, 143–149, 151–163, 165–173, 175
CHT Peace and Coordination Council, 111, 129
CHT people, 46, 49, 50, 63, 71, 74, 89, 110, 124, 126, 129, 130, 132, 146, 147, 170
Circle, 46, 47, 51, 52, 54
citizens, 7, 21, 23–25, 29, 58, 68, 79, 104, 189
civilian regimes, 139
civil servants, 114
civil service officers, 117
civil society, 12, 74, 98, 105, 127, 143, 170, 171
classical liberalism, 21
classical realism, 21, 22, 138
classical realists, 21
clauses, 2, 7, 68, 73
Cold War, 136, 139
collective (common) ownership, 7, 49
colonial style, 114
Committee of Revenue report (1874), 43
commodification of land, 49
common property, 48
Communist Party of Bangladesh, 97
community, 2, 3, 5, 6, 15, 28, 50, 53, 57, 59, 60, 64, 70, 73, 79, 111, 119–122, 126, 132, 133, 136, 142, 144–147, 158, 159, 161, 167, 168, 170, 198
community property, 50
community rights, 51
confidence and trust, 113
confidence-building, 144, 149, 168
conflict, 1, 2, 7, 9, 13, 14, 23, 29–33, 36, 41, 42, 61–63, 67–69, 81, 111, 116, 124, 126, 138, 146, 153, 172–174, 176
conflicting primary parties, 171
conflict resolution, 173
Congress, 51
consensus, 33, 35, 89, 108, 119, 151, 156, 170–172, 189, 199
constituencies, 35, 105, 106, 155, 166
constitution, 57, 58, 62, 64, 79, 100, 102, 197
constitutional autonomy, 14, 42, 64, 153
constitutional supremacy, 15
Constitution of Bangladesh, 7, 14, 42, 57–59, 64, 79, 97, 100, 103, 104, 153
Constitution of Pakistan, 42, 52
Council of Hill Peoples, 111
coup, 59
Cox's Bazar, 5
cultivable land, 54, 64
cultivation, 48, 53, 55, 64, 71
Cyril Radcliffe, 51

D
debt-bondage, 49
defence, 108, 109, 123
deforestation, 61, 148
demands, 2, 14, 19, 20, 39, 42, 48, 51, 57, 59, 62, 64, 79, 90, 99, 103, 104, 114, 124, 131, 139, 154, 167
democracy, 23, 52, 61, 144
democratic government, 139
demographic, 54, 155
demographic changes, 105
demographic composition, 3, 105
dependent variables, 34, 162

Deputy Commissioner (DC), 5, 45–47, 50, 51, 60, 80, 113, 115
descent, 5
development, 11, 22, 25, 29, 52, 53, 55, 56, 62, 70–72, 79, 82, 84, 88, 99, 109, 115, 142–147, 149, 153, 157, 160, 189, 198, 199, 201
development activities, 71, 72, 83, 120, 168, 198
development projects, 42, 60, 64, 109, 147
Dewan, Moni Swapan, 101, 122, 139, 183
dialogue, 59, 64, 69, 98, 127, 142, 146, 148
diaspora, 37, 67, 69, 143
Dighinala, 59, 88, 203
displacement, 53, 54, 61
district, 3, 5, 43, 53–55, 60, 62, 63, 71, 79, 84–86, 88, 104, 114–116, 130, 146, 166, 197–200, 203, 204
District Council, 60, 71, 72
District Forests (DFs), 50
divide and rule policy, 110
domestic issues, 2
domestic politics, 20
dominance of power, 111
dominant, 22, 33, 36, 106, 120

E
early liberal thinkers, 21
East India Company, 44
East Pakistan, 51, 52
economic, 3, 6, 7, 9, 16, 22, 26, 34, 44, 50, 58, 64, 69, 95, 107, 111, 141, 154, 157, 158, 160, 161, 165, 172
economic benefit, 44, 111
economic development, 29, 102, 129, 144, 145, 189

economic expenses, 107
economic exploitation, 53
economic gains, 48
economic growth, 29, 96, 171
economic interests, 8, 15, 33, 35, 44, 117, 153, 157, 167
economic marginalisation, 32, 48
economic policies, 53
economic rights, 68, 189
economic system, 48
education, 109, 144–146, 201
election, 32, 35, 62, 104–106, 117, 139, 155, 166, 198, 199
electoral roll, 104
electoral voters' list, 104
empirical discussion, 15, 152
empirical experience, 12
empirical field, 11
empirical study, 15, 152
English School, 23, 172
environment, 48, 98, 201
Ershad, Hussain Muhammad (H.M.), 59
ethnic cleansing, 59
ethnic communities, 3, 5, 15, 41, 108, 121, 128, 132, 145, 146, 167
ethnic conflict, 48, 70
ethnic groups, 28, 43, 123, 126, 137
ethnic identity, 48
ethnic minorities, 2, 62, 79
ethnolinguistic people, 3
European Commission (EC), 136, 144
European Community, 144
European Parliament, 141, 142, 144, 170
European Union (EU), 144, 146–148
excluded area, 47, 52
executive, 25, 35, 47, 58, 63, 82, 114, 115
executive power, 98, 114

exploitation, 29, 57
exploratory, 11
extortion, 126

F
faction, 8, 36, 37, 103, 120–123, 125–127, 132, 158, 166, 170
factionalism, 36
factional rivalries, 120, 126, 130
factors, 12, 14, 31, 32, 54, 56, 64, 67–69, 73, 91, 95, 96, 99, 106, 110, 116, 119, 138, 144, 148, 156, 160, 168, 175
failed state, 168
fallow, 48
Feni, 4
financial, 47, 54, 60, 63, 69, 85, 107, 148
forest, 4, 42, 50, 51, 55, 60, 61, 80, 81, 110, 153
forest resources, 50, 51, 64, 110
fragile state, 33
Free Aceh Movement, 16, 174
Fruit Tree Working Circle, 55

G
general amnesty, 70, 72, 199, 202
General Officer Commanding (GOC), 109, 141, 157
geopolitical, 137, 139, 140
globalised society, 15, 20, 37, 149
Gono Forum, 97
Gonotantry Party, 97
government's reluctance, 98, 127
Government of Bangladesh (GoB), 2, 7–9, 12, 14, 15, 19, 33, 35–38, 57, 58, 61, 63, 64, 67–69, 73, 77–79, 81, 82, 85, 90, 91, 95, 96, 98–101, 104, 108, 112, 125, 126, 135, 136, 139, 142, 144–146, 148, 149, 151, 152, 154, 156, 158–161, 163, 165, 167–172, 175
Government of India Act of 1935, 47
Government Reserve Forest, 50
Governor-General-in-Council, 47
Greater Nagaland, 174
group dynamics, 15, 120, 131
group rivalries, 120, 122, 125, 127, 131–133, 158–160, 162, 174
guerrilla, 57, 72, 107

H
Hasina, Sheikh, 62, 73, 74, 89, 99, 100, 105, 111, 116, 142, 143, 149, 160, 171
Headman, 47, 50, 52
health, 60, 109, 144–146
hegemony, 7, 110
High Court Division, 103
Hill allowance, 110
Hill communities, 2, 14, 15, 36, 42, 43, 45, 47, 49, 50, 53, 63, 121–123, 132, 159, 165
Hill District Council (HDC), 68, 70–72, 80, 82, 83, 104, 196–198, 203
Hill District Local Government Council Act of 1989, 70
Hill ethnic communities, 2, 5, 43, 44, 53, 56, 63, 92, 109, 122, 158
Hill ethnic people, 2, 57, 59, 123, 153, 158
Hill groups, 126, 127, 143
Hill people, 2, 5–9, 14, 15, 19, 33, 35–37, 39, 41–45, 48–50, 52–54, 56–59, 61, 63, 64, 69, 72, 79, 81, 90–92, 95, 97, 99, 101–103, 105, 106, 109–111, 115, 120, 124, 129, 131, 132, 136–138, 141, 143, 144, 148, 149, 153, 158–160, 162, 165–169, 171

INDEX 213

Hill People's Council, 123
Hill Students' Council, 123
Hill Tripura, 43
Hill Tripura Raj Dynasty, 43
Hill Women's Federation (HWF), 123, 143, 182
Hindu, 5
historiography, 42
homeless, 54, 61
House of Lords in London, 141, 160
Huda, Nazmul, 100
human rights, 2, 10, 15, 20, 32, 34, 37, 39, 59, 67, 69, 112, 136, 137, 140–144, 146, 149, 160, 184
human rights organisations, 69, 135, 136, 143, 149

I
idealism, 22
identity, 57, 85, 91, 123, 124, 132, 138, 158, 199
implementation of peace agreement, 10, 14, 19, 30–32, 173
implementation policies, 2, 36, 96, 120, 155–158, 166, 170, 173, 175
implementation process, 1, 2, 15, 31, 35, 41, 70, 73, 74, 88, 90, 95, 96, 101, 111, 112, 117, 121, 124, 129–132, 152, 172
implementing a peace agreement, 10, 20, 30, 173
implementing the agreement, 31, 33, 35, 36, 86, 90, 92, 95, 97, 100, 101, 105, 116, 119, 126, 147, 151, 156, 166, 170, 171, 175
income-generating business, 109, 157
independence, 7, 51, 56, 102, 121, 139, 140, 153, 174
independent variables, 34, 152

India, 5, 6, 12, 37, 44, 51, 54, 56, 58, 61, 64, 72, 85, 90, 101, 120, 135–141, 149, 152, 159–161, 168
Indian Forest Reserve Act, 50
Indian government, 138–140, 159, 174
Indian involvement, 140
Indian military, 138
Indian secessionist groups, 138
Indian subcontinent, 42, 44
Indian Union, 174
India-Returnee Tribal Refugees, 85
India's changing strategy, 67, 69
India's north-eastern states, 136, 138, 139
indigenous people, 3, 8, 47, 54, 77, 105, 111, 124, 128, 138, 147–149, 153, 159, 160, 174
Indonesia, 16, 174
Indonesian military, 174
industrial, 46, 53
influence, 20, 26, 50, 158, 166, 170, 175
influential, 8, 20, 26, 69, 112, 115, 117, 127, 140, 144, 147, 151, 162
institutional, 22, 92, 115, 144
institutional liberalism, 22, 160
institutions, 8, 12, 22, 25, 35, 47, 50, 52, 63, 71, 80, 82, 92, 95, 96, 98, 101, 102, 106, 112–115, 117, 120, 126, 127, 132, 145, 147, 154, 156, 157, 163, 167, 169, 170, 174, 199, 201, 203
insurgency, 59, 101, 108, 113, 119, 121, 139, 156
insurgent groups in Nagaland, 174
integration, 28, 29
inter-community, 120, 128, 129
interdependence liberalism, 22
interest of assuming power, 10, 33

interests, 7–10, 14–16, 20, 33–35, 37, 44, 53, 92, 101, 106, 107, 109, 113, 115–117, 120, 122, 129, 130, 136, 140, 147–149, 152, 153, 155–158, 160, 161, 163, 165–168, 172–175
internal feuds, 174
Internally Displaced People (IDPs), 68, 85, 90, 138, 182
internal situation, 135
international actors, 2, 9, 10, 15, 19, 20, 32, 34, 37, 39, 69, 90, 135, 144, 149, 159, 161, 162, 165, 166, 168, 171
international anarchy, 22
international community, 2, 8, 10, 20, 31, 33, 34, 37, 135, 137, 141, 149, 151, 160, 161, 163, 165
international donor, 109, 136, 142, 153
international factors, 135, 136
international level, 8, 13, 14, 20, 34, 35, 37, 38, 152, 161, 162, 168
international networks, 2
international politics, 20, 34, 136
international pressure, 61, 99
International Society, 23, 172
International Society theories, 19
international sphere, 10, 21, 27
International Work Group for Indigenous Affairs (IWGIA), 136, 140
intervene, 161, 163, 168, 171
interview, 12, 54, 97–100, 105, 108, 110, 111, 113, 114, 116, 121, 124–128, 137, 139, 140, 144, 147, 148, 185
interviewees, 10–13, 36, 96, 117, 122, 127, 131, 143, 148, 156–159, 169, 170, 175, 185
intra-community, 120
intra-group conflict, 116, 127, 129
intra-group rivalries, 127, 174
intra-tribal, 8, 15, 36, 152, 160, 163
Islamabad, 43

J

Jallal Khan, 43
Jamaat-e-Islami (JI), 100, 102, 103
Jatiya Party (JP), 97, 100, 102, 103
Jatiya Samajtantrik Dal, 97
Jatiya Sangshad, 102
jhum, 48–51, 61
jhum cultivation, 48–51, 55, 61, 63, 64, 153
jhumias, 49
judicial, 47, 63
Jumma, 48, 85
Jumma nation, 48
Jumma People's Network in Europe, 143
Jyotirindra Bodhipriya Larma, 7, 12, 63, 74, 121, 182, 204

K

Kapas Mahal, 43
Kaptai dam, 54, 55, 123
Kaptai Hydro-electric Project, 54, 64, 80, 148, 153
Kaptai Lake, 71, 80, 82, 110
Kaptai village, 54
Karbari, 47
Karnafuli, 4
Karnafuli Paper Mill, 53
Karnafuli river, 54
Kassalong, 4
key informant interview (KII), 11, 13
Khagrachhari, 3–5, 54, 59–61, 106, 110, 116, 124, 128, 166, 182
Khagrachhari Hill District Council (KHDC), 82, 182
Khaleda Zia, 61, 100, 141
Khan, Ayub, 52

Khan, Shaista, 43
Khasia, 51
khas land, 61, 80
Kheyang, 5
Khumi, 5, 197
Khyoungtha, 6
Kingdom of Arakan, 42
knowledge, 10, 12, 25, 130, 140, 175
Kuchbihar, 51
Kukis, 43

L

land, 3, 5–7, 42, 46, 48–51, 53–55, 59–62, 64, 68, 72, 77, 80, 81, 85, 86, 90–92, 97, 104, 105, 108, 113, 114, 116, 123, 124, 129, 130, 146, 153–155, 166, 167, 200, 201
Land Commission, 72, 86, 87, 99, 105, 111, 154, 200
land dispute, 72, 87, 90, 91, 175, 200
Land Dispute Resolution, 77, 87
land issue, 77, 154
landless, 54, 72, 86, 166
land of cotton, 43
language, 3, 5, 6, 12, 42, 58, 70, 79, 204
Larma, Manobendra Narayan (M.N.), 57
Larma, Santu, 7, 12, 74, 101, 105, 113, 114, 120–122, 130, 149, 154
law and order, 28, 72, 88, 108, 125, 157, 198, 203
leaders, 12, 51, 52, 56, 57, 59, 60, 64, 91, 98, 101–103, 113, 121, 124, 129, 130, 138, 147, 159, 169
leftist political parties, 97
legislature, 14, 25, 42, 57, 59, 64, 153
level of influence, 9

liberal idealism, 21
liberalism, 10, 13, 14, 19–23, 37, 38, 172
liberal thinkers, 21, 22
Liberation Tigers of Tamil Eelam (LTTE), 174
liberation war, 56
literacy, 122, 146
loans, 49, 148, 199, 201–203
local administration, 52, 71, 82, 112
Local Government Councils (LGCs), 60, 62, 197
local level, 8, 14, 34, 112, 132, 157, 160, 171, 174
local-level leaders, 174
Local Trust-Builders Network, 146
Long March, 143, 168
Lushai, 5
Lushai hills, 46

M

Manipur, 6, 138
marginalisation, 9, 14, 41, 42, 44, 48, 51, 56, 63, 64, 122, 153
marginalised ethnic people, 1
marginalised groups, 2, 48
market economy, 48
Marma, 5, 6, 43, 51, 53, 121, 197
Marma Development Council, 110
Marma Unnayan Sangsad, 110
martial law, 58
Matamuhuri, 5
media awareness, 149
media influence, 144
media resources, 125
Meghalaya, 6
Members of Parliament, 12
migration policy of Bengalis, 59
militarisation, 59
military, 56, 58, 60, 64, 68, 77, 88, 91, 92, 98, 105, 107, 108, 116,

127, 129, 137–139, 141, 159, 160, 170–172, 203
military and Bengali settlers, 141
military camps, 89, 92
military coup, 58, 138
military forces, 107
military power, 7
military professionalism, 107, 117, 157, 167
military regime, 52, 139
military withdrawal, 124
militia, 57
ministerial line, 113, 117, 158, 167
Ministry of Chittagong Hill Tracts Affairs (MoCHTA), 11, 13, 68, 77, 80, 89, 92, 98, 100, 101, 112, 114, 115, 117, 139, 145, 147
minorities, 59, 137
Mir Qasim Ali Khan, 44
Mizo and Nagaland's peace initiatives, 16
Mizo National Front, 138, 174
Mizo Peace Agreement, 174
Mizoram, 5, 6, 61, 137, 138, 174
mode of agriculture, 48
mode of production, 153
Mogh, 46
moneylenders, 49
Mongolian, 5
Mong Raja, 56, 204
Mong Revenue Circle, 46
motivate, 36, 116, 161, 168, 171
Mouza, 46, 47
Mrung, 5
Mughal, 41–44, 63
muktibahini (freedom fighters), 56
multi-ethnic state, 1
multi-party, 61, 62
Murong, 121
Muslim, 129, 158
Muslim Bengali, 129

Muslim League, 51
mutiny, 138
Myani, 4
Myanmar, 5, 43, 51, 54

N
Nagaland, 6, 140
National Awami League, 97
National Committee on Chittagong Hill Tracts (NCCHT), 2, 62, 70, 95, 189
national development, 53
national elections, 104, 105
national government, 22, 148, 161
national human rights institutions, 137
national identity, 58
national integration, 53, 96
national integrity, 64
nationalism, 57
national level, 13, 34, 119, 201
National Parliament, 58, 62, 73, 74, 89, 102, 105, 123, 130, 147–149, 168, 170, 171
national security, 21, 102, 108
National Socialist Council of Nagaland, 174
nation-state, 58
natural resources, 53, 64, 96, 153, 154, 171
negative peace, 28, 29
negotiation, 14, 29, 32, 41, 42, 61–64, 67–69, 128, 135, 139, 149, 154, 159, 169, 171
neoliberalism, 14, 19, 20, 22, 23, 37, 168
neoliberals, 23
neorealism, 14, 19–21, 23, 138
neorealist, 23
Nikhil Kumar Chakma, 109
non-cooperation, 83, 98, 101
non-cooperation movement, 98

non-governmental organisations
 (NGOs), 8, 37, 68, 69, 135,
 137, 141, 149, 198
non-implementation, 1, 11, 12, 54,
 56, 64, 98, 110, 114, 127, 137
non-state actors, 8, 14, 15, 37, 135,
 149, 152, 159, 160, 171
normative approach, 21
north-eastern India, 6, 16, 174
north-eastern insurgents, 139
north-eastern states, 168

O

Operation Dabanol, 88, 108, 157
Operation Wildfire, 88, 108, 157
opposition, 7, 35, 36, 52, 97,
 100–102, 130, 142, 156
opposition political parties, 8, 15, 35,
 39, 90, 96, 103, 141, 170
oral traditions, 42
ownership, 6, 50, 72, 87, 91, 92, 97,
 105, 113, 114, 116, 129, 130,
 146, 147, 154, 200
own interests, 10, 34, 39, 117, 132,
 152, 154, 158, 161, 168, 171,
 172

P

Pahari, 2, 129, 130
Pahari Chattra Parishad (PCP), 123
Pahari Gono Parishad (PGP), 123
Pakistan, 42, 51–53, 56, 64, 81, 138,
 140, 153
Pakistan army, 56
Pakistan government, 53–55
Pakistan regime, 6, 14, 41, 56
Pankho, 5
Para, 47
parallel administrative structures, 47
Parbattya All Party United
 Organisation, 128

Parbattya Gano Parishad (PGP), 111,
 128, 129
Parbatya Chattagram Jana Samhati
 Samiti (PCJSS), 2, 7, 8, 11, 12,
 14, 15, 20, 33, 35, 36, 39,
 57–64, 67–70, 72–80, 82–92,
 98, 99, 101, 104–106, 108–110,
 116, 120–127, 129–132,
 135–139, 141, 143, 148, 149,
 151, 154–156, 158, 159, 161,
 162, 167–172, 175, 184, 189,
 190
Parbatya Zilla Parishad, 71
Parbatya Zilla Sthanio Sarkar Parishad
 Ayin, 1989, 70, 190, 196
Parliamentary Caucus on Indigenous
 Peoples, 128, 147, 149, 160, 183
parliamentary committee, 61, 62
parliamentary forms of democracy, 64
parliamentary forms of government,
 67, 69, 139
partial (or weak) implementation, 2,
 9, 16, 34, 98, 99, 116, 117, 132,
 153, 161–163, 168, 172
participation, 106, 145
peace, 2, 10, 14, 19, 21, 22, 27–29,
 31, 33, 34, 38, 83, 91, 111, 121,
 127, 135, 140, 143–148,
 173–175
peace agreement, 1
peace agreement beneficiaries, 173,
 174
peace agreement implementation, 9,
 10, 13, 19, 21, 33, 38
peace agreement's signing parties, 1
peace and conflict, 27
peace and development, 145
peace and progress, 21
peacebuilders, 1
Peace Force, 7, 57
peace initiatives, 39, 120, 136, 170,
 175

peace-making, 172
permanent residents, 104, 204
plantations, 46, 51, 53, 201
plough, 48
plough cultivation, 48–50
police, 45, 59, 71, 82, 126
policy formulation, 83, 173
policymakers, 69, 172, 173, 175
policy outcomes, 112
policy recommendations, 16, 163, 166, 169, 172
political analysis, 22
political and strategic interests, 149, 159, 161
political autonomy, 43, 63, 105
political consensus, 116, 165
political culture, 2, 37
political discourse, 10
political economy, 26, 42, 49, 63, 153
political integration, 22
political interests, 8, 11, 15, 153, 169, 175
political paradigms, 175
political party, 8, 15, 35, 36, 96, 97, 100, 102, 105, 117, 122, 123, 132, 155, 156, 158, 166, 167, 170
political philosophy, 24
political science, 20, 24–26
political selection, 116
political support, 116, 155
political tactic, 156
political theory, 25
political thinkers, 20, 25, 26
politico-administrative changes, 42, 52
politico-military organisation, 120
politics, 8–10, 13, 14, 16, 19–21, 24–27, 33, 34, 38, 41, 51, 54, 56, 58, 63, 64, 68, 73, 90, 96, 112, 116, 119, 122, 132, 152, 153, 155, 156, 166, 171, 173

politics of interest, 2, 3, 7, 10, 173
polls, 105
population, 3, 5, 6, 29, 51, 54, 103, 121, 128, 155, 156, 166
positive peace, 28, 29
post-Agreement, 73, 103, 120, 136, 173
post-Agreement CHT developments, 122
post-conflict societies, vii
post-development phase, 9
post-Second World War liberalism, 22
poverty, 29
power, 1, 6, 8, 14, 15, 19–23, 25–27, 31, 35, 36, 44, 45, 47, 50, 52, 53, 58–60, 63, 71, 72, 92, 95, 97, 98, 101, 104–106, 108, 111–117, 126–128, 132, 140, 151, 153–156, 158–161, 163, 166, 167, 169, 170, 172
powerful, 20, 26, 174, 197
power politics, 22
power struggle, 91, 114, 165, 172
pre-colonial period, 14, 41, 42, 48, 63
pre-industrial mode of production, 48
pressure, 2, 37, 54, 69, 97, 136, 137, 139, 143, 144, 148, 149, 168, 170, 171
primary actors, 1
primary signatory parties, 14, 68, 77, 151
primitive method of agriculture, 48
Priti group, 121
Priti Kumar Chakma, 120
private property, 61
private rights, 50
pro-PCJSS, 123
property, 50, 141
Protected Forests (PFs), 55
protests, 52, 97, 103, 106, 130

provisions, 1, 2, 10, 14, 29–32, 35, 45, 57, 60, 68, 70–74, 77, 78, 80, 84, 87, 89, 91, 95, 98, 100, 101, 103, 106, 115, 116, 120, 121, 123, 137, 151, 154, 155, 168, 169, 172, 174, 200
Prue Chai Chowdhury, 56

Q
quasi-military, 64, 138, 139

R
Rahman, Sheikh Mujibur, 57
Rahman, Ziaur, 58, 100
Raja, 47
Rajapaksa, Mahindra, 174
Ramgarh, 45, 46
Rangamati, 3–5, 43, 45, 46, 54, 59–61, 73, 106, 109, 125, 148, 166, 181, 204
Rangamati Hill District Council (RHDC), 82, 99, 126, 181, 204
razakars, 56
realism, 10, 13, 19–22, 38, 104, 172
realist thinking, 22
realist view, 8, 15, 19, 20, 33, 39, 138, 161
rebellion, 59
refugees, 32, 37, 61, 72, 85, 135–141, 149, 154, 159, 160, 168, 200
regional political party, 122
regional power politics, 140
regions, 7, 32, 52, 96, 136, 201
rehabilitation, 54, 68, 70, 72, 77, 79, 85, 90, 199, 200
religion, 4, 5, 96
religious group, 129
repatriating Bengali settlers, 105, 156
republican liberalism, 22

Research and Analysis Wing (RAW), 121
Reserve Forests (RFs), 50, 61, 64, 81
restrictions, 51, 55, 60, 64
revenue, 42, 49, 108
rights, 3, 7, 8, 25, 43, 45, 47, 50, 53, 60, 62–64, 72, 87, 91, 92, 99, 101, 105, 110, 116, 121, 123, 124, 128–130, 132, 141, 142, 148, 149, 158, 166, 167, 171, 172, 200
rivalries, 8, 15, 119, 120, 123, 129, 146, 152, 161, 163, 166, 167
root causes of the conflict, 41, 42, 45, 175
Roy, Raja Devasish, 12, 137, 184
rubber, 53, 201
rules, 27, 35, 36, 44, 45, 47, 83, 87, 113, 154
Ruma, 88, 203

S
Sanders, Douglas, 140
Sangue, 4
satellite, 80
secessionist, 174
sections, 2, 7, 9, 11, 14, 16, 19, 20, 23, 24, 29, 33, 35, 36, 38, 39, 41, 42, 50, 51, 67–72, 74, 77–79, 81, 87, 90, 91, 95, 97, 113, 120, 121, 136, 144, 151, 152, 154, 155, 157, 158, 160, 166, 169, 172, 175, 190, 196
security, 22, 23, 44, 58, 64, 107, 111, 137, 138, 201
security forces, 59, 62, 68, 107, 154
security problem, 127
separatist, 138–140, 159, 168
settlement, 31, 46, 47, 54, 60–62, 68, 69, 77, 80, 87, 90, 91, 104, 109, 129, 139, 141, 154, 156, 200
Seven Sister States of India, 138, 139

Shah, Fakhruddin Mubarak, 43
Shanti Bahini (SB), 7, 57, 59, 69, 107, 120, 122, 138–140, 154, 159
Shoi Prue Chowdhury, 56
Shri Ushatan Talukder, 99, 184
slash-and-burn farming, 48
social, 7, 11, 26, 28, 29, 42, 49, 50, 123, 130, 141, 144, 147, 189
social justice, 29, 71, 82
social power, 3, 7
social sciences, 10, 25, 26
sociological liberalism, 22, 160
Softwood Working Circle, 55
Sonargaon, 43
South Asian, 139, 174
special status, 52, 116
Sri Lanka, 16
stakeholder, 10, 12, 90, 91, 96, 141, 149, 160, 170–173
state actors, 8, 14, 15, 37, 135, 152, 160, 163
state interests, 21
state level, 1, 8, 14, 15, 20, 29, 33–35, 38, 95, 119, 132, 151, 152, 155, 158, 160–163, 166, 167, 172
State Minister, 72, 98, 113, 114, 147, 197
state sovereignty, 21, 102, 103
strategic interests, 34, 160
strategy, 35, 44, 46, 60, 90, 92, 96, 101, 102, 107, 139, 140, 153, 160, 173
struggle, 7, 8, 14, 72, 97, 124, 126, 137
subordinate, 115
Sultanate in Bengal, 43
supremacy, 16, 20, 102, 126, 168, 173, 174
Supreme Court, 103, 184
survey, 72

Survival International (UK), 136
swidden agriculture, 48

T
Tamil crisis, 16
Tanchangya, 5, 197
tax, 43, 44, 47, 49, 50, 63
temporary army camps, 89, 108
territory, 5, 6, 22, 26, 27, 30, 43, 103, 139
Thana, 45
theoretical approaches, 13, 19, 20, 23, 38, 152
theoretical discourse, 172
theoretical framework, 19
theoretical perspective, 119
theoretical politics, 24, 25
third-party interests, 132
Totally Excluded Area, 47
Toungtha, 6
trade, 43, 55
traditional, 3, 21, 47, 48, 50, 52, 54, 61, 63, 92, 112–114, 117, 145, 157, 158, 167, 170
Transfer of Abandoned Lands, 76
transhipment, 140, 168
transit, 140, 168
transnational relationships, 22
tribal area, 44
Tribal Convention, 59
tribal-inhabited region, 70
tribal people, 2, 45, 62, 72, 79, 84, 119, 120, 131, 132, 175, 199, 200
tribal refugees, 68, 77, 85, 90, 199–201
Tri Dev Roy, 56
Tripura Development Council, 110
Tripura, N.B.K., 100, 122, 147, 183
Tripura state, 5, 6, 46, 51, 58, 61, 63, 85, 121, 122, 137–141, 149, 159, 160, 197, 199

Tripura Unnayan Sangsad, 110
trust and confidence, 36, 127, 170, 175
two-nation theory, 51

U
Unclassified State Forests (USFs), 51
UN Commission for Human Rights in Geneva, 143
uni-cultural, 58
uni-lingual, 58
union, 26, 51
unitary state, 58, 64
United Nations Development Programme (UNDP), 37, 135, 136, 144–149, 152, 159, 160, 168
United Nations (UN), 3, 8, 37, 137, 141, 149
United Nations Working Group on Indigenous Populations (UNWGIP), 142
United People's Democratic Front (UPDF), 8, 12, 14, 33, 36, 101, 116, 123–127, 129–132, 143, 151, 158, 159, 161, 162, 167, 170
United People's Party of CHT, 2
UN Sub-Commission of Prevention of Discrimination and Protection of Minorities, 142

Upajati, 2, 3
Upazila, 125
Ushatun Talukder, 73
usufruct, 50

V
valley, 4, 5
verbal agreement, 155
viable policies, 175
village, 50
Village Defence Party (VDP), 88, 108, 203
violence, 28–31, 146
vote, 104, 123, 197
vote bank, 133, 155, 156, 170
voter, 35, 104, 155
voter list, 104, 105, 116

W
war, 21, 23, 29, 30, 32, 34, 68
Western donor, 68, 69, 109, 142
West Pakistan, 52
withdrawal of temporary army camps, 68, 77, 90, 99, 154
women, 22, 79, 123, 145, 146, 176, 197
Workers Party of Bangladesh, 97
Working Group on Indigenous Populations (WGIP), 8
World Bank, 148

Printed by Printforce, the Netherlands